Web Design
DeMYSTiFieD®

DeMYSTiFieD® Series

Accounting Demystified

Advanced Statistics Demystified

Algebra Demystified

Alternative Energy Demystified

Anatomy Demystified

ASP.NET 2.0 Demystified

Astronomy Demystified

Audio Demystified

Biology Demystified

Biotechnology Demystified

Business Calculus Demystified

Business Math Demystified

Business Statistics Demystified

C++ Demystified

Calculus Demystified

Chemistry Demystified

College Algebra Demystified

Corporate Finance Demystified

Data Structures Demystified

Databases Demystified

Differential Equations Demystified

Digital Electronics Demystified

Earth Science Demystified

Electricity Demystified

Electronics Demystified

Environmental Science Demystified

Everyday Math Demystified

Forensics Demystified

Genetics Demystified

Geometry Demystified

Home Networking Demystified

Investing Demystified

Java Demystified

JavaScript Demystified

Linear Algebra Demystified

Macroeconomics Demystified

Management Accounting Demystified

Math Proofs Demystified

Math Word Problems Demystified

Medical Billing and Coding Demystified

Medical Terminology Demystified

Meteorology Demystified

Microbiology Demystified

Microeconomics Demystified

Nanotechnology Demystified

Nurse Management Demystified

OOP Demystified

Options Demystified

Organic Chemistry Demystified

Personal Computing Demystified

Pharmacology Demystified

Physics Demystified

Physiology Demystified

Pre-Algebra Demystified

Precalculus Demystified

Probability Demystified

Project Management Demystified

Psychology Demystified

Quality Management Demystified

Quantum Mechanics Demystified

Relativity Demystified

Robotics Demystified

Signals and Systems Demystified

Six Sigma Demystified

SQL Demystified

Statics and Dynamics Demystified

Statistics Demystified

Technical Math Demystified

Trigonometry Demystified

UML Demystified

Visual Basic 2005 Demystified

Visual C# 2005 Demystified

XML Demystified

Web Design
DeMYSTiFieD®

Wendy Willard

New York   Chicago   San Francisco   Lisbon   London   Madrid   Mexico City
Milan   New Delhi   San Juan   Seoul   Singapore   Sydney   Toronto

The McGraw·Hill Companies

Cataloging-in-Publication Data is on file with the Library of Congress

McGraw-Hill books are available at special quantity discounts to use as premiums and sales promotions, or for use in corporate training programs. To contact a representative, please e-mail us at bulksales@mcgraw-hill.com.

Web Design DeMYSTiFieD®

1 2 3 4 5 6 7 8 9 0   DOC DOC   1 0 9 8 7 6 5 4 3 2 1 0

ISBN   978-0-07-174801-8
MHID   0-07-174801-6

Sponsoring Editor Roger Stewart	**Copy Editor** Lisa McCoy	**Illustration** Glyph International
Editorial Supervisor Patty Mon	**Proofreader** Carol Shields	**Art Director, Cover** Jeff Weeks
Project Manager Tania Andrabi, Glyph International	**Indexer** Karin Arrigoni	**Cover Illustration** Lance Lekander
Acquisitions Coordinator Joya Anthony	**Production Supervisor** Jean Bodeaux	
Technical Editor Chrissy Rey-Drapeau	**Composition** Glyph International	

I first learned web design from a fabulous instructor, Lynda Weinman, while in college. I was privileged to be among the first students in the United States to learn how to design for webpages, and I have been smitten ever since. This book is dedicated to students everywhere who are finding their life's passions in classrooms all over the globe.

About the Author

Wendy Willard is a designer, consultant, writer, and educator who has been involved in web design for about 15 years, after obtaining a degree in illustration from Art Center College of Design in Pasadena, California. She is the author of the bestseller *HTML: A Beginner's Guide*, now in its fourth edition, and has written additional books and articles on the topics of Photoshop, web design, and Mac O/S.

About the Technical Editor

Chrissy Rey-Drapeau has been working with the Web since 1995 when she gave up animal wrangling for programming. Concentrating on Adobe Flash and web application development, she loves to teach what she knows. As the lead developer at Pongo Interactive, Chrissy works with such clients as the American Association for the Advancement of Science, Marriott International, Beaconfire Consulting, reZOLV Creative Solutions, and Swim Design.

Contents

Acknowledgments

I'd like to send out a special thanks to my technical editor, Chrissy. Even though I had written a ton about web design before, Chrissy really challenged my thought process throughout the course of writing this book. As a result, the content is much stronger, more succinct, and more clearly explained. Chrissy—you have truly made this a better book. Thank you!

And as always, I must thank my family for sticking by me even when I said (for the tenth time), "I just need to finish this chapter and then we can go…" ☺ *Psalm 100*

Introduction

When I started creating the outline for this book, I had just finished teaching a semester-long web design course for a local community college. That experience couldn't have come at a better time because it helped me refine my approach to teaching web design. I took my years of experience creating websites and writing about that process, and tweaked it a bit to tailor it for students. The result is *Web Design DeMYSTiFieD®*.

Who Should Use This Book

Even though this book is jam-packed with information, it is not meant to be the only resource for learning web design. It is, however, intended to be the perfect companion to instructor-led courses, either online or in the classroom.

You'll likely get the most from this book if you know a little about the following:

- **Your computer** Can you open, close, and move files around fairly easily? Do you have a web browser and Internet connection you feel comfortable using?
- **Design** Do you know what styles, layouts, and so on appeal to you? Can you express those in terms of color, shape, and texture?
- **HTML** Do you know what it is used for? Have you ever used it to create a basic webpage?

If you can't answer in the affirmative to at least two of the preceding questions, you can still use this book as an introduction to web design, but you'll want to pay special attention to the tips, hints, and notes throughout the book. Many of these list resources where you can find additional information about a particular topic, such as graphic design.

How to Use This Book

The chapters are organized based on a typical web design project and the steps taken to complete such a project. Within each chapter are learning objectives to help frame the content discussed in that section.

There are ten chapters in this book, each of which builds upon the one before it. When I wrote the book, I intended for each student to move through the chapters consecutively. However, individual chapters can also be used as a reference at a later date.

A ten-question quiz can be found at the end of every chapter. The purpose of this quiz is to help solidify key concepts identified in the material covered. Answers to each quiz can be found in the back of the book.

Finally, a 75-question exam is included after Chapter 10. This exam poses questions from all the material covered, in a random order, to verify you've retained the most important aspects of what you've learned. The exam answers are also included in the back of the book.

chapter **1**

Getting Started

To get started in web design, we need to first make sure we're all on the same page. Specifically, I will use this chapter to outline the steps involved in a typical web design process, as well as who completes each step and what tools are used to do so. By the end of this chapter, we'll be ready to switch gears a bit to discuss how web design differs from print design.

CHAPTER OBJECTIVES

In this chapter, you will

- Differentiate between the various aspects of web development teams
- Recognize the tools and technologies used by web development teams
- Identify the steps involved in planning a website
- Identify ways to document the web development process

What Is Web Design?

Prior to the mid-1990s, you might have wondered if web design was an activity reserved for spiders, like the one made famous by the movie *Charlotte's Web*. These days, it seems like everyone knows someone who designs webpages.

So what exactly does a web designer do? If you've picked up this book, you're probably interested in the answer to this question. Or, perhaps, you're taking a required web design course in school and need some help figuring out the basics. In either case, you've come to the right place. This book is meant to provide an introduction to modern web design concepts and technologies. With that said, it is not the be-all and end-all of web design instruction. Rather, I seek to touch on all key aspects and then provide references to online sources for additional information.

In its most basic form, web design covers the creation of any content viewed over the Web. Indeed, Wikipedia describes web design as "the skill of creating presentations of content (usually hypertext or hypermedia) that is delivered to an end-user through the World Wide Web, by way of a web browser or other web-enabled software like Internet television clients, microblogging clients, and RSS readers" (http://en.wikipedia.org/wiki/Web_Design).

In the business world, a professional web designer can take on a variety of different tasks, from planning the way a site's information will be presented, to designing that information and building the code used to display it. As you learn about web design, you may find a certain aspect appeals to you more than another. That can work to your benefit because many web designers specialize in very specific areas. For example, you might be drawn to how content is structured on a site and move toward the specialty called information architecture. Or, you might prefer making content interactive with tools like Adobe Flash and decide to focus your efforts on becoming proficient in such tools.

Regardless, I hope this book gives you a firm foundation in the basic aspects of web design as you start your journey.

Design vs. Development

You've probably heard both "web design" and "web development" used to refer to the creation of content for the Web. In fact, you may even be enrolled in a web design class within a web development curriculum and wonder how the two fit together.

Many people consider web design to be what happens to the *front-end* of a website, while web development might refer to the work on the site's *back-end*. The front-end of a site typically involves any customer-facing aspects of the site, such as the layout, navigation, graphics, and text. By contrast, the back-end comprises the behind-the-scenes code and technologies that make the front-end work. This frequently includes databases to store content, scripts to process web forms, and other programming to display content.

This book focuses on the creation of the front-end of a website, which we are referring to as web design.

Teams and Tasks

I just threw out a couple of different specialties within the overarching title of web design. When working on a large web design project, you may encounter one of each of these specialties, plus a few more. If you're working by yourself on a smaller project, you will probably dabble a bit in each of the following categories:

- Project management
- Information architecture
- Design
- Coding/programming
- Animation
- Copywriting/editing
- Testing
- Search engine optimization
- Maintenance

Project Management

Project management is an important aspect of any website project. Tasks that fall into this category might include:

- Evaluating the project goals and objectives
- Recognizing potential problem areas
- Communicating with client(s) about the project
- Identifying the site's target audience

- Collecting the site's content
- Scheduling the project and its milestones
- Keeping everyone on schedule
- Educating the client about the project's process and the site's maintenance

If you end up working for a design agency, the project management role will likely fall to an individual who manages several projects at once. As such, project managers must be extremely organized and task-oriented people. When the tasks in this category fall to you, either as the project manager for a larger web team or as the do-it-all web designer, it is important to stay focused on meeting the project goals and managing the steps along the way.

To learn more about project management for the Web, here are a few additional resources:

- *Managing Interactive Media Projects* by Tim Frick (Delmar Cengage Learning, 2007)
- *Making Things Happen: Mastering Project Management (Theory in Practice)* by Scott Berkun (O'Reilly, 2008)
- Effective Project Management for Web Geeks (http://articles.sitepoint .com/article/project-management-web-geeks)
- Project management, collaboration, and task software: Basecamp (www .basecamphq.com)
- Web Design: An Introduction to Project Management from Wikiversity (http://en.wikiversity.org/wiki/Web_Design/An_introduction_to_ Project_Management)

Information Architecture

In web design, information architecture involves organizing the content in the most effective and efficient manner for the end user. Tasks that fall into this category might include:

- Labeling the site's content areas
- Organizing the content
- Developing an efficient, user-centered structure for the site's content
- Creating wireframes (or storyboards) to track a user's progress through the site

- Ensuring the navigation meets the end-user requirements
- Documenting the site map

NOTE   *You will notice there is some overlap among the categories, in that some tasks are included in multiple categories. This is not a mistake! Web design teams vary greatly according to the people and projects involved, and sometimes tasks are shared.*

The information architect's ultimate goal is to organize the content in such a way that people can find what they want, when they want it. Moving through the site should be intuitive for end users, yet also make sense for the business owner. This can be particularly challenging, as much of the success of the website lies here. In other words, if the information architecture fails, the site fails. If people can't find the content they seek, the plain and simple truth is that they will go elsewhere. Therefore, it is important not to overlook the tasks in this category. Even if you are the only person on your web team, spend ample time at the beginning of the project figuring out the best way to organize the site's content. Look for more on this in Chapter 2. In the meantime, here are some additional resources you might check out:

- *A Project Guide to UX Design: For User Experience Designers in the Field or in the Making* by Russ Unger and Carolyn Chandler (New Riders Press, 2009)
- *Content Strategy for the Web* by Kristina Halvorson (New Riders Press, 2009)
- Jakob Nielsen on Usability and Web Design (www.useit.com)
- User Interface Engineering (www.uie.com)

TIP   *UX is an acronym for "user experience." In web design, UX is often used to refer to anything that affects a user's perception of the website. UX specialists often have experience in psychology, as well as design and computer science.*

Design

The design tasks of the site… it's what you're reading this book for, right? The overarching topic of design covers everything in this chapter, but the more specific design-related tasks typically include:

- Creating comprehensive designs (comps or mockups) for key sections/pages/screens of the project
- Translating those comprehensive designs into working prototypes

- Developing supplementary graphic content as needed
- Identifying the transitions between sections/screens/pages
- Coding the designs to display in web browsers

I cover more details about these tasks in the following chapters, so I won't discuss those in depth here. In addition to these tasks, the designer may or may not also be involved in the coding or programming of the site. Keep reading for more on what those tasks entail.

Coding/Programming

A website is nothing without the code to make it happen. For smaller website projects, the code needed is typically basic enough to be coded by the designer. But for larger or more complex projects, a programmer is an important addition to the team. This member of the team might perform tasks such as:

- Designing and maintaining appropriate databases, servers, testing environments, security procedures, networks, and so on
- Coding the designs to display in web browsers

Most people—myself included—consider coding and web design to go hand-in-hand. Even if a web designer isn't the one coding the pages, he needs to have a firm understanding of how the code works in order to create an appropriate web design. A large portion of this book will be spent discussing how to translate your designs into code. Even so, you'll likely need additional resources to solidify your coding knowledge. Here are a few options:

- *HTML: A Beginner's Guide, Fourth Edition* by Wendy Willard (McGraw-Hill/Professional, 2009)
- *HTML & CSS: The Complete Reference, Fifth Edition* by Thomas A. Powell (McGraw-Hill/Professional, 2010)
- HTML Source: HTML Tutorials (www.yourhtmlsource.com)
- World Wide Web Consortium (W3C)—the organization that develops and maintains HTML (www.w3.org)
- HTML Goodies: The Ultimate HTML Resource (www.htmlgoodies.com)
- HTML and CSS Tutorials (www.htmldog.com)
- HTML & CSS Tutorials (www.w3schools.com/sitemap/sitemap_tutorials .asp)

Animation/Multimedia

When a website project involves any type of animation, it's best to add a team member experienced with animation design. When web design was still in its infancy, designers often created static images as well as animated ones. But the level of design and complexity in web animation has grown such that animation design is truly a specialty. Tasks left to web animators might include:

- Designing key sections/pages/screens of the animation
- Developing the animation between frames/screens
- Coding/programming the animation

I often have students ask whether they should learn how to create web animation. If you're considering focusing your skills on web animation or multimedia, you'll want to spend some time learning Adobe Flash, as that is the de facto standard for animation and multimedia on the web. For additional information about web animation and Flash, check out these resources:

NOTE *Each of the books listed is available for users of Flash CS3, CS4, and CS5 (as of this writing). Select the book that corresponds to whichever version of the software you plan to use.*

- *Adobe Photoshop Classroom in a Book* by Adobe Creative Team (Adobe Press, 2010)
- *Adobe Flash Classroom in a Book* by Adobe Creative Team (Adobe Press, 2010)
- *How to Cheat in Adobe Flash: The Art of Design and Animation* by Chris Georgenes (Focal Press, 2010)
- Inspiring Flash Design (http://naldzgraphics.net/inspirations/45-excellent-examples-of-flash-websites-design)
- Flash Kit: A Flash developer resource site (http://www.flashkit.com)
- Smashing Magazine: Flash (http://www.smashingmagazine.com/tag/flash)
- About.com Flash Web Design (http://webdesign.about.com/od/flash/Macromedia_Flash.htm)
- Tutorialized Photoshop and Flash tutorials (http://www.tutorialized.com)
- Newgrounds Flash tutorials (http://www.newgrounds.com/collection/flashtutorials.html)

Copywriting/Editing

When businesses first develop websites, they often try to reuse content that was originally created to be viewed as a printed piece. This is not the ideal situation for the end user, who is accessing the content on a screen instead of paper. In the best-case scenario, a copyeditor is involved to write (or rewrite) the content specifically for web readers. Tasks in this category typically include:

- Working with an information architect and/or designer to label the site's content areas
- Developing the site's text content
- Reviewing and editing the site's text content for web readability

A copywriter isn't always in the budget for small design projects, but that doesn't mean these tasks aren't necessary. On the contrary, if there isn't an official copywriter on the project, it's up to the remaining team members to pick up the slack and ensure the content is edited for web readability. I touch on this more in Chapter 2. In the meantime, here are some additional resources to help you learn about copyediting for the Web:

- *Web Copy That Sells: The Revolutionary Formula for Creating Killer Copy That Grabs Their Attention and Compels Them to Buy* by Maria Veloso (AMACOM, 2009)
- *Content Strategy for the Web* by Kristina Halvorson (New Riders Press, 2009)
- *Do the Web Write: Writing for and Marketing Your Website* by Dan Furman (Self Counsel Press, 2009)
- The Web Developer's Copywriting Guide (http://articles.sitepoint.com/article/developers-writing-guide)
- Web Content and Writing for Web Sites (http://websitetips.com/webcontent)
- Copywriting 101: An Introduction to Effective Copy (http://www.copyblogger.com/copywriting-101)

Testing

The technical term for the process of testing a web project (or just about any project for that matter) is quality assurance, or QA for short. Although software development companies have whole departments devoted to QA, the tasks in this category may fall to the designer or other team members (or, more likely, *all* of the team members). Those tasks might include:

- Clicking every link to ensure that each one works as expected
- Completing every web form to check the functionality
- Testing the usability of the website to determine how well users can access the content
- Verifying that all text and graphical data display as expected in the target browsers and on all target platforms
- Coordinating with the appropriate team member to fix any errors found during testing

Testing is key to any website project, for obvious reasons: If you have a broken link (or worse, a broken page) that never gets fixed, your business loses credibility and maybe even some customers. Nevertheless, this category of tasks often falls through the cracks for many independent web designers. To avoid that trap, build time for testing into your project schedule from the very beginning. Make sure you spend time confirming that the site you built actually works. If you're trying to make a living doing this, you'll be taking the first step toward gaining repeat businesses from this customer and maybe even new business from someone who accesses the site.

For more on website testing, check out these resources:

- *Rocket Surgery Made Easy: The Do-It-Yourself Guide to Finding and Fixing Usability Problems* by Steve Krug (New Riders Press, 2009)
- *Handbook of Usability Testing: How to Plan, Design, and Conduct Effective Tests* by Jeffrey Rubin, Dana Chisnell, and Jared Spool (Wiley, 2008)
- The Ultimate Testing Checklist (http://articles.sitepoint.com/article/ultimate-testing-checklist)
- UITest.com (http://www.uitest.com)
- BrowserShots (http://www.browsershots.org)
- Litmus Testing Software (http://www.litmusapp.com)
- Adobe BrowserLabs (http://browserlab.adobe.com)

Search Engine Optimization

When a website is launched, most people want to know how soon it will be on the first page of Google's search results. Yeah, right! Search engine optimization

(SEO) is the process of making webpages easily understood and interpreted by search engines. Contrary to popular belief, this is not simply a to-do item you check off your project schedule after a site has gone live.

Instead, SEO is best tackled throughout the entire web development process. In fact, the tasks in this category can become so involved that large web development teams often include a person (or people) who specialize in this area. Here are examples of the types of tasks this person may perform:

- Cross-linking pages to ease navigation and increase visibility
- Reviewing and editing the site's content to add relevant keywords and phrases
- Submitting the site to search engines
- Checking the site's listing in key search engines
- Identifying potential changes to the site that may increase its visibility and/or popularity
- Blocking private pages from being listed with search engines
- Advertising with search engines to increase visibility

For more about SEO, check out these resources:

- *Search Engine Optimization: An Hour a Day* by Jennifer Grappone and Gradiva Couzin (Sybex, 2011)
- *Search Engine Optimization for Dummies* by Peter Kent (For Dummies, 2010)
- Patrick Gavin's SEO Blog (www.patrickgavin.com)
- Search Engine Watch (www.searchenginewatch.com)
- Search Engine Journal (www.searchenginejournal.com)
- Google's Website Optimizer (www.google.com/websiteoptimizer)

Maintenance

Who will take care of the website after it is launched? The answer to this question is often overlooked, but needs to be identified at the start of the project. If the site maintainer is a nontechnical employee of the client, the site needs to be built in such a way that a nontechnical person can maintain it, without needing to learn a programming language. Or, if the site is a personal blog, the technical skills of the blog owner will likely dictate which blogging software is used to build the site.

Regardless, it's important to consider what happens to the site after it's launched, so you can better understand the technical limitations involved in building it. Typical maintenance tasks are:

- Updating press releases and news
- Adding new content
- Posting jobs
- Updating the staff listings
- Keeping the calendar current

I cover the topic of website maintenance more in Chapters 9 and 10.

Technologies and Tools

Now that I've covered the basic tasks within a web development team, let's move on to the technologies and tools used to complete those tasks.

HTML and CSS

The most basic of all web technologies and the easiest to learn is HTML, which stands for Hypertext Markup Language. Essentially, HTML tells the web browser how to display content and link to related information.

Pretty much all webpages use HTML in some way, shape, or form. Even if you haven't noticed them before, there are likely lots of little HTML "tags" floating around behind the scenes of the webpages you visit. To see what I mean, open your web browser and choose View | Source, View | View Source, or View | Page Source (depending on your browser). This gives you a glimpse of the code used to create the page being viewed.

HTML was originally designed to *mark up* text and its structure (titles, headings, lists, and so forth), as opposed to dictate page layout. Technologies such as cascading style sheets (CSS) are better at handling page layout. Both HTML and CSS will be discussed in this book, as both are indispensible for web designers.

So what exactly does HTML do? It provides instructions to the browser regarding how to display content. For example, you might use a certain bit of HTML to indicate where paragraphs start and finish:

```
<p>This is a paragraph of text.</p>
```

Now that doesn't look so difficult, does it? All tags use brackets to separate them from the other content on the page. In the previous example, you can see that brackets surround both the opening and closing paragraph tags. The <p> tells the browser this is the start of a new paragraph, and the </p> tells it to end that paragraph. (To end or close a tag, you reuse the tag, but with a forward slash after the first bracket.)

NOTE　*Officially, the p portion of the code here is called the* **element***, while the p is referred to as a* **tag** *when surrounded by the brackets: <p>. However, in most cases, the two terms—element and tag—are used interchangeably.*

We use HTML like this to structure the page, telling the browser which pieces of content are paragraphs, which are lists, and so on. Then, we add some CSS to specify how to style each content area. We'll work with each of these—HTML and CSS—throughout much of this book.

Beyond HTML and CSS

When you want to move beyond basic page layout and content styling, you'll likely need to invoke some other web technologies and tools. Typically, we break those down into two categories:

- Client-side
- Server-side

When the action happens on the user's system (within the browser), it's referred to as being "client-side." Conversely, code that is processed before it reaches the user's system is said to be "server-side."

TIP　*Server-side scripts are stored on the server and sometimes require additional software to be installed there. Client-side scripts do not interact with the server and, therefore, do not require any additional software to be installed on the server.*

Suppose you want to offer your website in both English and Spanish, but you don't want the hassle of maintaining two separate versions of the site. You could store all the text content of the site in a database or plain-text files, and then reference those files within your HTML code using a server-side script. Then, when the user selects a language from the home page, the server-side script builds the pages on demand, importing the English or Spanish text segments

Still Struggling

There are thousands, if not millions, of online resources for each of the technologies mentioned in this chapter. For some tips and tricks with JavaScript, HTML, ASP, PHP, or any of the other types of web programming, check out http://www.devarticles.com. Or, try the Google Code University by visiting http://code.google.com/edu.

as needed. This is a great example of how a *server-side* script can really benefit a web developer.

To help you understand how a *client-side* script might work, consider forms you fill out on the Web. Have you ever clicked the submit button on such a form, only to be told you missed a required field? This type of form field confirmation is accomplished through a client-side script. When the submit button is clicked, the script tells the browser to make sure any required fields are complete before sending the form content to its final destination. Nothing goes back to the server until the content is verified at the client (user) level. Once the content of the form does get sent back to the server, a server-side script is called upon to process the form.

Table 1-1 lists some popular scripting choices in each of the two categories I've discussed. It should be noted, however, that JavaScript, VBScript, and AJAX all have server-side capabilities as well.

TABLE 1-1 Popular Scripting Choices	
Client-side	**Server-side**
JavaScript	ASP/ASP.NET
AJAX	ColdFusion
Jscript	Java
VBScript	Perl
	PHP
	Ruby
	SMX

Web design students can sometimes become overwhelmed by the sheer number of technologies listed in Table 1-1. If that sounds like you, take heart because no one really knows how to use *all* of those technologies well. Most people choose to focus on one or two that complement each other. Then, you might work with other developers who specialize with alternative technologies when those are needed for a particular project.

Design Tools

If you've already looked at a list of design applications, you've undoubtedly recognized a few names on that list. The most popular design applications are all owned by Adobe, who is a world leader in graphics and imaging software.

Photoshop is probably best known for its image manipulation capabilities. Sometimes a copy of Photoshop Elements (the scaled-back, but still fabulous, version) is included with the purchase of new scanners or digital cameras, and home users are introduced to it. But by and large, Photoshop is the go-to program for professional designers.

To really become accomplished as a web designer, you'll need to be proficient in a design application. If you already know a little about Photoshop, I would encourage you to continue down that path. If you're new to design and are wondering which application to learn, check out my suggestions in Table 1-2.

All of the tools listed have free demo versions available. I encourage you to download and try them before investing in any new software. In addition, if you're a student or teacher, be sure to check for academic pricing when you purchase. An academic discount can often save quite a bundle, particularly for the more expensive software packages.

TIP   *Looking for help building websites with a combination of Adobe's applications? Check out Joseph W. Lowry's book,* **Adobe CS4 Web Workflows: Building Websites with Adobe Creative Suite 4** *(Wiley, 2009).*

Flash

While I could have listed Adobe Flash (www.adobe.com/flash) in Table 1-2, it really is a breed of its own for a couple of reasons. First, Flash is both a design application and a full-fledged animation tool. Second, the Flash program

TABLE 1-2 Common Tools Used to Design Webpages

Application	Pros	Cons
Photoshop (www.adobe.com/photoshop)	Powerful, professional–grade design tool Integrates well with Adobe Dreamweaver (see Table 1–3) and Flash Includes web graphics features, plus tools for graphic design, video production, and photography Scaled–down and less expensive version is available	Full version is expensive Animation options are clunky at best Potentially steep learning curve if you're new to design
Fireworks (www.adobe.com/fireworks)	Powerful tool built specifically for web design Seamlessly integrates with Dreamweaver (see Table 1–3) and Flash Less expensive than Photoshop Supports web animation	Potentially steep learning curve if you're new to web design Only capable of using red, green blue (RGB) color graphics Images developed with Fire–works are not intended for commercial printing
Illustrator (www.adobe.com/illustrator)	Powerful, professional–grade illustration tool Includes web graphics features, plus tools for drawing and painting Integrates well with Flash	Expensive Software is geared more toward illustration and line art than web design Steep learning curve No photo editing
Paint Shop Pro (www.corel.com/ paintshoppro)	Low price Includes advanced photo–editing features Integrates a media storage component	Software is geared more toward digital camera users than web designers Lacks animation support
GIMP (www.gimp.org)	Free Available for Mac, Windows, and UNIX It is open–source, but this means there is a community of people updating and refining it	Lacks support for some of the more advanced features found in the other tools listed Tends to be a bit "buggy" or "quirky" sometimes

includes its own scripting language, so you really can build fully functional websites with it. Plus, as of this writing, Flash doesn't really have a whole lot of competition, although that may change as HTML5 and Microsoft's Silverlight (www.silverlight.net) gain support among web designers and browsers alike.

NOTE   *Web browsers must have a Flash player installed in order to view Flash files, but thankfully the player is free and widely distributed. (One notable exception has to do with mobile, web-enabled devices, many of which are not capable of displaying Flash files.)*

Flash's scripting technology is called ActionScript, which can be used on the server side or the client side, depending on what you're trying to do. This makes Flash a highly customizable, flexible solution that is hugely popular among web developers.

Refer to the additional resources listed in the Animation section (p. 7) for places to learn more.

Coding Tools

The software used to code a website depends on a variety of factors, the most important of which is the technologies used. For example, if you're building a site purely in HTML, you can use something as simple as NotePad or TextEdit (free text editors that can be downloaded and installed in minutes). Other web tools can handle HTML in addition to more complex technologies.

Table 1-3 lists some of the popular tools available to help you identify which might be suitable for your needs. Of course, this is not an exhaustive list, but is included merely as a starting point. As with the design tools, these typically can be downloaded and tested for free. Be sure to try a couple of different options before settling on your preferred tool.

TIP   *WYSIWYG means "what you see is what you get." These types of editors don't require users to know HTML. Instead of looking at the code in your pages, you view and edit a "preview" of how the page will look in the browser, simply dragging and dropping pieces of your layout as you see fit.*

TABLE 1-3 Common Tools Used to Design Webpages		
Application	**Pros**	**Cons**
Amaya (www.w3.org/Amaya)	Free Open-source Available for Mac, Windows, and UNIX Includes spell-checker WYSIWYG visual editor	No browser preview No multiuser editing
BBEdit (www.barebones.com)	Free and paid versions available Text-based editor capable of handling many popular programming languages, including C, C++, CSS, Java, JavaScript, JSP, Perl, PHP, Ruby, HTML, SQL, and XML	Mac only
CoffeeCup (www.coffeecup.com)	WYSIWYG visual editor Includes spell-checker, browser preview, and file transfer protocol (FTP) upload Comes with templates	Windows only
Dreamweaver (www.adobe.com/dreamweaver)	WYSIWYG visual editor Available for Mac and Windows Integrates seamlessly with design applications like Photoshop and Fireworks Very popular among coding and design pros	More expensive than some other options Complex enough to scare away some beginning users
Expression Web (www.microsoft.com/expression)	WYSIWYG visual editor Integrates with Expression Studio (for design) and Visual Studio (for more complex programming)	More expensive than some other options Windows only May be confusing for beginners
NoteTab (www.notetab.com)	Free and pro versions available Text-based editor Pro version is highly customizable and includes features such as a spell-checker, plus templates	No browser preview Windows only
Visual Web Developer (www.microsoft.com/express/vwd)	Free WYSIWYG visual editor Includes FTP upload, spell-checker, and browser preview Comes with templates Supports server-side scripting and multiuser editing	Windows only

Planning a Site

When you begin any web development project, it's important to spend some time planning. Although this section of the book is quite small in comparison to the part devoted to the layout and style of the site, the planning part of the project is nevertheless significant. In fact, I would go so far as to say it is one of the most important aspects of the project.

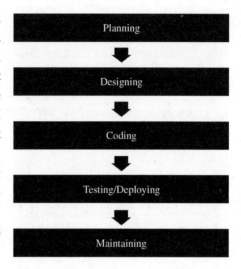

To get started, let's take a look at where planning fits into the lifecycle of a typical web project, as shown in this illustration.

Your first task should be to identify the goals of the project. Why are you creating this website? If you're working in a professional capacity, you might have received a formal Request for Proposal (RFP) from a client. An RFP is a company's way of stating its project needs so that the information is easily broadcast to a variety of potential bidders, who then respond with a written proposal specifying how they intend to meet the client company's project needs.

If you're not responding to an RFP, you still need to know some basic information about the project, including:

- Description and objectives of the website (What will the site do?)
- Explanation of the hosting environment (Where will the site live?)
- Required content, components, and functionalities (How will the site work?)
- Description of the target audience (Who will the site serve?)
- Proposed timeline (When will the site go live?)

Even though you may be developing the site for a family member or a friend, you still need to get everything down on paper to ensure a smooth development process. In addition to the list you just read, here are a few things you might want to remember while trying to assess the project's needs.

- *Get to know the company profile and background.* What are its strengths and weaknesses? Who are its competitors, and where do they stand in regard to comparable products?

- *Get to know the contact person.* What is her experience level with the Web and similar projects? What comparable sites does she like and dislike?
- *Get to know the company's brand.* Is there an existing logo, or do you need to create one? Can the visual design be an extension of the current "look and feel," or must it be a complete redesign?

After considering this information, you'll likely be in a better position to identify the goals of the site. A few examples of site goals might be:

- Sell products/services
- Increase public awareness of a company/product/service
- Acquire employees
- Entertain
- Educate
- Communicate with customers
- Disseminate information
- Provide updates to products/services

Now let's look more closely at the where, who, and how of planning the project.

Hosting

The hosting of the site answers the *where* question posed previously. Before you can build any site, you must know where it will be stored on the Web. During development, the site may be housed on your own personal computer, but it can't stay there when the site goes live. All public websites must be transferred or uploaded to a host computer with 24-hour access to the Internet. Businesses pay monthly fees to companies who *host* (or store) webpages so they can have 24/7 availability to web surfers.

A variety of web hosting options exist, from free, personal site hosting to paid, business site hosting.

Personal Site Hosting

If you have an e-mail account with Google (Gmail), you're halfway to setting up your own personal site hosting. Google offers free webpages to its users, specifically targeting those who want to create sites for clubs, families, and other social groups. This type of situation is perfect if you aren't concerned about having a custom domain name (such as www.wendywillard.com). Visit http://sites.google.com to get started.

NOTE *Other sites that offer free personal site hosting include Bravehost (www .bravenet.com/webhosting) and Tripod (www.tripod.com). Also, check with your e-mail or Internet service provider to see if you already are eligible for free hosting space with your existing account.*

Because these sites are largely targeted to beginners, they make uploading and maintaining your webpages a breeze. Most use web-based tools to help you create a site, so you don't need to purchase or install any software.

Business Site Hosting

Most businesses cannot take advantage of free hosting, because many of those tools prohibit use by for-profit companies. For the majority of businesses, paid offsite hosting is therefore the most effective and popular solution. Hosting like this might either be on a shared or dedicated server. While a shared server can be significantly less expensive than one dedicated to your needs, it may not be possible in all situations. For example, if your site runs custom web applications, requires a high level of security, or needs a large amount of hard drive space, a dedicated server is preferred.

TIP *If a dedicated server is not in the budget, a* virtual *private server (VPS) might be adequate.*

Even within the category of paid offsite hosting there are many different service levels. If you do a search online for "website hosting" you will be overwhelmed with choices. So how do you decide which one to select? Here are a few questions to ask when looking for business hosting:

- How much hard drive space is included?
- How much traffic can the site generate per month? (Ask for some average traffic rates for similar sites to compare.)
- How many e-mail accounts are included?
- What kind of access is permitted? (You want to make sure you have FTP access to upload files.)
- What kind of support is offered, and when is the support team available?
- How often are backups made? How are they accessed?

- What sort of site statistics are measured? (You want to have access to traffic reports, for example.) How are they accessed?

- Do they allow third-party/custom applications to be installed? (This is important if, for example, you want to add shopping cart software.) Are there any such applications pre-installed in your servers?

- What kind of server-side languages and database servers are supported? (You may want to install a particular third-party application that requires ASP.NET, for example.)

In the end, you'll probably get the best ideas about which hosting provider to use by asking friends and business associates. In that vein, here are a few of my suggestions:

- Site5 (www.site5.com/in.php?id=37181)

- DreamHost (www.dreamhost.com)

- BlueHost (www.bluehost.com)

- Hostway (www.hostway.com)

- Media Temple (www.mediatemple.net)

NOTE *Another option for personal and business users alike is a blogging tool. Believe it or not, many popular blogging tools offer to host their clients' blogs as well. Google's Blogger (www.blogger.com) and WordPress (www.wordpress.com) both enable users to create hosted websites using their blogging software. Both offer tutorials to help you get started, as well as tons of templates for customizing the look of your blog. I'll talk a bit more about blogs in Chapter 8.*

Domain Names

I would be remiss to finish a section on hosting without discussing domain names. As a web designer, you will often be asked to give advice about selecting domain names. Many people underestimate the power of a guessable and memorable domain name.

When talking about this, I frequently use the example of a company called Acme Landscaping Incorporated. While it may seem logical to its business owners to purchase the domain name alinc.com, it's probably not the first thing a potential customer would try. The name acmelandscaping.com would be my first guess, but if that were already taken I might try acmelandscapers.com or acmelawns.com. Then, I'd probably add another domain that doesn't have the business name, but instead provides a good search engine tag.

In the case of a summer camp website I created, we were able to register thebestsummercamp.com in addition to a domain name with the organization's name. While thebestsummercamp.com isn't the Uniform Resource Locator (URL) listed on the business cards, it has proven to be a valuable marketing tool for the organization as it reaches out to new members of the target audience.

TIP   *You can register a domain name either through your hosting company or independently through a site like Go Daddy (www.godaddy.com).*

Target Audience

Now that we've answered the *where* question, it's time to move on to the *who*. If you're creating a website for a business, a group, or an organization, you're most likely targeting people who might buy or use the company's products or services. Even if your site is purely for the purpose of disseminating information, you must be targeting a certain audience.

Knowing that audience can significantly affect how you design and develop the site. For example, if you're developing a site to sell a new game for Mac users, you know you can target the Mac operating system and browsers. Conversely, a site selling products for both Mac and PC users needs to be built and tested to function well on both platforms. Or what about a site whose target audience frequently uses web-enabled phones to access the site? Such a site would require coding and testing on a variety of web-enabled phones, in addition to traditional desktop browsers. When considering your site's target audience, also consider how it affects such things as:

- **Target platforms**   The computer through which the site is accessed
- **Target browsers**   The software through which the site is accessed
- **Target screen area/resolutions**   The "window" through which the site is viewed

PROBLEM 1-1

I've been asked to create a website for my company, but it's not the typical marketing site. My boss wants a site just for the employees of the company, to share documents and other information. How do I plan for this type of audience?

 **SOLUTION**

It sounds like you've been asked to help create an intranet site, which is a private site only accessible to qualified users. Creating a site for such a narrow audience will enable you to tailor the look and feel to the needs of your company's employees, which probably all have similar computers, monitors, browsers, and access speeds. However, you must also consider whether employees will access the site from home computers or mobile phones, which will likely have different requirements than your typical office computer. Talk with your boss to determine whether the site will be accessible to both home and office users, and then plan accordingly.

Each of these affect design decisions you make, such as which fonts to use, how wide to make the graphics, and which layout works best. I discuss this a bit more in the next chapter.

In the meantime, here are a few sites that provide online demographics and market research helpful to web designers. These sites offer details about technical demographics such as browsers, access speeds, hardware, traffic patterns, and site performance, as well as consumer demographics, such as advertising trends and purchasing decisions.

- http://www.access-egov.info/learn.cfm?id=demo&xid=MN
- http://www.internetnews.com/stats
- http://www.thecounter.com/stats
- http://www.gvu.gatech.edu/research
- http://en-us.nielsen.com/tab/industries/media/online_publishers

TIP *Whenever possible, try to speak to members of the site's target audience. Inquire about their online usage to determine what they might look for at the proposed website. I like to walk them through a sample scenario, asking first how they might try to find the site, and then what they might like to do there.*

Information Architecture

Another aspect of the site that is important to plan ahead of time is the way the content is structured, or the information architecture. Of course, there is no perfect way of organizing content, at least not one that works for everyone. Instead, you must look at all the possible ways of arranging the content on the site and select the method that works best for your project's goals, as well as the needs of the target audience.

Suppose you were designing a site for the youth group at your church. The proposed content for the site includes event listings, trip details (and any associated paperwork), staff bios, information for parents, links to social networking sites, and general information for students. Once you have identified the content categories, it's time to figure out how best to structure them within the context of a website to then identify how users move through the site.

All-in-One

You could just put all the information on a single page. For sites with only a little bit of content, or those that serve primarily as a way to access information on other sites (through links), this is a good choice. But for the youth group site? Probably not.

Flat

Another option is to have all the pages at the same level, where each page is accessible from every other one. This is probably the most common method of organizing content for small businesses and organizations (like our youth group). You've probably seen sites like this a lot, where you visit the home page and find links to pages titled "About Us," "Contact Us," "Our Services," and "Home." Sites organized like this may or may not have a "site map" or "index page" as an additional resource for quick linking.

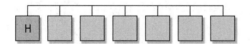

Hub-and-Spoke

Sometimes you need a way to structure content so that certain sections are separate from others, and each one follows a linear structure. One example might be an online training site, where you return to your "desk" after watching a class lecture or taking a test.

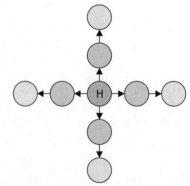

Strict Hierarchy

What if you wanted to offer several sections geared toward the different people who might visit the site? For the youth group site, those might be "Parents" and "Students." With a strict hierarchical structure, visitors to the Parents section would only be presented with information for parents. They'd have to go back to the home page and switch to the Students section to see that information.

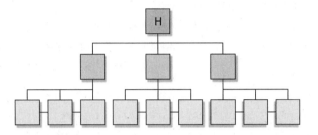

Multidimensional Hierarchy

This type of structure is similar to a strict hierarchy, but with one key difference: In this case, it is possible to access content from a different section without first returning to the home or gateway page. Multidimensional hierarchy has become a really popular way to lay out content on large, complex websites. A great example of this might be a large online bookstore that lets you view books by title, author, subject, or even keyword. The content can be reached by any of these methods.

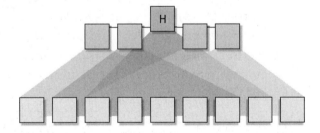

NOTE   *A great resource for learning more about web development is Web Design from Scratch (www.webdesignfromscratch.com), which is run by a web design agency in London called Scratchmedia. The information architecture classification system I used here was based on Scratchmedia's research and included with their permission.*

Documentation

Finally, I want to spend a few minutes talking about how to document your project. Typically, this does not come easy to designers. We often focus on the more creative aspects of a project and sometimes neglect the more mundane tasks. Having said that, I encourage you to come up with a method of documenting your projects that meets the needs without being cumbersome. The easier you make documenting the project, the more likely you are to do just that.

What needs to be documented? Anything that might affect how the site will ultimately function. The most commonly documented aspects of a website project include:

- **Structure** A site map might be used to document the information architecture of the site before it is built (see Figure 1-1).
- **Layout** A wireframe document might outline where a particular page's elements might be placed (see Figure 1-2).
- **Navigation** A storyboard can be used to document a target user's ideal path through the site (see Figure 1-3).
- **Style** A mockup or comp is typically created in a design program and used to figure out the site's look and feel (see Figure 1-4).

Aside from these documents, which are typically produced during the beginning phases of a project, there are several other types of documents that may be created even before a project has really begun. When a project is either being pitched or just getting off the ground, the web team likely will create some sort of proposal to the client to explain how the site will be built. After a project has been officially contracted, a Statement of Work is created to spell out what work is being performed for what price.

If the site is complex, particularly if it requires coding or programming beyond basic HTML, a technical specification should also be included in the documentation. This document identifies the technologies to be used and how the site's functionality will be achieved with each one.

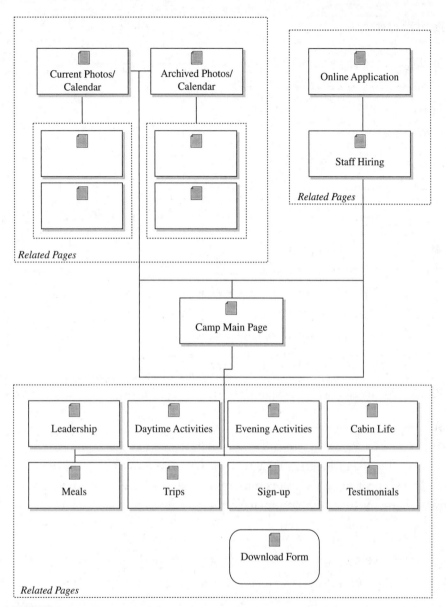

FIGURE 1-1 • This sample site map was created using Microsoft Visio, but you can develop similar outlines with a graphics program or even some word-processing tools.

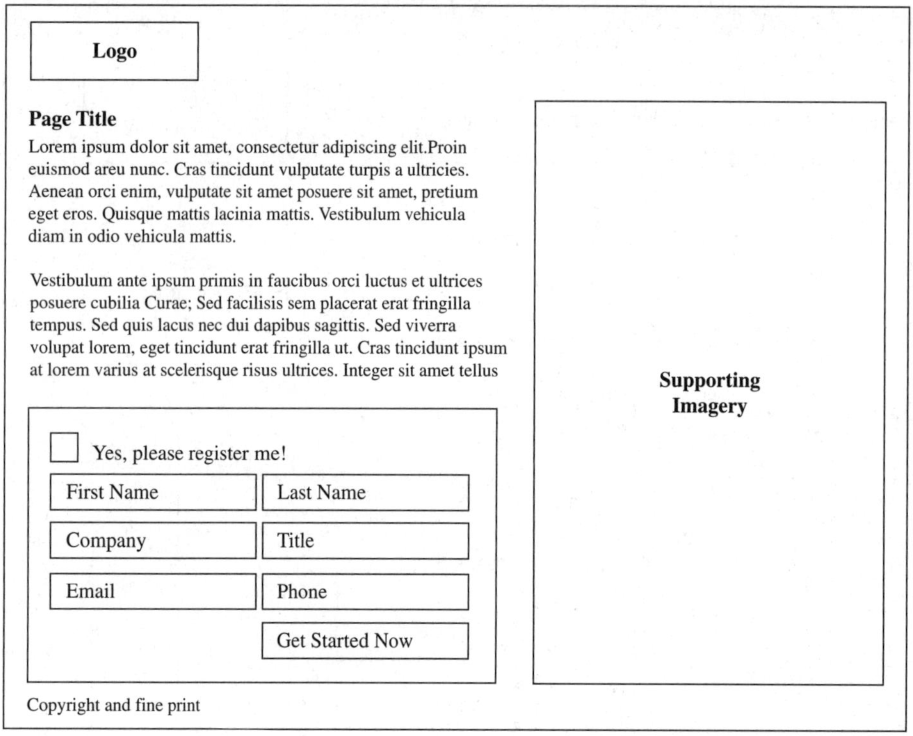

The wireframe contains the following labeled areas:

Logo

Page Title

Lorem ipsum dolor sit amet, consectetur adipiscing elit.Proin euismod areu nunc. Cras tincidunt vulputate turpis a ultricies. Aenean orci enim, vulputate sit amet posuere sit amet, pretium eget eros. Quisque mattis lacinia mattis. Vestibulum vehicula diam in odio vehicula mattis.

Vestibulum ante ipsum primis in faucibus orci luctus et ultrices posuere cubilia Curae; Sed facilisis sem placerat erat fringilla tempus. Sed quis lacus nec dui dapibus sagittis. Sed viverra volupat lorem, eget tincidunt erat fringilla ut. Cras tincidunt ipsum at lorem varius at scelerisque risus ultrices. Integer sit amet tellus

☐ Yes, please register me!

First Name	Last Name
Company	Title
Email	Phone
	Get Started Now

Supporting Imagery

Copyright and fine print

FIGURE 1-2 · The goal of a wireframe like this is to identify page layout before a lot of time is spent on the look and feel.

With all of these documents floating around, the project management aspect of any web project becomes even more important. Thankfully, there are some great online tools to help you manage this process.

- Basecamp (http://www.basecamphq.com)
- FreelanceSuite (http://www.freelancesuite.com)
- Zoho Projects (http://projects.zoho.com)

TIP *If none of those online project management tools seem to fit into your ideal workflow, consider using Google Docs (http://docs.google.com) as an online repository. Although it doesn't include an official project management tool, it does make it easy to collaborate and share files.*

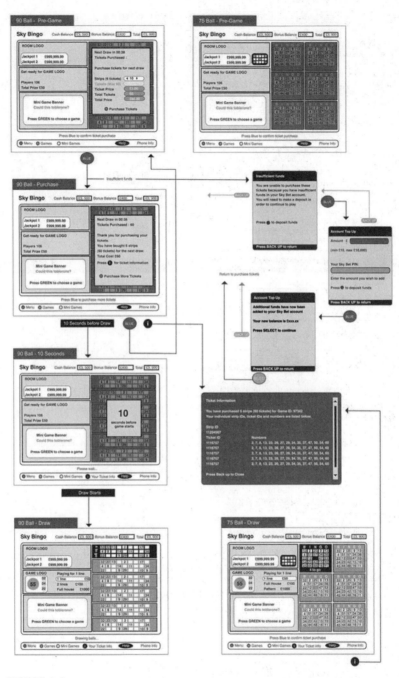

FIGURE 1-3 · This sample storyboard shows how a user might move through the site (reprinted with permission from www.paultrow.com).

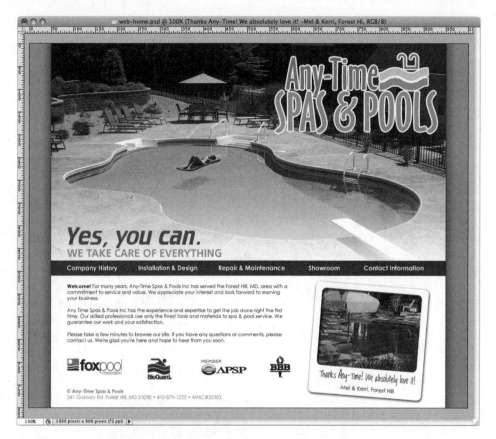

FIGURE 1-4 · This mockup is an example of how a site's style is worked out in a graphics program before any code is typed.

Chapter Summary

This chapter helped set the groundwork for the web development process by discussing the teams, technologies, tools, and documentation commonly used. Next, we'll move on to those aspects of design that are unique to web design, and begin the page layout process.

QUIZ

Choose the correct responses to each of the multiple-choice questions.

1. **Which is not typically considered part of the "front-end" of a website?**
   A. Text
   B. Graphics
   C. Database
   D. Navigation
   E. Page layout

2. **Which task is considered part of the *information architecture* role within a web development team?**
   A. Labeling the site's content areas
   B. Scheduling the project and its milestones
   C. Coding the designs to display in web browsers
   D. Creating mockups for key sections/pages/screens
   E. Completing every web form to check the functionality

3. **Which task is considered a key part of the *programming* role within a web development team?**
   A. Labeling the site's content areas
   B. Scheduling the project and its milestones
   C. Coding the designs to display in web browsers
   D. Creating mockups for key sections/pages/screens
   E. Completing every web form to check the functionality

4. **Completing every web form to check the functionality ideally falls under which role within a web development team?**
   A. Design
   B. Coding
   C. Animation
   D. Quality assurance
   E. Search engine optimization

5. **Developing supplementary graphic content ideally falls under which role within a web development team?**
   A. Design
   B. Coding
   C. Animation
   D. Quality assurance
   E. Search engine optimization

6. **What does HTML stand for in web development?**
   A. Human Text Markup Link
   B. Host Terminal Modal Link
   C. Hypertext Markup Language
   D. High-speed Transmission Meta-Language

7. **What do we call a script that runs on the user's system?**
   A. Host-side
   B. Client-side
   C. Server-side
   D. Browser-side
   E. Database-side

8. **Which type of information architecture might be called "flat"?**
   A. All pages are at the same level, where each is accessible from every other one.
   B. Pages are grouped into sections and each one follows a linear structure.
   C. Pages are grouped into sections, and within each section the various pages are always accessible; a user must return to the home page to jump to a different section.
   D. Pages are grouped into sections, and within each section the various pages are always accessible; a user can access other sections without returning to the home page.

9. **Which type of information architecture might be called "hub-and-spoke"?**
   A. All pages are at the same level, where each is accessible from every other one.
   B. Pages are grouped into sections and each one follows a linear structure.
   C. Pages are grouped into sections, and within each section the various pages are always accessible; a user must return to the home page to jump to a different section.
   D. Pages are grouped into sections, and within each section the various pages are always accessible; a user can access other sections without returning to the home page.

10. **How is the layout of a website typically documented during the planning phase of the project?**
   A. With a mockup
   B. With a site map
   C. With a wireframe
   D. With a storyboard
   E. With a technical specification

Designing for Screens

Now that we're all on the same page with regard to who does what in a typical web development project, let's focus a bit more on the designer's role. If you're antsy to get into your favorite graphics editor to start designing, great! But before you do, let me bring to your attention a few key design issues first.

CHAPTER OBJECTIVES

In this chapter, you will

- Identify those design issues that are unique to screen design, particularly as they relate to devices, browsers, bandwidth, color, navigation, and transitions
- Create design mockups that meet the project goals
- Determine the best method of sharing design mockups for your needs

What's Unique About Screen Design?

Whenever you begin a new web design project, you must consider how the user will ultimately view your design. When the Web was in its infancy, users could only view webpages through web browsers on computers. But now people can access the Web from mobile phones, game systems, TVs, and even refrigerators! The one thing all of those have in common is this: Each has a screen on which content is viewed. Beyond the fact that each one has a screen, however, there are plenty of differences.

To ensure you understand those differences, let's look more closely at some of them.

Devices

The most obvious difference between how users view webpages is in the device itself. Is your target audience accessing the site from a traditional computer (desktop or laptop) or a mobile, handheld device (such as a phone, game console, or MP3 player)? In all likelihood, the answer will include both categories. So how do you accommodate traditional computer users as well as mobile users?

Let's take a look at how some other sites have handled this issue. First, check out Figures 2-1 and 2-2 to see how Target deals with a target audience accessing their site from various different devices. Figure 2-1 shows how www.target.com displays in a typical web browser, while Figure 2-2 shows that same site on an iPhone.

A 2009 Pew Internet research report found that at least 33 percent of Americans access the Internet on mobile devices. If you're part of that 33 percent, you know how hard it can be to view websites on mobile devices versus traditional computers. More often than not, it can be difficult to view and navigate complete webpages when viewed on the small screens that come with most mobile devices. Thankfully, there's a way to create a customized version of your site, just for mobile users.

Figure 2-3 shows the customized Target site that displays for most mobile users. Target's developers have included a script on the web server to "sniff out" mobile users and serve the appropriate pages. Notice how you can view the entire page at once without zooming or squinting.

TIP   *If you expect moderate mobile use, create a mobile-friendly style sheet for your site. This is discussed in more detail in Chapter 6.*

FIGURE 2-1 • Target.com viewed in Firefox on a traditional computer

Screen Area

Speaking of zooming and squinting, do you know the resolution of your screen? Or, put a different way, what is the total amount of viewing space available on your monitor, regardless of the monitor's physical size? Table 2-1 lists typical screen areas for common monitor sizes. Also, check out www.screenresolution.org for additional information.

The screen area is important when you're dealing with how much content can realistically fit onto a single webpage. Unlike pages printed on paper, where everyone sees a design at the same size (perhaps 8.5 × 11 inches), the designed webpage will vary in size according to the screen area of its viewer.

TABLE 2-1 Typical Screen Areas for Common Monitor Sizes	
Monitor Size	**Typical Screen Area**
14–15 inches	640 × 480 800 × 600
17 inches	800 × 600 1024 × 768
21 inches	1024 × 768 1152 × 870 1280 × 960 or 1280 × 1024
Laptops	Varies widely; typically 1024 × 768 or 1280 × 960
Handheld devices	Varies widely, from 150 × 150, to 320 × 240 or 320 × 480 (iPhone)

You can experiment with different resolution settings on your personal computer to see how the available screen area affects the page. One way to easily compare is to use the Web Developer toolbar for Firefox. As you can see in Figure 2-4, this highly functional toolbar includes all sorts of ways to make a web designer's life easier, not the least of which is the Resize function.

FIGURE 2-2 • Target.com viewed in Safari on an iPhone

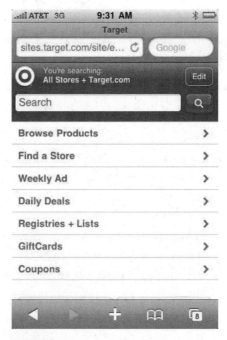

FIGURE 2-3 • A customized mobile version of Target.com viewed on an iPhone

FIGURE 2-4 • The Web Developer toolbar is a great addition to Firefox for web designers.

Choose a different screen resolution from the drop-down menu to cause the browser to be resized to fit within the selected screen size. This allows you to see how much of a design remains visible at different screen resolutions.

TIP   *If you use Internet Explorer 8, you will find these same developer options built into the browser. Choose Tools/Developer Tools to access these features. For the resizing tool, you then need to select Tools/Resize, followed by the desired screen area.*

The biggest area of concern with regard to screen sizes of traditional computers is how much horizontal space is available for content. In the early days of the Web, designers focused on the lowest common denominator (640 × 480). This means the most important content was designed to fit within a width of about 600 pixels. (The extra 40 pixels are taken up by the browser chrome—menus, scroll bars, etc.—and the operating system.)

Now, however, designers typically opt to create liquid pages, which grow and shrink according to the available screen area on the visitor's monitor. This means you must design a page that looks good both at 800 pixels wide and 1200 pixels wide, which isn't always easy to do. To help in that regard, here are some quick tips:

- Photographs don't easily scale. So if your page includes large photos, figure out how to handle the space around them as the page grows. Likewise, don't make the photos so large that they cause other important content to be hidden on smaller screens.

- Text is difficult to read when contained within really wide columns. As such, I suggest using a fixed width for text areas and filling in the surrounding space as necessary with other elements.

- Really wide pages don't typically translate well into really small spaces. Consider creating a maximum layout width so your pages don't get unwieldy and difficult to read.

- Don't forget the "fold," which refers to the point at which users will have to scroll vertically. Be sure the most important content is located "above the fold" for your target screen sizes.

TIP *To find the Web Developer toolbar shown in Figure 2-4, open the Firefox web browser and visit https://addons.mozilla.org/en-US/firefox/addon/60. Then click the Add To Firefox button to install.*

But what about designing for mobile screens? While you can add custom sizes to the Resize function within the Web Developer toolbar, it's not a true indication of how your pages will display because the web browsers used on mobile devices are so different. (More on how the browsers affect the page display shortly.) The best way to plan your designs for display on mobile screens is to work with the correct sizes when creating your mockups. For example, design tools like Photoshop allow you to create new documents according to common screen sizes. You can even choose from a list of popular mobile device screen sizes, as shown in the following illustration.

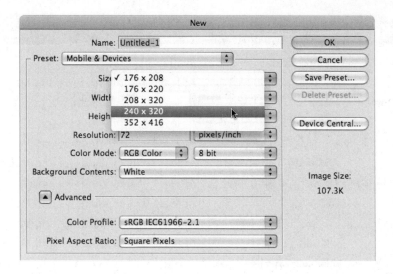

Fonts

Another consideration is that fonts are typically device-dependent. So, while Arial might be a default sans-serif font for Windows computers, Helvetica is more popular on Macs. If you select a font that is not available on your user's system, what happens? That depends on how the font is specified.

If you use a font that will ultimately be included inside of an image (such as a file saved as a JPG or GIF), you don't have to worry about the font selected. That's because the text itself ends up being saved as a picture and loaded into the webpage. But if you want to use a particular font for text that will be rendered by the browser, you must be careful about which fonts are selected.

The reason is that text generated by the browser can only be displayed using fonts loaded on the user's system. So if you specify that a section of text should display using Gill Sans, but some users don't have that font, the text will not display as you expect. In your HTML or CSS, you can actually specify a cascade of fonts, which is a list of fonts you'd like to use for the text, in order of preference. We'll cover that in more detail in Chapter 5. For now, you just need to be aware of which fonts you're selecting while designing. Table 2-2 lists the most popular fonts already loaded on the typical user's system.

Not only are the font faces themselves an issue, the size at which they display is also a variable. Text displayed on a Macintosh system typically appears smaller than its counterpart on a Windows-based PC. Many of the browsers' latest versions do help combat this problem by offering Mac users the option of displaying

TABLE 2-2 Popular and Widely Supported Web Fonts

Font Name	Example Text	Availability
Arial	ABCdefg 123456 !?@	At least 99% of Windows and Mac systems
Times New Roman	ABCdefg 123456 !?@	At least 98% of Windows and Mac systems
Verdana	ABCdefg 123456 !?@	At least 98% of Windows and Mac systems
Courier	ABCdefg 123456 !?@	At least 97% of Windows and Mac systems
Arial Black	**ABCdefg 123456 !?@**	At least 97% of Windows and Mac systems
Comic Sans MS	ABCdefg 123456 !?@	At least 96% of Windows and Mac systems
Courier New	ABCdefg 123456 !?@	At least 96% of Windows and Mac systems
Trebuchet MS	ABCdefg 123456 !?@	At least 96% of Windows and Mac systems
Georgia	ABCdefg 123456 !?@	At least 95% of Windows and Mac systems
Impact	**ABCdefg 123456 !?@**	At least 95% of Windows and 84% of Mac systems
Helvetica	ABCdefg 123456 !?@	At least 88% of Windows and 99% of Mac systems
Tahoma	ABCdefg 123456 !?@	At least 88% of Windows and 55% of Mac systems
Times	ABCdefg 123456 !?@	At least 87% of Windows and 99% of Mac systems
Arial Narrow	ABCdefg 123456 !?@	At least 84% of Windows and Mac systems
Century Gothic	ABCdefg 123456 !?@	At least 80% of Windows and 60% of Mac systems

type at Windows sizes, but that doesn't change the fact that they are different by default. This means text set to display at 12 points doesn't look the same on all systems. To compensate, make sure there is room in your designs for font sizes to change from system to system.

In summary, it's important to know the types of devices used among your site's target audience and design accordingly.

 **PROBLEM 2-1**

The list of fonts in Table 2-2 seems really limited. Are you sure there are no other fonts I can use for text in my web designs?

✓ SOLUTION

You can always create images for headlines that work better in nontraditional fonts. Image-based text doesn't require specific fonts to be loaded on a user's system because an image is essentially a "snapshot" of the text. But text contained in graphics isn't searchable or accessible by nonimage-based browsers. In addition, images are harder to maintain and update because they must be edited with a graphics program and then reuploaded to the server.

Another option that is not yet widely used but remains full of possibility, is a Flash-based font-replacement tool. Check out Mike Davidson's sIFR for one such tool that replaces plain browser text with text rendered in your typeface of choice, regardless of whether users have that font installed on their system: www.mikeindustries.com/blog/sifr.

Browsers

After identifying a few target screen sizes to design for, you also have to consider the browsers used within those screen sizes. Browsers behave differently according to the type of browser and the device used for viewing. This means not all versions of Internet Explorers (IE) are alike. In fact, Microsoft is up to at least version 8 of IE for traditional Windows-based computers, but the company never got past version 5 of the same product for Macs. The features within the browsers—even for the different Windows versions of the software—vary greatly.

TIP *To keep current on statistics about browser use, visit http://en.wikipedia.org/ wiki/Usage_share_of_web_browsers.*

IE is the most widely used browser as of this writing, but a few other standouts are definitely worth testing your designs under. Specifically, Mozilla Firefox, Apple Safari, and Google Chrome are all considered standard test browsers for me before I launch a new web design. If a site works well in each of those four browsers, I feel comfortable it will behave appropriately for the majority of traditional computer users.

When designing for multiple browsers, here are a few things to keep in mind:

- **Provide alternatives**   Some web browsers on mobile devices are text-only. That means anyone using these browsers won't see the graphics in your webpages. Therefore, if any critical information on the site is included in graphics, you must make alternative text-only options available.

- **Use standard code**   As you become more familiar with HTML, you'll learn that some elements are handled better by certain browsers, and some tags are completely ignored by other browsers. Try to stick with standard HTML as specified by the World Wide Web Consortium (W3C—www.w3.org), and you'll be more likely to reach the widest audience.

- **Test, test, and test some more**   Don't assume your page looks good in Firefox just because it works well in IE. Confirm it.

NOTE   *Chapter 9 talks more about testing sites in different browsers and using various devices.*

Bandwidth

Another aspect of web design that is unique is bandwidth. When designing an advertisement for a magazine, you don't have to consider how many kilobytes the file is. (That's a good thing because most print ads end up being many *megabytes* in file size!) Unfortunately, website visitors are definitely concerned with the size of your files.

The term bandwidth refers to the speed at which web users access the Internet. Users who log on to the Internet from computers using telephone modems (yes, many people still do) often access at speeds of 28.8 to 56 Kbps (kilobits per second), while cable and DSL (digital subscriber line) users' speeds increase significantly to an average of 2 to 3 Mbps (megabits per second) or 2000 to 3000 Kbps. Anyone using FiOS can see speeds double that of cable. And mobile users' bandwidth can run the entire gamut: Stationary users can see speeds similar to cable and DSL users, while those in a moving vehicle only receive about 350/Kbps.

With such a varied bandwidth selection, you must design your graphics accordingly. The larger the size of your graphic files, the longer they'll take to download onto a user's screen. Sit in front of your web browser and slowly count to ten. Are you willing to wait that long for a webpage to download? Many people wait less than ten seconds before giving up and moving on. Therefore, you have precious little time with which to grab someone's attention and invite him to stay longer.

To estimate the size of a webpage, you must add together the sizes of the text (the HTML and CSS files) and the images (the GIFs and JPEGs). Using Table 2-3, a page totaling 500K in content might take five seconds to download over a 3G network in a moving vehicle, but less than a second if the same user were stationary or accessing the page from a desktop computer connected through FiOS.

If you're creating webpages for the general public, a good rule of thumb is to limit your main content pages to around 200K in size. HTML and CSS files typically weigh in at around 1 to 3K, so that leaves the vast majority of the total for other content such as graphics. This guideline can often restrict you to using the most important and necessary graphics on a page. There will always be exceptions to this, particularly for pages with a designer's portfolio or a video archive.

Color

Right from the start, screen-based color is unlike print-based color because they use two unique color palettes. All color used in screen-based designs is created with the RGB (red, green, blue) color palette, as opposed to the print-standard CMYK (cyan, magenta, yellow, black) palette. In addition, while graphics created for the printed page look relatively the same to all who view them, web graphics may look vastly different from one computer to the next. This variation

TABLE 2-3 Average Download Speeds for Popular Connection Types	
Connection Type	**Average Download per Second**
T1/T3 network	1000 to 40,000 Kbit+
FiOS	5000 to 30,000 Kbit
Cable/DSL/3G (stationary)	2000 to 5000 Kbit
3G (moving)	100 to 350 Kbit
Modem/dial-up	6 to 7 Kbit

in color can be caused by distinctions in another type of color palette—the one that ships with the computer's operating system—as well as lighting and gamma issues related to the user's monitor.

In fact, only 216 colors will display uniformly across all Mac and Windows systems (but even those colors can be affected by lighting and gamma issues). Those 216 colors are commonly referred to as "web-safe" colors.

TIP   *Refer to www.visibone.com/color/chart_847.gif for a visual representation of a web-safe color chart, complete with RGB and HTML values for each color.*

In the past, web designers were leery of using anything but web-safe colors, for fear their choices wouldn't be available on every user's system. When colors weren't available, the browser sometimes displays those areas of the page with completely different colors. This often caused webpages to look awful on some systems, even though they were beautiful on others. But as computer systems and monitors have gotten better, the risk that web users will not be able to see a particular color on a webpage has decreased. Because of this, most web designers now ignore the web-safe palette altogether in favor of whatever color looks good.

Still Struggling

If you feel a bit green when it comes to color theory, you can easily learn a few key concepts by visiting some excellent online color resources like http://www.colormatters.com/colortheory.html and http://en.wikipedia.org/wiki/Color_theory.

Contrast

Even though you can use any of the colors in the RGB color spectrum, there are certain considerations in regard to which colors you select. Perhaps the most important color consideration for screen design is contrast. Whatever colors you select, you need to make sure the page offers enough contrast to allow any text to be readable, regardless of the user's lighting. This is especially true when mixing hues with similar values. While it can be beautiful to mix a mid-tone blue with a mid-tone green, some people just won't see the difference.

So what creates contrast? Here are a few ideas:

- **Change the hue**   Place a red box next to a yellow one, and you've achieved contrast because of the difference in hues.

- **Change the value**   White text on a black background causes a distinct contrast because of the variation in value (shade) of the colors.

- **Change the pattern**   A striped background next to a solid color background creates contrast because of the divergent patterns.

- **Change the movement**   Good design moves your eyes around a page according to what's most important. Contrast in movement occurs when you design with the intention of gently moving the user's eye down the page, perhaps with a gradation of color, and then abruptly stop them with a different shape, filled with a different color.

Contrast can be good when it succeeds in helping you focus the user's attention; but it can also be bad. Bad contrast typically happens when the designer loses focus on what's important—that is, creating a readable site that fulfills its goals.

While you're thinking about the contrast of your designs, don't forget about the text color—both foreground and background. Yes, even I choose colored background behind text from time to time, but the truth is that white is usually the best color for backgrounds behind big chunks of text. Let's face it: It's often easier to read dark text on a light/white background than the opposite. White text on dark/black backgrounds can be beautifully moving, but is not typically appropriate for large areas of text (i.e., anything more than a few sentences of text).

TIP   *When it comes to smaller bits of text, such as in navigation or headlines, it can be quite beneficial to use dark backgrounds to add contrast and draw attention.*

Contrast is of particular interest to anyone who is colorblind. A few online tools can help you visualize what people who are colorblind see when viewing certain colors. Check out www.newmanservices.com/colorblind/default.asp to see one example. Or you can download a desktop-based tool to help you analyze the contrast of your designs: www.stainlessvision.com/projects/colour-contrast-visualiser and www.vischeck.com/vischeck/vischeckURL.php are good options.

If you're using a graphics editor such as Photoshop to build your design, one method of quickly checking the contrast of a design is to switch temporarily to grayscale color mode. Viewing colors in grayscale can help identify problem areas. Another more low-tech method of spot-checking color contrast is to squint your eyes while looking at the design. Areas with little contrast tend to blur when viewed with squinted eyes. While this may be okay for color meant only as a background texture, it's not appropriate for body copy or headlines.

Color Tools

If you need some inspiration to create harmonious color schemes, you'll find a lot of online tools to help. Consider one of the following to get you started:

- http://www.colorschemedesigner.com
- http://www.colourlovers.com
- http://kuler.adobe.com

Navigation

Obviously, navigation is a big part of any screen design. Print designers don't have to worry about making buttons available to access additional information (although it could be argued that a link to a company's website and other contact information might be considered the "navigation" of a print advertisement, but I digress…).

The navigation of a site includes links to related content. So the first thing you need to do is identify all the links your pages need to include, starting with the home page. Not every page on a site needs to be accessible from the home page, so you must figure out which ones should be included, and then of those, which are the most important. You can usually divide the links into level of navigation: primary, secondary, tertiary, or supporting.

Primary navigation is typically included on every page of the site. These are the most important links that must be accessible everywhere. In many cases, these are the navigation bars found across the top of webpages.

Secondary navigation commonly houses the department-level navigation that is included only in certain sections of the site. So if you had your primary navigation across the top of the page, as shown in this illustration, you might include the secondary navigation down the left side.

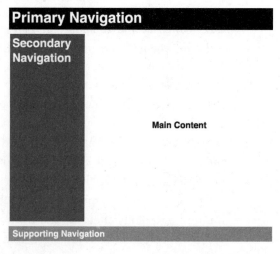

Then, the tertiary or other supporting navigation might include miscellaneous pages that don't clearly fit into the department-level or primary navigation. Commonly included in this type of navigation are pages like Privacy Policy and Terms of Use. Many designers also include text links to key sections of the site for easy access.

Complex sites can often include many levels of navigation on the same page. The trick is getting them all to work together to offer plenty of options without being overwhelming. Let's take a look at a large, complex site to see exactly how this might be accomplished. Visit www.amazon.com, then review Figure 2-5 to see how I've labeled the different types of navigation to make them easier to discuss.

- Block A links to all the departments on the site. This is the *hierarchical navigation block* that links to the site's structure, since this site is primarily organized by department. For this website, the hierarchical navigation block acts as the primary method of navigation. (Refer back to Chapter 1 for explanations on the different ways you can organize content.)

FIGURE 2-5 · Amazon.com page with navigation blocks outlined

- Block B is what I call the *dynamic navigation block*, because the resulting pages (search results, cart contents, and so on) are different for each visitor. On Amazon.com, dynamic navigation is a secondary navigation method.
- Block C is commonly referred to as *local navigation*, in that those links are local to the particular section currently being browsed (in this case, the Kindle Store). Note that these links will not appear when another section of the site is being viewed. This e-commerce site depends on its local navigation as an important tertiary method of navigation.
- Block D shows *shortcut navigation*, which offers one-click access to essential functions of the site. For Amazon, the Buy Now button is perhaps the most important link available. Shortcut links are typically included in a variety of places on the site and don't live in just one department or section.
- Block E, *reference* or *related navigation*, is a different type of navigation that is custom to each page, as related content is pulled from a database behind the scenes. For the Amazon page, that's a display of items other customers also bought after purchasing the book currently being viewed.

TIP *Another commonly used navigation method is* **breadcrumb navigation.** *Sites with deep local navigation often use "breadcrumb trails" to help orient users and provide easy access to pages along their path in the site.*

The Amazon site is certainly filled with plenty of options for the user. Most likely, your first few websites will be much less complex in nature. So let's look at the navigation for a sample small business, which is at the opposite end of the spectrum in terms of navigation. Visit www.lawnscape.us and refer to Figure 2-6 to see a page on this site with a few very basic methods of navigation.

After you identify the levels of navigation, you need to figure out how to visually represent each bucket of links. Things such as underlined text and tabs work well because everyone understands these as you can click for more content. If you spend any amount of time on the Web, you'll probably see a lot of the same types of visual navigation metaphors, such as:

- Tabs
- Vertical navigation bars docked to the left side of the screen, with each link on a separate line
- Horizontal navigation bars docked to the top of the screen, with links separated by characters such as the pipe (|), dash (–), bullet (•), and forward slash (/)

FIGURE 2-6 • Lawnscape.us page with navigation blocks outlined

- Graphical buttons
- Text directory of links
- Inline text links that appear within the content itself
- Form elements, such as drop-down menus and search boxes
- Collapsible and flyout menus, where clicking a closed section opens it and reveals additional links

- Tag clouds (check out http://en.wikipedia.org/wiki/Tag_cloud for a visual explanation of these)
- Sliders, where additional options can be accessed by clicking buttons on the right and/or left of the current option

TIP *Looking for some creative navigation ideas? Check out http://patterntap.com/tap/collection/navigation.*

When you sit down to design a site, consider the content and its target audience to help determine which type(s) of navigation works best for your particular situation.

Transitions

Finally, I don't want to finish this section on unique aspects of screen design without mentioning webpage transitions. A transition refers to what happens when a user attempts to access a new piece of content. Does the entire page change? Does the new content appear in place of the old content, using the same layout and structure? Or is the new content placed in a new "layer" floating on top of the current page? What about pages that appear in completely new (pop-up) browser windows?

If you have a Facebook account, you've probably seen a variety of transition methods. For example, when new posts are flowed into the news feed, only the content within the news feed changes (older posts move down the page). And when someone posts a link to a YouTube video, you initially see a small preview of that movie. When you click the preview, the video grows to full size and the content around it adjusts accordingly. These are all effective ways of transitioning between content without requiring additional user input.

Because transitions affect how a user accesses content, it's important for the design to incorporate a transition plan for the site.

Layout

In Chapter 1, I mentioned that a wireframe document can be used to help refine a webpage layout before the page is actually designed in a graphics editor. A good web layout addresses the user's needs while fulfilling the site owner's goals.

Obviously, this can be done in a variety of ways, so there is no one "right" way to lay out a webpage. But here are a few guidelines to consider:

- Provide consistent navigation (as discussed in the preceding section).
- Keep content accessible and relevant.
- Orient the user (help the user recognize what page he's viewing within your site's structure), usually with a relevant page title.
- Maintain an appropriate content hierarchy.

With regard to the final bullet point, the most important thing you can give your users is reliable, relevant, up-to-date content. With this being the case, the content should always be the first priority within the structure of the page, and it should serve to achieve the business objectives for that page and for the entire site.

I remember my graphic design instructors in art school repeating over and over again: "What's the first thing you want viewers to notice on your page?" That should be the same question you ask yourself when developing the content structure for webpages.

Remember that, as the designer, you're in the driver's seat when it comes to prioritizing what users see on the page. While it might be tempting to make every element on the page animated, moving, glowing, or brightly colored, use these extras sparingly. Usability study after study shows viewers are drawn to the real meat of the site, much more than the glitz and glamour, and it's the content that keeps them coming back.

Also, when designing the page structure, think about how you look at a webpage. You'll probably agree that you look at the center first, and then move your eyes around the page according to what jumps out at you. Other common first glances include the top-left portion of the screen (close to those back buttons!) and the right edge (near the scroll bar). Check out www.useit .com/eyetracking for some eye-tracking studies on where people look when viewing webpages.

In journalism, you typically put the most important details in the beginning of a story, as not all readers will make it to the end. The Web is the same, at least in that not everyone makes it to the bottom of the screen. Therefore, the top portion should contain enough details to encourage users to keep reading, but not so much that they are overwhelmed and don't know where to look.

Creating Design Mockups

Well, you've read all about the unique aspects of designing for screens, but you may still be wondering exactly how to get started. Suppose you read through the first chapter and did some planning and are now ready to begin work in a graphics editor. You may have some ideas as to the colors you'd like to use, or maybe you have a particular navigation method in mind. Hopefully, you've spent some time sketching possible layouts and have selected one or two to move forward with. That's all great. Now it's time to cement those ideas with a comprehensive design mockup (also called a comp).

I typically start in Photoshop, with a new file that's roughly 1000 pixels wide by 800 pixels tall, at 72 dpi (dots per inch). This is a good size for most of my projects (as of this writing, I am typically targeting a screen resolution of at least 1024 × 768), as it is large enough to give me some room to work. Consider your target audience before selecting the size of your page.

After you create your blank file, begin by importing all of the various page elements, such as the logo and any existing company graphics. Because your file will probably grow to contain many layers, I suggest taking advantage of the organization options in your graphics program. For example, if you're using Photoshop, Figure 2-7 shows how you can gather related layers into groups to help keep your layers palette uncluttered.

NOTE *Learning a graphics program like Photoshop is beyond the scope of this book, but I will offer related tips as much as possible. Refer back to some of the outside resources mentioned in Chapter 1 to learn more about Photoshop and other graphics editors.*

From time to time, there may be aspects of the page that you need to import from other sources. That might include stock media (which is discussed in the next section), sample text, or placeholders for elements to be created by the browser. For example, if your mockup shows a page that contains form elements, you could take screen captures of those elements and paste them into the mockup to give a client an idea how it will look when it's all finished. Or, you can download copies of all sorts of form elements from a site like www .webdesignerstoolkit.com.

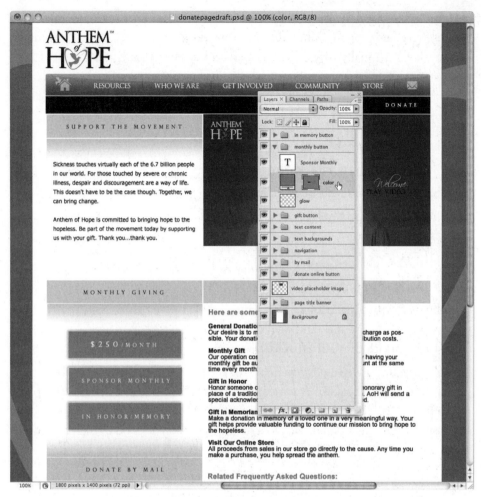

FIGURE 2-7 · Photoshop lets you organize layers into groups.

Stock Media

The use of photography and multimedia can often add a sense of professionalism to a website, but many businesses don't have the budget to hire photographers or artists. Thankfully, plenty of stock companies offer royalty-free media that can be used for almost any purpose, except for resale.

TIP   *Royalty-free does not mean the item is free. But it does mean you (the purchaser) are permitted to use the item multiple times without having to pay an additional fee beyond the original purchase price. Read the license to determine for what types of projects you can use a particular item.*

Tempted to search for "free" images using Google or another search engine? Just because you find a photo online that fits your project perfectly doesn't mean it's fair to use it, especially if your project is for a business. While you may find free media online, those are typically restricted to noncommercial use only. If you can't get permission from the owner, it's best to move on and look for something else.

Here are a few places where you might find suitable stock media:

- http://www.istockphoto.com
- http://www.shutterstock.com
- http://office.microsoft.com/clipart
- http://www.gettyimages.com
- http://www.fotosearch.com
- http://punchstock.com
- http://www.photos.com
- http://www.clipart.com

Sharing Copies of Your Mockups

If you're creating a website for someone else, you undoubtedly have to show that person your design mockups at some point. There are plenty of ways to accomplish this, but you want to make sure you have a way of managing the mockups in case the site owner wants to refer back to a previous version later on in the project.

As a freelancer, I typically use one of two methods to manage this process:

- **Create a mini-site on my personal site**   Sometimes I create a page on my website where I store and track design mockups. Figure 2-8 shows an example of how I handled this for one client. The client could click the links to display each mockup within the browser to see how the final page will look surrounded by the browser chrome.

- **Use an online document storage location**   Other times (depending on the nature of the project), I simply create a folder for the client files on my online document storage site. I use Drop Box (www.dropbox.com), but you can use whichever online storage site you're comfortable with. I love Drop Box because as soon as I add a file to a shared folder, it alerts the other users of that folder to the presence of the new or updated file. (And hey, it doesn't hurt that the first 2GB of storage space is free. Plus, if you signup using this referral link, we both get 250 MB of extra space, free: www.dropbox.com/referrals/NTM4ODE5OTE5.)

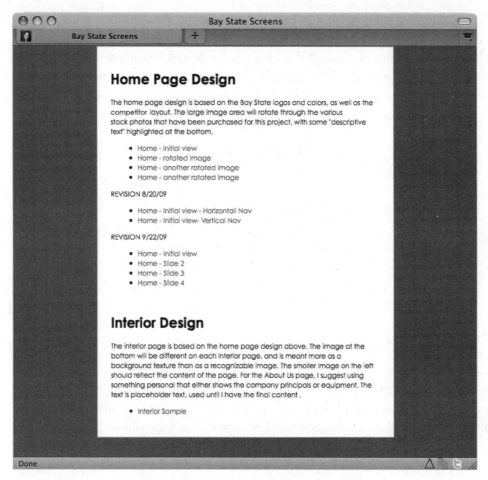

FIGURE 2-8 • One method of sharing mockups is to create a mini-site like this.

TIP *I don't suggest managing a project through e-mail only. It's too easy to lose e-mails and overwrite files.*

Alternatively, you can use an online document or project management tool to share and manage not only your mockups but also any related client communication. Some popular packages include:

- Basecamp (http://www.basecamphq.com)
- FreelanceSuite (http://www.freelancesuite.com)
- Zoho Projects (http://projects.zoho.com)

Finally, it might make sense to collaborate with clients and/or team members through a tool such as Google Docs (http://docs.google.com). One of my clients prefers this method of communication to track deliverables, tasks, and deadlines. We even use a shared spreadsheet for tasks. About nine team members have access to the spreadsheet, and we each can mark tasks as complete or add new to-dos. Best of all, it's free and requires no HTML coding for anyone involved.

I encourage you to check out each of the options I've listed to determine the method that best fits your work style.

TIP   *To show someone how a mockup will look when viewed in a browser without requiring the person to view the mockup inside of a browser window, consider including a copy of the browser window within your presentation. You can download free browser templates from www.webdesignerstoolkit.com.*

Chapter Summary

When it is time to create page mockups for a web development project, you must consider how the delivery method affects the design process. In this chapter, I outlined several of the ways in which the process is affected. Specifically, devices, browsers, bandwidth, color, navigation, and transitions were covered. As the designer, you will need to determine how each of these affects your particular project and what you can do to ensure the end users receive the content as you intend.

In the next chapter, we move on to breaking apart the mockups into text and image files, and then preparing them for storage on the web server.

QUIZ

Choose the correct responses to each of the multiple-choice questions.

1. **What is a typical screen area for a web-enabled, handheld device such as an iPhone?**
   A. 100 × 76
   B. 320 × 480
   C. 640 × 480
   D. 800 × 600

2. **What does it mean to create liquid webpages?**
   A. The page layout can be customized by the user.
   B. The page content can be customized by the user.
   C. The page layout grows and shrinks according to the available screen area.
   D. The page content grows and shrinks according to the available screen area.

3. **Which is *not* a font commonly found on at least 95 percent of Windows and Mac systems?**
   A. Arial
   B. Verdana
   C. Trebuchet
   D. Century Gothic
   E. Times New Roman

4. **Which is the most popular web browser for traditional computer systems?**
   A. Safari
   B. Firefox
   C. Chrome
   D. Internet Explorer

5. **What is the most important reason to use standard code recognized by the W3C?**
   A. To meet federal guidelines
   B. To address all of the site goals
   C. To conform to web regulations
   D. To reach the widest possible audience
   E. To take advantage of the newest features

6. **Which best describes the phrase *audience bandwidth,* with regard to web design?**
   A. The rate at which content uploads
   B. The rate at which content downloads
   C. The speed at which designers access the Internet
   D. The speed at which web users access the Internet

7. Which connection type has an average download speed of 350 Kbps?
   A. FiOS
   B. Cable
   C. 56K modem
   D. 3G (moving)
   E. 3G (stationary)

8. How many colors are contained within what is commonly referred to as the "web-safe" palette?
   A. 64
   B. 216
   C. 256
   D. 1024
   E. Millions

9. Which statement best describes how shortcut navigation might be used on a website?
   A. It provides access to content customized for each user.
   B. It offers one-click access to essential functions of the site.
   C. It provides related content typically pulled from a database behind the scenes.
   D. It helps orient users and provides easy access to pages along their path in the site.

10. Which best describes the term *transition,* as related to web design?
   A. Launching a new browser window
   B. How a user determines which link to click
   C. What happens when a user attempts to access a new piece of content
   D. The method used to display multimedia content without launching a new window

chapter **3**

Building the Pages

After you've completed a mockup, with everything looking just how you'd like it to display in the browser, what's next? Wouldn't it be great if we could wiggle our noses and have the graphics editor do all the dirty work to make the file web-ready? Yes, and no.

Most web graphics editors do include some options to speed up the process and make it almost effortless, but you'll undoubtedly need to do a bit of tidying up around your files to get them in tip-top shape for web viewing. That's exactly what this chapter focuses on: the basics of building pages to be viewed in a browser.

CHAPTER OBJECTIVES

In this chapter, you will

- Identify web-friendly file formats for images
- Determine how the compression method affects the image
- Slice mockups for efficient web delivery
- Select the best method of exporting images and text for your project
- Identify basic HTML header and body content
- Recognize basic CSS content

Web File Formats

First, let's spend a few minutes covering exactly which types of files can be viewed in a browser. If you've ever tried to open a Photoshop (.psd) or Flash (.flv) file in your browser, you've probably found out that doesn't work very well. Those file formats are used for building pages in Photoshop and Flash, but not for viewing in a browser. In effect, .psd and .flv files contain more information than the browser needs. So, you need to flatten and condense those files in a way that is suitable for display in a browser.

Key Terms

Image files are typically saved as one of three browser-friendly formats: .jpg, .gif, and .png. (Flash files are typically exported as .swf files, but can also be saved in a variety of other web-friendly formats, depending on the project.) Before we cover the details about GIFs, JPEGs, and PNGs, I need to define a few new terms that relate to those file formats.

Compression Methods

Web graphic file formats take your original image and compress it to make it smaller (in file size) for Web and e-mail delivery. Two basic types of compression methods are used for web graphics: lossy and lossless.

Lossy compression requires data to be removed permanently from the image to compress the file and make it smaller. Typically, areas with small details are lost as the level of lossy compression is increased. Lossless compression is the opposite of lossy, in that no data is lost when the file is compressed. In these cases, the actual data looks the same whether it's compressed or uncompressed.

NOTE *While lossless compression does not result in a loss of data, the file can change in appearance if colors are removed during compression. I comment more on this in the section about GIFs.*

Color Mode

All web images are displayed in the standard screen-based RGB (red, green, blue) color mode. But when you compress an image to make it smaller in file size, it can be helpful to remove some of the colors.

For this reason, some web file formats have smaller, more restricted color palettes. Others are capable of handling millions of colors, and instead shrink the file size in other ways. Table 3-1 (shown after the "Key Terms" section) identifies the number of colors available in each web file format discussed.

Transparency

When you view an image and are able to see through parts of it, that image is said to have transparency. Some graphics editors show this transparency by displaying a gray and white checkerboard behind the image, as indicated in the following screen capture taken from Photoshop.

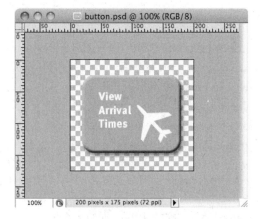

TIP   *When a web graphic contains transparency, the webpage's background color or background image shows through in the transparent areas.*

File types that support transparency fall into two categories: binary and variable. Binary transparency means any given pixel is either transparent or opaque. Variable transparency, also known as alpha channel, allows pixels to be partially transparent or partially opaque; therefore, it is capable of creating subtle gradations.

Certain file types don't support transparency at all. If the image shown in the previous illustration were to be saved in a format not supporting transparency, the areas shown in a checkerboard would be filled in with a solid color.

Interlaced/Progressive

Have you ever viewed a webpage and noticed that a web graphic first appeared blocky or fuzzy before gradually coming into focus? If you frequently access the Web via high-speed connection, you probably haven't encountered this as much as you might have with a slower connection, or as much as you might with a web-enabled mobile device.

When you save web graphics, you have the option to make them interlaced or progressive (depending on the file format), which essentially just means the graphic is displayed at multiple levels of clarity, from blurry to clear.

Noninterlaced/nonprogressive images must be fully loaded before the browser displays them in a webpage. If you have a large image on a page accessed with a slower connection, users may see only blank space while the file is downloading. If it takes too long, users may leave your site. For this reason, it is helpful to web users if designers save web graphics as interlaced or progressive.

GIF

Originally designed for online use in the 1980s, GIF uses a compression method that is well suited to certain types of web graphics. This method, called LZW compression, is lossless. Even though that means no data is lost when the file is compressed, the nature of the GIF file format is such that it does not support more than 256 colors. Compare that to other graphics file formats that support millions of colors, and you can see how this lossless format isn't completely lossless.

NOTE *GIF is officially pronounced with a soft g.*

Because GIFs are limited to a certain number of colors, the following types of images lend themselves to being saved in this format:

- Text
- Line drawings
- Cartoons
- Flat-color graphics

JPEG

The JPEG file format (pronounced jay-peg) was created by the Joint Photo-graphic Experts Group, who sought to create a format more suitable for com-pressing photographic imagery than GIF.

One major difference between GIFs and JPEGs is that JPEGs don't contain an exact set of colors, but are capable of displaying as many colors as are neces-sary for the file. However, when you save a photograph as a JPEG, you might consider all the colors in the file to be merely *recommended*, because the lossy compression could require some colors to be altered. In addition, all web JPEG files must be in the RGB (red, green, blue) color mode, as opposed to the print standard of CMYK (cyan, magenta, yellow, black).

The JPEG format is well suited for the vast majority of your photographic web images.

PNG

PNG (pronounced P-N-G or ping) stands for Portable Network Graphics and is the newest and most flexible of these three graphic file formats. Many designers consider PNG to be the "best of both worlds" as it offers some advantages over GIFs and JPEGs.

NOTE *PNG was recognized as an international standard in late 2003.*

My favorite aspect of the PNG format is its ability to save files with alpha transparency. This feature (which is not available with GIFs or JPEGs) means you can place an irregularly shaped image on top of a multicolored background seamlessly. In other words, you could have one image fade into another without an obvious edge between them.

An additional benefit of PNG is its gamma correction. The PNG file format has the capability to correct for differences in how computers and monitors interpret color values. However, as of this writing, no browser has yet to support this feature.

So… why isn't this the only file format I'm discussing if it's so good? Because PNG wasn't an original web file format, users of older browsers needed to download a plug-in to view web graphics saved in the PNG format. Even though all modern browsers support the basic characteristics of PNGs, web designers have been slow to uniformly adopt this feature-packed file format.

Still Struggling

Want to read more about how the PNG file format compares to GIF and JPEG? Check out http://en.wikipedia.org/wiki/Portable_Network_Graphics.

TABLE 3-1 Web File Format Characteristics

	GIF	JPEG	PNG
Color Mode(s)	8–bit (Restricted to no more than 256 exact colors)	24–bit (Millions of colors)	8–bit 24–bit 32–bit (24–bit plus alpha channel)
Compression Method	Lossless	Lossy	Lossless
Animation	Supported	Not supported	Not supported
Transparency	Supported (Binary only)	Not supported	Supported (Variable/alpha)

Table 3-1 compares the basic characteristics of each of these three file formats. Regardless of which one you select for a particular situation, remember to test your files to ensure they perform to your satisfaction in all your target browsers.

TIP *The 32-bit color format is similar to 24-bit color because it also has millions of colors. However, 32-bit color has an additional masking channel, which can be used for alpha transparency. (An alpha channel is essentially a place within the file where you can store extra information about it.) Be sure to thoroughly test any pages using PNG alpha transparency, as it is not supported by some browsers.*

Slicing Designs

A lot of beginning designers try to save their entire designs as single images for the webpage. While this might be the easiest way to get a design from a graphics editor to the browser, it is not the best for our site's visitors for a couple of reasons. First, a single large image will undoubtedly be quite hefty in file size, which translates to longer download times for users. Second, a single large image isn't flexible enough to work well in the variety of different viewing conditions discussed in the previous chapter.

In addition, text is best left to the browser to render, to allow the user to increase or decrease the font size as needed. Text rendered by the browser is also searchable (whereas text contained within an image is not) and easily linked to related information.

For all these reasons, it is best to slice your design up into individual images and chunks of text to be put together by the browser. The good news is that all the graphic editors I mentioned previously contain slicing tools to make this task easier.

Using Guides

To get started, you can draw "guides" across an image to help you identify where each individual piece begins and ends. This is important because every image on your webpage is, ultimately, saved in a rectangular box. No, you can't save a triangular-shaped GIF. All GIFs, JPEGs, and PNGs must have four sides and must be rectangles. You can use transparency to make things look like they aren't rectangular but, in reality, everything is contained within some sort of box.

Because everything is contained in those boxes, you might need to break some elements up across several boxes to achieve the desired result. These pieces likely are going to be put back together with code. Think of it as a tic-tac-toe game, in which each element on the page is placed in a different square of the game. When you draw guides on your design, you're drawing the edges of those game squares.

TIP *While the exact steps vary according to the graphics editor being used, most allow you to simply drag from the horizontal or vertical rulers in to wherever you want the guide to be located.*

Creating Slices

Just like drawing guides, the specific steps necessary to create slices depend on which graphics editor is being used. In Photoshop and Fireworks, the steps are essentially the same: You use the Slice Tool to create slices. After selecting this tool from the tool palette, draw boxes around each of the elements to define slice borders. Figure 3-1 shows a design mockup that is sliced and ready to be exported.

In Figure 3-1, notice I only drew two slices on the page, but Photoshop displays at least seven. Because everything must fit into a "grid," the application basically fills in the gaps around my slices (which it refers to as "user-slices") with its own slices.

I created this slice to contain
the top banner image.

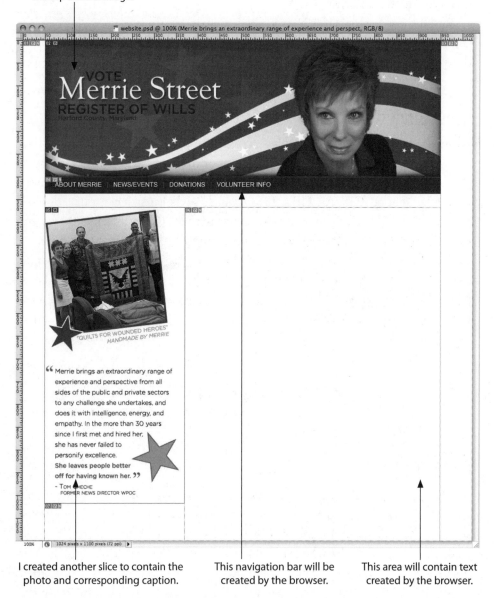

I created another slice to contain the
photo and corresponding caption.

This navigation bar will be
created by the browser.

This area will contain text
created by the browser.

FIGURE 3-1 · Sample design mockup that has been sliced in Photoshop

TIP   *If you're using Fireworks CS4 or CS5, you can quickly create slices by SHIFT-selecting page elements and then right-clicking (or CTRL-clicking for Mac) to select Insert Rectangular Slice.*

Naming Slices

After you've created all the necessary slices, it's time to name them. Here are the basic steps to do that in the two most popular web graphics programs:

- In Fireworks, you can do this in two different places. You can select the slice and name it in the Property Inspector, or you can add the name after clicking the web layer in the Layers panel. (If you don't see the Property Inspector, choose Window | Properties.)
- In Photoshop, you use the Slice Selection tool to double-click the slice and access the Slice Options dialog box.

Regardless of which program you use, it's important that you come up with an appropriate naming convention for your site's assets (supporting files) before you start naming. Here are a few guidelines to consider:

- *Use descriptive filenames that might increase your site's search traffic.* For example, suppose each news article on the site displays a photograph of the article's author. You might name each photo something like "article1-photo." While that works great to help you identify which photo goes where, it doesn't actually tell you much about the contents of the photo. An alternative might be "joesmith-photo." Not only does this identify the image as being a photo of Joe Smith, but it allows anyone searching for "joe smith photo" to find the image.
- *Avoid numbering slices unless they will be used on a page that will never need to be updated.* It's very tempting to name images with schemes such as "home-01.jpg," "home-02.jpg," and so on. The main problem with this type of convention comes in the site maintenance. Suppose you need to add an image in between 02 and 03. Do you use 02b? It can get real confusing, real fast.
- *Use dashes instead of underscores.* Underscores have been a common way to separate words in filenames, because spaces aren't allowed. A better choice is the dash, because it is more easily recognized when the filename is linked (and underlines by default).
- *Be consistent with regard to case.* It's fine to mix cases, as in JoeSmith-photo, provided you can remember your naming convention and stick with it. If you name a file JoeSmith-photo and then link to joesmith-photo, you'll end up with a broken link.

NOTE   *Your web graphics program may include the option to automatically name each slice (such as slice01, slice02, and so on). While this can be helpful if you need to name a lot of slices, it works best if you customize the settings so you have a better idea what each slice contains. In other words, AboutUs01 and News01 make more sense than slice01 and slice02.*

Exporting Designs

After you've named your slices, it's time to optimize them. This means you select the desired file format (GIF, JPEG, or PNG) and the appropriate settings (number of colors, dithering, and so on). Here are a few tips to help you through that process:

- **A smaller color palette makes GIFs smaller**   Remember that images saved as GIFs have a limited number of colors (no more than 256). The fewer colors present, the smaller the file size. Therefore, it's important to only use as many colors as is necessary to accurately display the image. Few GIFs actually need all 256 colors. Try reducing the number of colors all the way down to 8 or 16, and work your way back up as high as you need to go to make the image look acceptable.

- **Dithering adds file size**   When you reduce the number of colors in an image's palette, the program must know what to do with the areas that contain the colors being removed. If you tell the program to use dithering (you can specify the amount of dithering between 0 and 100 percent), it may use multiple colors in a checkerboard pattern in those areas to give the appearance of the color you removed. If no dithering is used, the removed colors are replaced with another solid color. Dithering can be useful in providing the appearance of gradations or subtle color shifts—but be forewarned that it adds to the file size.

- **Photographs don't usually require high-quality JPEG settings**   When you save an image as a JPEG, you choose between several quality levels. The highest level has the least amount of compression and, therefore, the least amount of data removed. The lowest-quality JPEG has the most data removed and often looks blotchy, blurry, and rough. I usually save JPEG images with a medium quality. Your decision will be based on the lowest quality you can use without compromising the integrity of the file: The lower the quality level, the lower the file size.

TIP *JPEGs are most commonly used for images of a photographic nature and those that feature color gradations.*

- **The PNG format is flexible enough to fit a variety of situations**   When saving a file as a PNG, you must first choose how many colors to include. Saving as a PNG-8 uses an exact palette of 256 colors or less, just like the GIF format. Alternatively, you can save with millions of colors (PNG-24), similar to the JPEG format. If you're working with an image that requires multiple levels of transparency, use the PNG-24 mode with the option for transparency selected, as shown in the following illustration. Remember that older browsers (particularly IE 6 and earlier) have trouble displaying transparent PNGs. Be sure to test your pages thoroughly if you take advantage of that feature.

Using PNG-24 transparency enables these coupons to float seamlessly on top of the webpage background. Photoshop uses a checkerboard pattern to indicate which areas will be transparent.

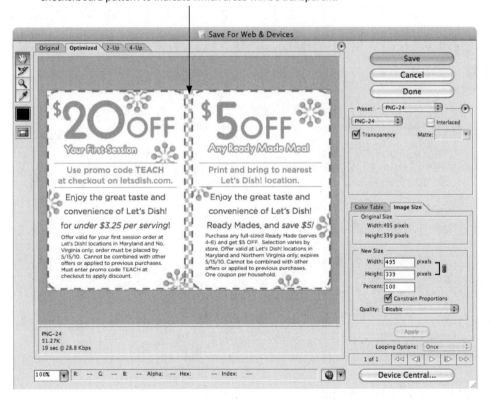

Choosing the best file format for your web graphics is a bit like shopping—you are looking for the format that looks the best but costs the least. In this case, the cost comes in download time for webpage visitors. Thankfully, any graphics program geared toward web design will let you visually compare how each format affects your file. In fact, most programs offer a way to compare all three formats at once.

Photoshop's Save for Web feature (shown in Figure 3-2) allows you to compare up to four versions of an image at once. Figure 3-2 compares the original image to three other versions, each using different export settings. In this example, the PNG-24 is the largest in terms of file size (6.773k), but is the only one that allows the shadow behind the button to fade to transparent.

The GIF version does include transparency, but it will only display appropriately if the background of the page matches the matte color (which in this case is white). This happens because GIF files only support one level of transparency. The JPEG

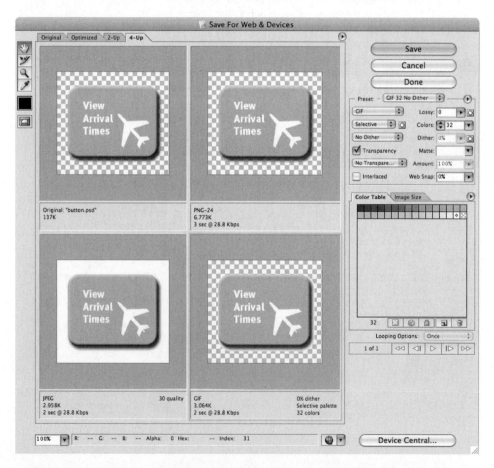

FIGURE 3-2 · Photoshop's Save for Web comparing GIF, JPEG, and PNG formats for a button

version is the smallest in file size, but shows the most pixilation and dithering that occurs with its file compression, particularly in areas of solid color.

There is not one format that is perfect for every file. In the end, you'll have to weigh the various options to determine which file format is appropriate in each situation. When all your slices are named and optimized, your final step is to allow the graphics program to do its part and save each file. You can export all the slices at once or individually if you prefer.

Exporting Slices

The steps for exporting slices vary slightly depending on which graphics program you're using.

NOTE *Many designers begin by designing in Photoshop, then switch to Fireworks to take advantage of the great web export options. If you decide to go that route, simple save your file as a .psd in Photoshop and then open that same .psd in Fireworks before continuing with the export options.*

- In Fireworks, you can quickly export a single slice by right-clicking (CTRL-clicking in Mac) the slice and choosing "Export Selected Slice." Or, if you are ready to export all the slices in your file at once, choose File | Export, and then specify where you want to save the file(s) before clicking the Export button.

- In Photoshop, the only way to access the Export options is to choose File | Save For Web & Devices. The resulting window contains options for naming and optimizing your slices (if you have not already done so). Then, if you want to export a single slice, select it with the Slice Select tool before clicking the Save button. The last step is specifying where the slice(s) should be saved. At that point, you can also tell Photoshop whether to output All Slices, All User Slices, or Selected Slice.

Still Struggling

Lots of online tutorials help walk you through exporting slices in whichever graphics program you're using. Check out http://snook.ca/files/sc-export.mov for a great video about exporting slices from Photoshop and Fireworks.

Exporting HTML

Both Photoshop and Fireworks will also write the HTML code to display your slices according to the layout you designed. Before you get too excited, this doesn't mean you're off the hook about learning HTML! If you plan to use a graphics program to write your code, it's still important for you to understand HTML. The reason is that these programs write code according to some pretty strict rules contained within them. If your layout doesn't fit into those rules, you will likely end up with buggy, inefficient code.

That doesn't mean you should never use code written by graphics programs either. Instead, I often suggest that beginners use this code to get started. I encourage you to see how the program wrote its code and determine what is working and what isn't. Don't feel bound to the outputted code, but consider it one possible way to code your design.

PROBLEM 3-1

Wait! I don't really understand HTML! How am I supposed to code the pages myself when I'm still learning the code?

SOLUTION

Don't worry—this is a common struggle for new web designers. But that's why you're reading this book, right? As I mentioned, it's okay to let the graphics editor write your code for you while you're learning, as long as you dig into this code and use it as a learning tool. Challenge yourself to move the navigation from the left side to the right, for example, after the code has been written for you. Be sure to save a copy of the original code, then go through the process of editing the code, saving it, and checking out the results. You will make a lot of mistakes, but we all do. It's the process of fixing those mistakes that helps you learn and understand how HTML does what it does.

From Photoshop

When you allow a graphics editor to create the necessary code for a design to display in a browser, you must specify the type of slice for every square pixel on the page. Because much of your page will likely be browser-generated text, you'll have to specify some of those areas as "No Image" slices.

This dialog box was reached by double-clicking
slice 01 with the Slice Select tool in Photoshop.

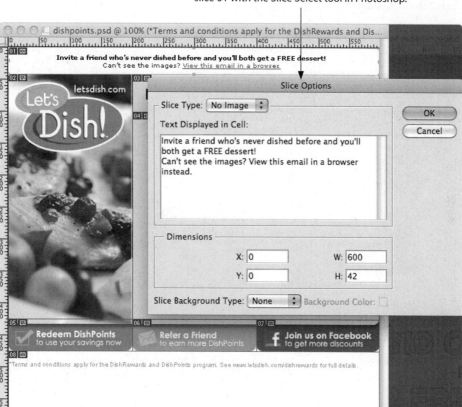

FIGURE 3-3 • "No Image" slices can contain text or HTML code to be rendered by the browser.

Figure 3-3 shows the spot in the Slice Options to enter the text for a "No Image" slice. You can type plain text (as I did) or HTML code in the space provided. Options for alignment and background colors are also available.

After you've accounted for each and every slice in the design, you can choose File | Save For Web & Devices and click the Save button to complete the process. When you reach the Save Optimized As dialog box (shown in the following illustration), be sure to select "HTML And Images" as the format and "All Slices" for slices.

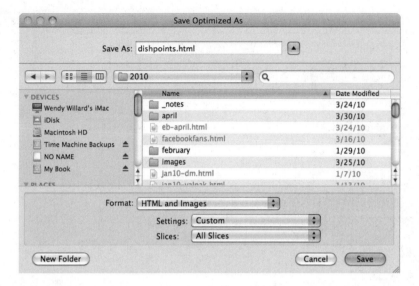

From Fireworks

As with Photoshop, Fireworks can easily create the HTML and CSS necessary to display your layout in a browser. While Photoshop calls any nonimage blocks "No Image" slices, in Fireworks you choose between two options for slices: Image and HTML.

After all of your slices have been named and optimized, you choose File | Export to reach the Export dialog box. At this point, you can select "HTML And Images" in the Export options, and adjust the remaining options as needed.

TIP   *The latest versions of Fireworks can do an incredibly good job at writing HTML and CSS, so much so that you may not even have a whole lot to edit after the code is output. It's definitely worth trying, especially since Fireworks can import fully layered Photoshop files. Here's a tutorial discussing how to integrate Photoshop and Fireworks for web design: http://addicted2webdesign.com/2010/03/create-a-website-fast-using-photoshop-and-fireworks.*

Layout Options

As you go through the process of exporting HTML from Photoshop or Fireworks, you'll encounter a few different layout options. These choices determine which type of coding methods will be used to place each element on the page. If you're not yet familiar with HTML and CSS, it can be a bit daunting to stare at a list of choices like "Generate Table" or "Generate CSS." At this point, you may even be wondering, "What's the difference?"

When HTML was first put into practice, the pages being developed were quite simple. At that point, "tables" were used to re-create tabular data, which is typically housed in spreadsheets. But then, web designers came on the scene and started using tables to lay out more complex webpages, placing different aspects of the page into each table cell and then hiding the table edges (borders) to make the design appear seamless.

Eventually a better solution became available: positioning with cascading style sheets (CSS). Thankfully, all modern browsers now support CSS for positioning, which is great news for web designers. CSS positioning requires less code than table-based page layouts and offers more flexibility. CSS layouts are also easier to maintain than their table-based counterparts.

Having said that, CSS positioning is not yet supported by most e-mail readers, as of press time. Because of that, most designers rely on table-based layouts for any pages created for e-mail.

Still Struggling

The layout options vary according to the graphics editor being used. So when you get to this point in the design process, it's a good idea to review some tutorials that address the specific export options available for your graphics editor. For Fireworks, try http://tv.adobe.com/watch/learn-fireworks-cs4/creating-cssxhtml-layouts. For Photoshop, try http://tv.adobe.com/watch/assets-in-motion/episode-4. To see how you can use Fireworks and Photoshop together to streamline the process, check out http://tv.adobe.com/watch/everyday-timesavers-web/quickly-transform-photoshop-layouts.

Coding the File Structure

When I first start the coding aspect of a project, I typically create a new folder on my hard drive to house all the related files. Then within that folder, I create a few additional subfolders. The most important of these is probably my images folder. It is a good idea to place all the images for a site within a particular folder instead of leaving them strewn about in various places. This makes it easier to locate and reference images later. Another folder I typically create is called "common" and contains all the non-HTML code files referenced by the web-pages, such as the style sheet (which is a .css file) and any JavaScript files (saved with a .js extension).

After you finish exporting the various elements of the design from your graphics editor and have them organized on your computer, it's time to switch to a coding tool. While you can definitely code HTML and CSS with any text editor, the vast majority of web designers use a professional, web-specific coding tool such as Dreamweaver or Expression Web.

If you exported code from your graphics editor, open it in your code editor and take a look at what you have. When you view HTML files in a browser, the code is translated behind the scenes to display the page accordingly. When you instead open that same file in a code editor, you see only the code. You might think of HTML files as being two-faced, in that they look completely different depending on how you approach them.

NOTE *Many code editors contain browser previews so you can see both "faces" of the HTML code from within one development tool. In Dreamweaver, the Code view displays the code only, while the Design view shows a browser preview.*

Basic Page Code

All HTML pages need to have the `html`, `head`, and `body` tags, along with the DOCTYPE identifier. This means, at the very least, your pages should include the following:

- A line containing information about which version of HTML is used
- A header section, containing descriptive information about the page
- A body section containing the page's actual content

NOTE *The required tags for HTML pages depend in part on the version of HTML currently being used. HTML4.01/XHTML1.0 was released as an official specification by the World Wide Web Consortium (W3C) in 1999. As of this writing, HTML5 is in development but is not expected to be completed for several years. Even so, some parts of the HTML5 specification may be supported by new browsers before the specification is finished. Therefore, it's a good idea to check the W3C's website (www.w3.org) for any updates. To read more about what's coming in the next versions of HTML and CSS, check out this article: http://www.pcworld.idg.com .au/article/345863/geek_101_html5_css3.*

Here's an example of a basic HTML document:

```
<!DOCTYPE html PUBLIC "-//W3C//DTD XHTML 1.0 Transitional//EN"
"http://www.w3.org/TR/shtml1/DTD/transitional.dtd">
<html>
<head>
    <title>My First Web Page</title>
</head>
<body>
This is the basic page code.
</body>
</html>
```

Version Information

The first thing every HTML document needs is a line that identifies which version of HTML is used to code the page. The HTML and XHTML specifications each include three document type definitions (or DTDs for short):

- **Strict**   Includes only those tags available in the current specification, and none of those that have been *deprecated* (retired)
- **Transitional**   Includes everything in the strict DTD, as well as some older tags
- **Frameset**   Includes everything in the transitional DTD, plus older tags used to create frames

The actual code used to tell the browser which DTD is being used tends to get quite long (as you may have noted by the first two lines in my previous example). Most people copy and paste the code from another source online to avoid any typos. Check out www.w3schools.com/tags/tag_doctype.asp for a complete list (including copyable code references) for each of these DTDs.

Header Content

As I mentioned, the header of the document contains information about the document, as opposed to actual page content. The header section is created by an opening and closing `header` tag. The other elements typically included in the header are:

- `<title>`
- `<meta>`
- `<base>`

- `<style>`
- `<script>`
- `<link>`

Title

The `title` element is required, as it tells the browser what to display in its title bar. First and foremost, you should always include some descriptive text that gives users an idea what the page is about. Many people also use this part of the page to help orient users to their location within the website.

Meta

The `meta` element is used to provide reference information such as the author of the page or its copyright details. Table 3-2 lists the most common types of `meta` tags. I also cover them a bit more in Chapter 9. Here's an example of header content that includes a title and relevant meta data:

```
<head>
<title>Amy's Flowers | Roses | Amy's Blooming Dozen Bouquet</title>
<meta name="author" content="Wendy Willard" />
<meta name="copyright" content="2010, Amy's Flowers" />
<head>
```

TIP *The* `meta` *element is one that does not have a closing tag. Tags like this are often referred to as* empty *tags. So to "close" tags like this one, you place the terminating slash before the final bracket, as shown in the previous code snippet.*

Base

The `base` element is used when it's necessary to identify a base URL for all links on the page. For example, if all the links on a page access files within

TABLE 3-2 Common Types of Meta Tags

Type of Meta Tag	Usage Example
author	`<meta name="author" content="name of author" />`
copyright	`<meta name="copyright" content="year, owner" />`
description	`<meta name="description" content="brief description" />`
keywords	`<meta name="keywords" content="list of keywords" />`
robots	`<meta name="robots" content="none" />`

someone else's website, it can save time to list the base part of that address (such as "http://www.address.com") in the base tag. Then, you only need to list the actual file location (such as "/downloads/party.pdf") in your links. In this case, the browser will understand the complete link to be "http://www.address .com/downloads/party.pdf."

Style

The style element is used to include internal or external style sheets (CSS). Style sheets are so important to the process, that I discuss them in much more detail later.

Script

The script element is used to add scripts, which are responsible for functionality not possible using basic HTML. You can add scripts in two ways. First, you can create separate script files, which are then linked from within the header content, as shown in the following example:

```
<head>
<title>Amy's Flowers - Our Services</title>
<script src="insertmovie.js" language="JavaScript" type="text/
javascript"></script>
</head>
```

Scripts can also be added to the header content, such that the script itself is placed between the opening and closing head tags. Here's an example where the script tells the browser to display an alert box when the page is loaded:

```
<head>
<title>Amy's Flowers - Our Services</title>
<script type="text/javascript">
function message()
    {
    alert("This alert box was created with JavaScript");
    }
</script>
</head>
```

Link

The link element can be used to establish relationships with other documents without requiring any user interaction. In other words, when a document is linked using the link tag, the relationship between the two is immediate. (By contrast,

Still Struggling

If you need help with figuring out how specific tags work, don't miss the W3Schools Tag Reference: www.w3schools.com/TAGS.

when a link created with the a element, which I discuss later, nothing happens until a user clicks the link.)

The `link` tag is most often used to reference external style sheets, as in:

```
<link rel="stylesheet" type="text/css" href="styles.css" />
```

Body Content

The rest of the code within an HTML file is contained within the body content. Everything that displays within the browser content area is somehow referenced in between the opening and closing `body` tags. Here's an example of some very basic body content:

The p tag is used to contain paragraphs of text on the page.

The h1 tag is used to contain the most important headlines on the page.

```
<body>
<h1>Amy's Flowers</h1>
<p>Located in Bel Air, MD, Amy's Flowers has been serving the
Harford County area for almost 20 years.</p>
<p><a href="products.html" title="View sample products">View
Sample Products</a> | <a href="contacts.html" title="Contact
Us">Contact Us</a></p>
</body>
```

The a tag is used to create links to other content.

As you review the preceding code sample, notice some tags have aspects you can customize. These options are called *attributes* and are placed after the element name in the tag, but before the final bracket. In the preceding example, `href` and `title` are attributes of the opening a tag (which, in this case, is used to create a link to another page).

Each attribute has a value, which comes after the equal sign and is placed within quotation marks. For the *View Sample Products* link in the example, "products.html" is the value of the `href` attribute and "View sample products" is the value of the `title` attribute.

The tags located in the body content area of a webpage are discussed in more detail in the following chapters.

Basic CSS Code

I've already mentioned the phrase "style sheets" a few times, but I haven't really given them a full explanation yet. Part of the reason is that style sheets weren't really a part of the earlier versions of HTML. The purpose of *cascading style sheets* (CSS) is to separate the *style* of a webpage from its *content*.

The current W3C specifications dictate that we use HTML only to identify the content of the page, and then use a style sheet to specify the presentation of that content. This not only makes webpages more accessible and usable to all users (regardless of their browsers, platforms, operating systems, physical limitations, and so forth), but also to search engines and other types of software.

TIP   *If you've ever used the style drop-down menu in some versions of Microsoft Word, you've already used a style sheet of sorts. The most basic style sheet might include a style called Body Text that specifies how the body text of the webpage should look—which font and color to use, how much space to leave around it, and so on.*

CSS offers three types of style sheets:

- **Inline**   Styles are embedded right within the HTML code they affect.
- **Internal**   Styles are placed within the header information of the webpage and then affect all corresponding tags *on a single page.*
- **External**   Styles are coded in a separate document, which is then referenced from within the header of the actual webpage. This means a single external style sheet can be used to affect the presentation on a whole group of webpages.

You can use any or all of these types of style sheets in a single document. However, if you do include more than one type, the rules of *cascading order* take over: These rules state that inline rules take precedence over internal styles, which take precedence over external styles.

In a nutshell, CSS styles apply from general to individual. This means a rule-set in the header section of a document overrides a linked style sheet, while a ruleset in the body of a document overrides one in the header. In addition, more local (or *inline*) styles only override the parent attributes where overlap occurs. We'll look at this more in Chapter 5.

Inline

Inline styles are enclosed in straight quotes using the `style` attribute with whichever tag you want to affect. For example, if you wanted to cause a paragraph of text to display using the Verdana font, you could use an inline style declaration like this:

```
<p style="font-family:verdana;">
```

If you also wanted to make that text blue, you can add another rule to do just that. (Rules are separated by semicolons.)

These are CSS *rules.*
The two rules together are considered a style *declaration.*

```
<p style="font-family:verdana;color: blue;">
```

TIP *Inline styles are best for making quick changes to a page, but aren't suited for styling an entire document or website. The reason is that when styles are added to a tag, they occur only for that individual tag and not for all similar tags on the page. To affect all similar tags on the page, use internal or external styles.*

Internal

When you want to change the font for all the paragraphs on a single page, you can use an internal (also called embedded) style sheet. Internal `styles` are added with the style element in the header content of the page. Here's an example of what an internal style sheet might look like:

These are called *selectors.*

```
<head>
<title>Amy's Flowers</title>
<style type="text/css">
h1 {font-family: georgia; color: blue;}
p {font-family: verdana;}
</style>
</head>
```

All rules end with semicolons.

The two rules together are contained within curly brackets.

With internal style sheets, a *selector* is placed before the declaration, which is enclosed in curly brackets. The selector tells the browser which aspect of the page you want to affect. In the preceding example, h1 and p are each used as selectors to tell the browser we want to change the appearance of the most important headlines and all paragraphs on the page.

Some people prefer to break internal rules over several lines to ease readability. That means the following example is just as valid as the preceding example:

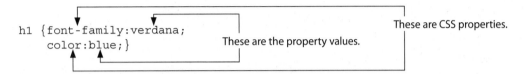

TIP   *You can use certain shorthand properties to reduce the amount of coding necessary. For example, instead of specifying both the font-family and font-size properties, you could simply use the font property, as in:*
```
h2 {font: verdana 12pt;}.
```

External

The third and final type of style sheet is not contained within the HTML page, but is housed within its own document and then referenced from within the HTML document. An external style sheet doesn't use the style tag, or contain any HTML tags at all, but simply includes a list of rulesets as instructions for the browsers. As such, an external style sheet might look like this:

```
h1 {font-family: georgia; color: blue;}
h2 {font-family: georgia, color: orange;}
p {font-family: verdana; font-size:12pt;}
```

After you create your external style sheet, save it as a text file with a .css filename extension. Then return to your HTML file and add the link tag to the header content to reference the external style sheet, as in the following example:

```
<head>
<title>Amy's Flowers</title>
<link rel="stylesheet" type="text/css" href="styles.css" />
</head>
```

This specifies the type of file being linked.   This specifies the file containing the external style sheet.

> **TIP** *External style sheets are best used to house all the styles for an entire website. Note these styles can be overruled by any internal or inline style sheets contained within individual pages.*

Coding Best Practices

If you view the source code for several different websites, you will see a few similarities. This is not a coincidence; according to the latest HTML specification, you should keep in mind the following etiquette rules as you code your pages:

- All tags should be lowercase.
- All tag values should be placed within straight quotation marks.
- All tags must be closed.

> **NOTE** *These rules come from the XHTML 1.0 specification, which is the latest published spec related to HTML that has been created by the W3C (as of this writing). When HTML5 is released, the rules may change.*

You also want to observe proper spacing within tags. Let's look more closely at some example code to identify where proper spacing should occur:

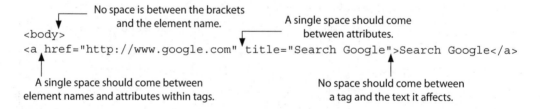

Finally, you must consider how to nest tags properly. The term *nesting* refers to the process of using one HTML tag inside another. The easiest way to understand this concept is to see it in action:

```
<strong><em>These tags are nested properly.</em></strong>
<strong><em>These tags are not nested properly.</strong></em>
```

You should always be able to draw semicircles that connect the opening and closing versions of each tag. If any of your semicircles intersect, your tags are not nested properly.

TIP   *When you look at other designers' code, you will likely see many lines of code are indented. People sometimes indent code to help organize it visually, but indenting has virtually no impact on the code itself.*

Naming Conventions

If you use a tool like Dreamweaver, the program will automatically prompt you to save in the correct file format. Even so, remember the following few points when saving your HTML files:

- You can use .html or .htm, but it's best to be consistent in whichever you choose.
- Some web servers are case-sensitive, so MyPage.html is different than mypage.html.
- Don't use spaces, punctuation, or special characters other than hyphens (-) and underscores (_).

Chapter Summary

Whew! This chapter covered a lot of the nuts and bolts required as you translate your designs from mockups to working webpages. Even if you ultimately decide to let your graphics editor do much of the work for you by exporting your designs and writing the code, it is important that you understand what is happening during that process. Knowing what's going on behind the scenes will make it easier to fix errors and customize the code to display exactly as you intended.

In the next chapter, I'll discuss the HTML used for page layout in more detail, and outline the code necessary to add headlines, paragraphs, lists, links, images, tables, and forms.

QUIZ

Choose the correct responses to each of the multiple-choice questions.

1. **Which file format is not suitable for web graphics to be viewed in a browser?**
    A. GIF
    B. PSD
    C. PNG
    D. JPEG

2. **What does a checkerboard pattern indicate when it is visible in a file viewed in a graphics editor?**
    A. dithering
    B. animation
    C. interlacing
    D. compression
    E. transparency

3. **Which file format is limited to no more than 256 colors?**
    A. GIF
    B. PSD
    C. TIFF
    D. JPEG
    E. PNG-24

4. **True or False: You can save a triangular-shaped GIF.**
    A. True
    B. False

5. **Which element is used to tell the browser which version of HTML (or XHTML) is used?**
    A. HTML
    B. VERSION
    C. DOCTYPE
    D. IDENTIFIER
    E. HTMLVERS

6. **Which tags surround the header content of a webpage?**
    A. <title></title>
    B. <head></head>
    C. <html></html>
    D. <body></body>
    E. <header></header>

7. **If the following code was added to the header content of a page, within which set of tags would it be contained?**

```
function message ()
     {alert("Hello World");}
```

   A. <link></link>
   B. <meta></meta>
   C. <style></style>
   D. <script></script>

8. **If the same CSS rule is defined in all three types of style sheets affecting a single webpage, which one takes precedence?**
   A. inline
   B. internal
   C. external
   D. embedded

9. **When multiple rules are included within a single CSS declaration, which character separates them?**
   A. colon
   B. period
   C. semicolon
   D. curly bracket
   E. quotation mark

10. **In the following style declaration, which is the property?**

```
h2 {font-family: verdana;}
```

   A. h2
   B. verdana
   C. font-family
   D. font-family: verdana
   E. h2 {font-family:verdana;}

chapter 4

All About the HTML

When moving from a graphics editor to an HTML editor, a lot of beginning designers get hung up in the intricacies of the code. It's no wonder, given that the two types of applications are so different from one another. You might relate it to the old "left brain vs. right brain" argument, where left-brain thinking is more analytical and focuses on the individual parts, while right-brain thinking is more intuitive and looks at the wholes.

In any case, the next few chapters focus on the individual parts of the design layout, as we put them back together with the code.

CHAPTER OBJECTIVES

In this chapter, you will

- Determine how the div element is used to organize content
- Use HTML to add headlines, paragraphs, and lists to webpages
- Differentiate between absolute and relative links
- Create basic tables and forms with HTML
- Understand how to add images and multimedia with HTML

Content Blocks

As was mentioned previously, each part of your designs must fit into a "block" within the overall layout. Even though you probably didn't think a whole lot about those blocks when you were creating the design, they become extremely important during the coding.

In fact, if you structure your content blocks appropriately, you'll be able to easily customize them later as needed. How? The secret lies in something I can't stress enough: the separation of the *style* of a webpage from its *content*.

Consider a design with four key content blocks: a header, some navigation, body copy, and a footer. If each of those blocks is first structured within the HTML and then styled with the CSS, you can actually format and move the blocks independently on the page without ever returning to the HTML code. Indeed, a great strength of style sheets is their ability to let you apply groups of formatting characteristics to whole sections of text.

The key to setting up those content blocks is the `div` element. Adding a simple `<div>` and `</div>` grouping to the code on your page will cause no outward change in appearance when the page is viewed in the browser. This element is merely used as a container, allowing you to manipulate its contents later with style sheets. As you begin coding your pages, you want to identify the most appropriate blocks, or sections, to house the content on the page.

Planning the Structure

The vast majority of webpages follow a similar structure, with a header, navigation, main content, and footer. That's not to say all webpages *look* the same, but just that many have a similar underlying structure. It's how you organize the structure on the page that is unique. Let's take another look at a site I sliced in Chapter 3 to see how this might work. Figure 4-1 shows the site's design, while Figure 4-2 shows how it might be broken up into content blocks.

In the code, we use the `div` element to separate content blocks, then add the `id` attribute to give each block a name (as I did with *header*, *mainContent*, *nav*, and *footer* in the following example). In the same way that a unique Social Security number is assigned as identification—ID—for each person

FIGURE 4-1 • Sample design mockup

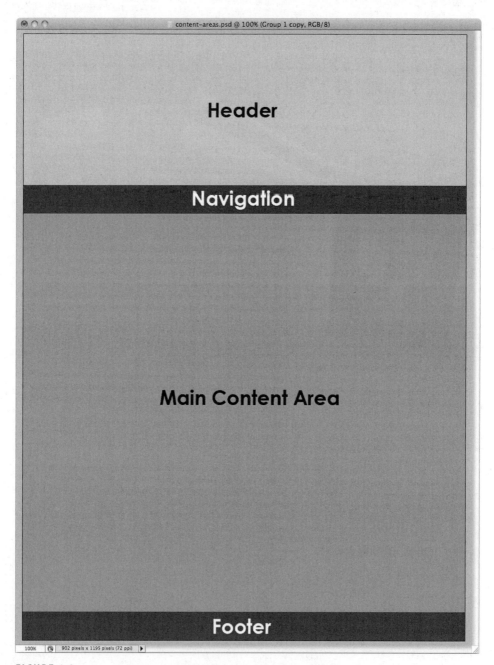

FIGURE 4-2 · Sample design mockup with main content blocks defined

living in the United States, so should a unique name be given to each block on a webpage.

```
<body>
<div id="header">
Header content goes here.
</div>
<div id="nav">
Navigation goes here.
</div>
<div id="mainContent">
Main content goes here.
</div>
<div id="footer">
Footer goes here.
</div>
</body>
```

Once you've named your content blocks, they can easily be formatted in the site's style sheet. Need to change the font style or even move a block from the top of your page to the bottom… on ten different pages? Not only is it easy to change that navigation bar, but you have to edit only the style sheet—and not the individual HTML pages—to do so. Here's an example showing how different styles can be applied to each content block:

```
#header {border:1px solid black;}
#nav {background-color:black; color:white;font-size:10px;}
#mainContent {font-size:11px;}
#footer {font-size:9px;}
```

In the style sheet, the # before each content block name is necessary because this is an *id* selector (and not a tag or element selector). Instead of using a *tag* as my selector, such as p, I've essentially made up my own selectors and given them names like *header* and *footer*. And because I used the id attribute to name them, I prefaced my selector name with a pound sign (#).

NOTE   *I cover more about CSS selectors in Chapter 5.*

Other HTML Containers

After you've organized your page into the key areas, you can further organize the content within those larger blocks using some basic HTML container elements. (We call these *container* elements because their main purpose is to *contain* page elements.) Each of the elements discussed in this section belong in one of two

TABLE 4-1 Differences Between Block-Level and Inline Elements		
	Block-Level	**Inline**
Formatting	Begin on new lines	Do not begin new lines
Contents	May contain other block–level elements as well as inline elements	May contain only other inline elements
White space	Can have margins, padding, and forced dimensions (width/height)	Cannot have margins or forced dimensions (width/height)
Positioning	Can be moved independently of the surrounding elements	Are treated as part of the normal flow of the document text and cannot be moved outside of that

categories: *block-level* or *inline*. Table 4-1 outlines the differences between these two types of HTML elements.

The `div` element is a commonly used block-level container because it helps designers define the overall structure of pages. Inside those, block-level containers might include the headlines, paragraphs, and lists. The element used to create links is an example of an inline container. Each of these is outlined in the following few sections.

To really make things interesting, it should be noted that you can actually force an element to be block or inline. This means you could force a link (which is normally an inline element) to display as a block-level element instead. I discuss this more in the next chapter, but at this point you only need to understand how being block-level or inline affects page content.

NOTE   *Block-level and inline elements are discussed more in Chapter 5, when styling the page.*

Headings

One of the earliest means of structuring text content were the heading elements, which are available in six levels of importance from `<h1>` down to `<h6>`. You use the heading elements to tell the browser which pieces of text function as headings, and then specify how to style them later with CSS.

```
<h1>About Us</h1>
```

Headings in HTML are similar to the headings you might use in a word processor like Microsoft Word. They are also similar to headings in outlines, because they should only be used in the proper order, from h1 down to h6. For example, you wouldn't create an outline that began with a small letter *a* and was followed by the roman numeral I. Instead, you would begin with the roman numeral I, follow that with a capital *A*, and so on. In like manner, an `<h1>` should be followed by an `<h2>`, as opposed to an `<h3>`.

While the heading element does change the size of the text contained by it, this element is primarily used as a structural element to identify the headings within various content areas. So at this point, don't try to change or alter the font characteristics of your headings. We'll do that with a style sheet in the next chapter.

Paragraphs

The next most basic method of structuring text content is with the paragraph element. HTML is different from traditional word processors because you cannot simply press the RETURN or ENTER key to end a paragraph, and then press the TAB key to indent a new one. Instead, you have to use tags to tell the browser where to start and end paragraphs, as well as any other types of breaks.

The paragraph element (which is coded as `<p>...</p>`) functions specifically as a container for paragraphs of text. This means you use an opening paragraph tag at the beginning of your paragraph, and a closing version at the end. Here's what this ends up looking like:

```
<p>CHOP POINT CAMP is a Maine summer camp combining a strong
residential camping program with the excitement of an adventurous
trip program. Each summer, 80 teenagers between the ages of 12
and 18 come to Chop Point from all over the world to have one of
the best summers of their lives.</p>
```

Even though the paragraph element's sole purpose is to contain paragraphs of text, it doesn't automatically indent them. That can be achieved through a style sheet, if desired. Instead, paragraphs created with `<p>` are separated by blank lines.

Line Breaks

Sometimes it's necessary to force a line break within a chunk of text. The line break element is an inline tag perfect for this purpose. Adding `<br />` to your code is the same as pressing SHIFT-RETURN or ENTER on your keyboard in a word processor. It causes the browser to stop printing text on that line and drop down to the next line.

Because this tag is not a container tag, in that it performs a function within the code but doesn't hold any other content, it has no closing version. This type of tag is also known as an *empty* tag. In situations like this, the closing slash is included right within the tag.

Lists

Many of us use lists to stay organized at home and work. Websites also frequently use lists to organize content on a page. As an added benefit, lists can help the usability of webpages because they make the text content more readable.

There are three basic types of lists in HTML, as outlined in Table 4-2. Remember the purpose of the list elements is not to style the content but to structure it. As such, if you'd like to change the color of the bullets or adjust the indentation, wait until you add a style sheet to the page for that.

TABLE 4-2 Types of HTML Lists

Type of List	Sample Code	Sample Browser Display
Ordered—each list item is preceded by a number or letter	```Homework: <ol> <li>Read pgs. 4-10</li> <li>Do the exercises on pg. 11</li> <li>Select a science fair project</li> </ol>```	Homework: 1. Read pgs. 4-10 2. Do the exercises on pg. 11 3. Select a science fair project
Unordered—each list item is preceded by a bullet	```Homework: <ul> <li>Read pgs. 4-10</li> <li>Do the exercises on pg. 11</li> <li>Select a science fair project</li> </ul>```	Homework: • Read pgs. 4-10 • Do the exercises on pg. 11 • Select a science fair project
Definition—contains terms, which are flush left, and definitions, which are indented	```<dl> <dt>HTML</dt> <dd>Hypertext Markup Language</dd> <dt>FTP</dt> <dd>File Transfer Protocol</dd> </dl>```	HTML Hypertext Markup Language FTP File Transfer Protocol

Links

Links are a huge part of any webpage. Without any links, a webpage is really just a dead end. Because they are so integral to webpages, links are typically sprinkled throughout the different content blocks of the page. Remember that links are inline elements (as opposed to being block-level), and can be placed anywhere within the body section of the code.

In HTML, a link has two ends (also called *anchors*) and a direction between them. One end—the *source*—is where it all starts, and the other—the *destination*—is the content being linked. The tag most frequently used to create links is the a element (short for *anchor*). Here's an example of what a link to CNN.com might look like using that tag:

```
<a href="http://www.cnn.com" title="Click to visit CNN.com">CNN</a>
```

In this code example, the opening a tag tells the browser the content in between the opening and closing tags is some sort of link. The href attribute, short for *hypertext reference*, tells the browser the direction, or destination, of the content.

The title attribute provides a brief description of the link. Some browsers display this description as a tool tip when the user's mouse hovers over the link, so it's a good idea to include it when you can.

Here are a few more attributes commonly used when creating links:

- **accesskey**   Used to assign a keyboard shortcut to the link
- **tabindex**   Used to customize the tab order of the link
- **target**   Used to specify the browser window in which a link should display

Still Struggling

Visit www.w3schools.com/TAGS/tag_a.asp and www.w3.org/TR/WD-htmllink-970328 for additional details regarding the anchor tag.

Relative vs. Absolute Links

When linking to other content, it's very important to properly format the hypertext reference. For example, to link to CNN's website, you must include the entire address, beginning with the http:// (which is called the *protocol*). This is called an *absolute* link because it leaves no doubt as to where the linked content is located.

By contrast, a *relative* link uses a path relative to the current page. This means the actual path taken to reach the file might vary depending on where you are in the file structure. Relative links are most commonly used when you want to link from one page to another within a single website. Here's an example linking from a file called quote.html to another one named benefits.html:

```
<a href="../careers/humanresources/benefits.html">Benefits</a>
```

In this example, the ../ at the beginning of the hypertext reference tells the browser to go up one level within the file structure from the current location. Then, the benefits.html file will be found in the humanresources folder within the careers folder at that level.

Then, if you wanted to link from the benefits.html page back to the quote.html page, the link might look like this:

```
<a href="../../contact/quote.html">Request a Quote</a>
```

The following illustration helps clarify the relationship between the two files.

TIP   *Most servers are also set up to recognize a single slash as a direct link back to the root directory of the server. So `<a href="/index.html">` links back to the main index page regardless of where the file you're linking from is located. This type of link is called a* **root-relative path**.

Interior Links

What about when you want to link to a section of content within a webpage, as opposed to the entire page? In this case, you must first define the destination by using the name attribute:

```
<h2 name="contact-form">Contact Form</h2>
```

You can either add the name attribute to an existing tag—as I did in the previous example—or you can use the a element to create the anchor anywhere on the page:

```
<a name="section1"></a>
```

When it's time to link to the section of the page, you need only to add the destination name (prefaced by a pound sign) to the end of the hypertext reference, like this:

```
<a href="/company.html#contact-form">Contact Us</a>
```

Other Links

It's important to note you can also use the a element to add links to e-mail addresses and multimedia files and a variety of other types of content. In each case, you need to follow the same basic structure:

```
<a href="destination">
```

So as already shown, an absolute link to another website would look like:

```
<a href="http://www.foxnews.com">
```

A link to an e-mail link would look similar, just with a different destination prefaced by the mailto protocol:

```
<a href="mailto:email@emailaddress.com">
```

Alternatively, a link to execute a bit of JavaScript code (which I'll explain more in Chapter 7) when clicked would be prefaced by the javascript protocol:

```
<a href="javascript:window.open('http://example.com','Window
Title','width=350.height=550')">
```

Tables

If you've spent any amount of time using a word processor or spreadsheet application, you're probably familiar with the concept of a digital table. Quite simply, a table is a section of information divided into columns and/or rows of blocks, called *cells*. To create tables with HTML, you need to know about four basic table elements, as described in the following list. With these elements in mind, you can create both basic and complex table structures.

- **<table></table>**   This is the container for every other element used to create a table in HTML. The opening and closing `table` tags should be placed at the beginning and end of your table.
- **<tr></tr>**   This creates a new table row. The opening and closing `tr` tags surround the cells in that row.
- **<td></td>**   This creates a new table cell. The opening and closing `td` tags surround the actual content of that cell.
- **<th></th>**   This optional element creates a new table header cell and is used in place of the `td` element for that cell. By default, the content in header cells is boldface and centered.

NOTE   *Tables are block-level elements.*

If you wanted to create a table with three columns, a header row, and two data rows, like this:

Row 1, Header Cell 1	Row 1, Header Cell 2	Row 1, Header Cell 3
Row 2, Data Cell 1	Row 2, Data Cell 2	Row 2, Data Cell 3
Row 3, Data Cell 1	Row 3, Data Cell 2	Row 3, Data Cell 3

Here's how you might code it:

```
<table>
    <tr><th>Row 1, Header Cell 1</th>
        <th>Row 1, Header Cell 2</th>
        <th>Row 1, Header Cell 3</th>
    </tr>
    <tr><td>Row 2, Data Cell 1</td>
        <td>Row 2, Data Cell 2</td>
        <td>Row 2, Data Cell 3</td>
    </tr>
```

```
    <tr><td>Row 3, Data Cell 1</td>
        <td>Row 3, Data Cell 2</td>
        <td>Row 3, Data Cell 3</td>
    </tr>
</table>
```

Perhaps the most confusing part of tables is the order in which they are coded. Many people just getting started with web design mistakenly assume they should create the columns and then the rows. That's true... sort of. While you are creating the column structure with the th and td cells, you must place all the cells of each row together within the corresponding tr tags.

TIP *To keep yourself in check, remember to code tables as you read English, from left to right, top to bottom.*

You can include nearly any type of content in a table cell that you might include elsewhere on a webpage. This content should be typed in between the opening and closing table cell tags. All elements used to format that content should also be included between those cell tags.

Tables, by nature of their design, have internal and external borders. By default, most recent browsers set the border size to zero, making those borders invisible. However, borders can be quite useful for making tables easier to read. Thankfully, there's a style sheet property for that (which we'll address in Chapter 5), as well as adjusting the space in and around each cell.

Forms

The last type of HTML container I want to discuss is the form. All forms have the same basic structure, which includes opening and closing form tags, input controls, and processing methods. The form tags surround the entire form, just as html tags surround an entire HTML document.

All the other form-related tags are then placed in between the opening and closing form tags. The parts of the form that allow for user input are referred to as *input controls*. The most basic type of input control is the single-line text field. This and other input controls are highlighted in Table 4-3.

Usually, text fields are preceded by descriptive text (also called the *label*) telling the user what to enter in the box. That text is enclosed within opening and closing label tags, with an associated for attribute to let the browser know

TABLE 4-3 Types of HTML Form Input Controls

Input Control	Description	Code Example
Single–line Text Field	Single–line, white spaces for text	`<input type="text" name="name" />`
Multiple–line Text Area	Larger text field, capable of handling multiple lines of text; width (cols) value is based on an average character width, and height (rows) value is based on the number of text lines	`<textarea name="comments" cols="20" rows="5"></textarea>`
Radio Buttons	Small, round buttons that enable users to select a single option from a list of choices	`<input type="radio" name="contact-method" value="Phone" />` `<input type="radio" name="contact-method" value="Email" />`
Check Boxes	Small, square buttons that enable users to select multiple options from a list of choices	`<input type="checkbox" name="interests" value="Graphic Design" />` `<input type="checkbox" name="interests" value="Illustration" />`

Select Menus	Expandable lists that enable users to select one or more options (using the multiple attribute)	`<select name="State">`
		`<option value="">Choose a State</option>`
		`<option value="AL">Alabama</option>`
		`<option value="AK">Alaska</option>`
		`<option value="AZ">Arizona</option>`
		`</select>`

File Uploads	Enables users to upload a file to be sent with the form's contents	`<input type="file" name="resume" />`
Submit Buttons	A clickable button that can be used to submit the form	`<input type="submit" value="Submit" />`
Image Buttons	A clickable image that can be used to perform an action in the form	`<input type="image" src="sendmessage.gif" name="Submit" alt="Send Message" />`

for which input control this is a label. Here's an example of how this might translate into code:

The value of the `for` attribute should be the same as the value of the corresponding input control's `id` attribute. Each `label` element can only be associated with one input control.

```
<form action="comments.php" method="post">
<label for="name">Name:</label>
<input type="text" name="name" id="name" />
<label for="email">Email:</label>
<input type="text" name="email" id="email" />
<label for="comments">Comments:</label>
<textarea name="comments" id="comments" cols="20" rows="30">
</textarea>
<input type="submit" value="Submit" />
</form>
```

Form Attributes

The input controls listed in Table 4-3 each have several attributes that really drive what's happening in the form. For example, several of those input controls are created with the `input` element. In each case, it's the value of the type attribute that determines exactly which input control is displayed. Table 4-4 outlines commonly used attributes and their possible values.

TABLE 4-4 Attributes for Form Input Controls

Attribute	Description	Values
type	Identifies the type of input control	type="text" type="checkbox" type="radio" type="password" type="submit" type="file" type="image"
name	Defines the name of the input control used when processing the form	name="firstName"
size	Defines the width of an input control (text fields are defined in average number of characters, while other fields are defined in pixels) or the number of items in a select menu that are visible when the page loads	size="20"
src	Defines the location (URL) of an image used in an input control	src="/images/button.gif"

TABLE 4-4   Attributes for Form Input Controls (*continued*)

Attribute	Description	Values
alt	Defines an alternative text description when an image is used in an input control	alt="Send this form"
checked	Specifies that an input control should be checked by default when the page is loaded (applies to check boxes and radio buttons only)	checked="checked"
disabled	Specifies that the input control cannot be used	disabled="disabled"
maxlength	Defines the maximum number of characters a user can enter in a text field	maxlength="40"
readonly	Specifies that a user can read, but not edit, an input control	readonly="readonly"
value	Defines the initial value of an input control when the page is loaded	value="(555)555-5555"
selected	Defines the option as selected when the page is loaded (applies to items in a select menu only)	selected="selected"
multiple	Enables users to select multiple choices in a select menu	multiple="multiple"
tabindex	Specifies the tab order for the input control	tabindex="1"
accesskey	Specifies the keyboard shortcut for the input control	accesskey="U"

Form Structure

After you've coded the form, you'll undoubtedly want to add some structure and style. We'll take care of the styling part in Chapter 5, but there are two more HTML elements we need to consider to help structure input controls more efficiently: fieldset and legend.

The fieldset element enables you to group related input controls and labels, and the legend element allows you to add a caption to that fieldset. Without any structure, the input controls and labels will simply flow together on the page. This occurs because unlike paragraphs and headings, input controls are inline elements that don't force line breaks by default.

Suppose you were creating a form for prospective employees to complete. It might contain three sections: personal information, employment history, and education. Each section then contains the input controls and labels to gather the necessary information:

```
<form action="application.asp" method="post">
<fieldset>
   <legend>Personal Information</legend>
   <label for="personal-name">Name:</label> <input type="text"
name="personal-name" id="personal-name" />
   <label for="personal-email">Email:</label> <input type="text"
name="personal-email" id="personal-email" />
   <label for="personal-phone">Phone:</label> <input type="text"
name="personal-phone" id="personal-phone" />
</fieldset>
<fieldset>
   <legend>Employment History</legend>
   <label for="employment-title-01">Job Title</label> <input type="text"
name="employment-title-01" id="employment-title-01" />
   <label for="employment-dates-01">Employment Dates</label> <input
type="text" name="employment-dates-01" id="employment-dates-01" />
   <label for="employment-company-01">Employer</label> <input
type="text" name="employment-company-01" id="employment-company-01" />
   ... more employment history ...
</fieldset>
<fieldset>
   <legend>Education</legend>
   <label for="education-degree-01">Degree</label> <input type="text"
name="education-degree-01" id="education-degree-01" />
   <label for="education-school-01">University</label> <input type="text"
name="education-school-01" id="education-school-01" />
   ... more education ...
</fieldset>
<input type="submit" value="Submit" name="submit" />
</form>
```

This creates a basic structure, which can then be customized with a style sheet. Alternatively, you can use a table to structure a form, where each input control and label are contained within cells of the table. That type of structure might look like this:

```
<form>
<table>
   <tr><td><label for="name">Name</label></td>
      <td><input type="text" name="name" /></td>
   </tr>
   <tr><td><label for="email">Email</label></td>
      <td><input type="text" name="email" /></td>
   </tr>
... more rows and input controls ...
</table>
</form>
```

You may be wondering which method of structuring forms—tables or fieldsets—is better. Well, each one has its pros and cons, depending on the situation.

Still Struggling

For more help with HTML forms, visit www.w3schools.com/html/html_forms.asp.

I recommend you have both in your arsenal to make the appropriate decision based on the specific table you're coding. After you've structured your table, it can easily be customized with a style sheet, as discussed in Chapter 5.

Form Processing

So what happens after you've created the form? Is the form's data e-mailed to the website manager or stored in a database somewhere? Is it, perhaps, written to another webpage on the site, such as occurs with blog comments? Many possibilities exist, and they ultimately depend on the purpose of the form.

Because HTML does not include form processing options, most web forms use some sort of scripting (such as ASP, PHP, or CGI) to process the data. When a user clicks the submit button, the contents of the form are sent to the script. The script then determines what to do with the data: send it, store it, or display it.

In many development teams, programmers typically handle the processing of web forms. If this responsibility falls to you, first check with the site's hosting provider because they may offer free scripts to customers. Or, you can search the thousands of free scripts available at sites like these:

- www.scriptarchive.com
- www.hotscripts.com
- www.cgi-resources.com

Pay attention to the documentation offered with each script, because it should tell you how to customize the script for your needs and how to install it on your server.

After you install and customize a script, you'll just need to reference it from within the form. That is accomplished with the addition of two attributes to the opening form tag, like this:

```
<form action="script.php" method="post">
```

The action attribute identifies the location of the processing script. The method attribute carries two possible values: get and post. With the get method, the form's data is added to the end of the script identified in the `action` attribute as it's being sent for processing. By contrast, the post method writes the form's data to the message body when it is sent for processing. The former method is used primarily for search forms, while the later method typically works for just about every other type of form.

Images

So far in this chapter, I've covered various ways you can organize and contain webpage content. For the most part, the HTML elements discussed pertain to text content. But we all know the Web is a lot more than just text content. There is one HTML element in particular that you need to understand in order to add images to your webpages.

The `img` element (short for image) is an inline, empty tag, in that it has no closing version. Instead, it has a few key attributes that tell the browser all about the image being displayed. The `src` attribute identifies the location of the image file, while the `alt` attribute provides a text description for nonvisual browsers. Just as with adding links, the `title` attribute can also be used to provide a tool tip for supporting browsers. Finally, the `height` and `width` attributes (specified in pixels) tell the browser how much space on the page to allot for the image. Here's how that might look in HTML:

```
<img src="/images/banner.jpg" width="600" height="200"
alt="Products Banner" title="Here are just a few of the products
we feature each month" />
```

Images can be placed within forms, inside tables, among paragraphs, and just about anywhere in your webpages. After you add them with this HTML code, you'll probably want to customize their display a bit with your style sheet. As you'll see in the next chapter, CSS can be used to cause images to display as block-level elements, and then align them, overlap them, add borders, adjust spacing, and even position an image in an exact location on the page.

Multimedia

When you want to incorporate multimedia—anything beyond static images added with the `img` tag—you can do so in two primary ways: You can *embed* media so it appears within the webpage, or you can *link* to it.

A link to a multimedia file is essentially the same as any other link. This means you can use the a element and href attribute, like this:

```
<a href="slideshow.mov" title="Click to see this slideshow">Watch
this student's slideshow.</a>
```

Users who click this link will be prompted to either download the file or view it now (in whichever application is set up to handle the file type).

Alternatively, you can cause the file to display directly within the context of your page. As long as the appropriate plug-in is installed on the user's computer, the file loads and plays along with anything else that might appear on that page. HTML's object element is perfect for embedding all sorts of multimedia, from Flash files to YouTube movies. Thankfully, YouTube (and other similar sites) provide lots of help for anyone trying to embed their files on other pages.

If you visit www.youtube.com and locate the video you'd like to embed, you'll find the necessary code for both linking to and embedding the file. Here's some code provided by YouTube, which we can use to better understand the object tag:

```
<object width="480" height="385">
  <param name="movie" value="http://www.youtube.com/v/FK-s2ek_5Cc&hl=en_
US&fs=1&rel=0"></param>
  <param name="allowFullScreen" value="true"></param>
  <param name="allowscriptaccess" value="always"></param>
  <embed src="http://www.youtube.com/v/FK-s2ek_5Cc&hl=en_US&fs=1&rel=0"
type="application/x-shockwave-flash" allowscriptaccess="always"
allowfullscreen="true" width="480" height="385"></embed>
</object>
```

In this example, the opening object tag has only the width and height attributes, used to tell the browser how much space to allot to the media file. Next, param tags (short for parameter) are used to specify the individual file characteristics. The most important one—and the only one we really need in this case—identifies the location of the YouTube video. The other two are proprietary Flash features.

Before the object element was the preferred method for embedding media files, some browsers used the embed element. In an effort to reach the widest possible audience (which may include users of very old browsers), YouTube includes an embed element with the same information as was already provided by the object and param elements. That way, if the page is viewed within a browser that

Still Struggling

The code required to embed multimedia files can sometimes be confusing because of the wide variety of media files available and each one's proprietary code. Luckily, plenty of online sites make this process easier. For example, you can use the Center for Instructional Technology's Embedded Media HTML Generator to write code for embedding Flash, Real Media, QuickTime, or Windows Media files: http://cit.ucsf.edu/embedmedia.

doesn't support the `object` element but does support the older `embed` element, the latter will be used instead.

NOTE *Because YouTube's code contains nonstandard code (specifically the `embed` element), it will not validate. If you are coding a page that absolutely must validate, try using a converter tool like www.tools4noobs.com/online_tools/youtube_xhtml to make YouTube's code follow the W3C specs.*

While you probably won't encounter a whole lot of users who need the `embed` element, you may come across those who can't access multimedia of any kind. With the number of folks accessing webpages from mobile devices growing exponentially each year, we need to be sensitive to people who either don't have the ability to download large media files or simply want to wait until reaching a larger monitor. Therefore, instead of adding an `embed` element before the closing `object` tag, you can actually add a static image and even some text to display if the media file doesn't. Here's how that might work:

```
<object width="320" height="240" type="application/x-shockwave-flash">
   <param name="movie" value="movie.swf" />
   <a href="http://www.adobe.com/products/flashplayer" title="You must
first install Flash to access this movie"><img src="movie-pic.jpg"
width="320" height="240" alt="Screen capture of movie - need Flash to
view" />Your browser is not capable of displaying this video right now.
</a>
</object>
```

PROBLEM 4-1

I want to include multimedia in my pages, but I don't know how to use Flash.

SOLUTION

A few years back, professional web designers were expected to be proficient in Flash as well as static web design tools. But then Adobe unveiled a much more robust version with Flash 5, and sent many traditional designers running for the hills (including me). The latest version is significantly more powerful as a delivery method for rich, interactive online content, but is also much more complex to use. As such, a new crop of Flash-centric developers has risen up, with traditional web designers acting in more of an art direction role for Flash projects.

So, what does that mean to you? I encourage you to explore Flash with Adobe's free 30-day demo. If it is something you enjoy using, take some additional classes and really dive into the product. You will find plenty of work as a custom Flash developer.

But if Flash isn't your thing, you have a few options. First, you could partner with a custom Flash developer. Second, you can purchase stock Flash files from sites like www.istockphoto.com and www.buystockflash.com. Third, you can take advantage of an intermediate tool that helps you create certain types of Flash files. For example, I like PulpMotion for making quick and easy Flash slideshows (www.pulpmotion.com) or SwishMiniMax for simple Flash banners (www.swishzone.com).

Chapter Summary

Do you feel comfortable with HTML yet? Don't worry if you don't, because it will come much more easily with a bit of practice. Before you know it, you'll be coding line breaks (<br />) in your sleep. But in the meantime, use the many online references mentioned in this chapter to stay up-to-date on the code and increase your skills.

Chapter 5 moves on to presenting the nitty-gritty of CSS, so you can style all the HTML you learned in this chapter.

QUIZ

Choose the correct response to each of the multiple-choice questions.

1. **Which tag is considered the key to setting up content blocks within HTML?**
   A. <p>
   B. <id>
   C. <div>
   D. <span>
   E. <body>

2. **Which is *not* true about block-level elements in HTML?**
   A. They begin on new lines.
   B. They may contain other block-level elements.
   C. They can have margins, padding, and forced dimensions.
   D. They are treated as part of the normal flow of the document and cannot be moved outside of that.

3. **True or False: Paragraphs created with <p> are automatically indented.**
   A. True
   B. False

4. **Which is *not* a block-level element?**
   A. <p>
   B. <ul>
   C.
   D. <h1>
   E. <table>

5. **Which attribute is used to identify the destination of a web link?**
   A. src
   B. href
   C. value
   D. name
   E. target

6. **www.google.com is an example of what type of link?**
   A. anchor
   B. interior
   C. relative
   D. absolute
   E. incomplete

7. Which is used to create a new row in an HTML table?
   A. <tr>
   B. <to>
   C. <td>
   D. <th>
   E. <tw>

8. Which is an input control used to create expandable lists in HTML forms?
   A. text fields
   B. text menus
   C. radio buttons
   D. check boxes
   E. select menus

9. To properly identify an input control's label, which attribute's value should be the same as the value of the corresponding input control's id attribute?
   A. id
   B. src
   C. for
   D. type
   E. value

10. Which is used to group related input controls and labels in an HTML form?
    A. <div>
    B. <select>
    C. <object>
    D. <fieldset>
    E. <formgroup>

chapter **5**

All About the CSS

After you've created the basic structure of the page with HTML, you can move on to formatting it with CSS. What exactly you do with your style sheet depends on the amount of formatting necessary. In the beginning, you might stick to the basics like changing font characteristics and colors. But as you grow more comfortable with CSS, you'll hopefully realize just how powerful those style sheets can be.

CHAPTER OBJECTIVES

In this chapter, you will

- Differentiate between various types of CSS selectors
- Recognize which style takes precedence when two styles are in conflict
- Style text, lists, links, and forms with CSS

Selectors

In Chapter 4, I briefly touched on selectors. With CSS, you use selectors to apply styles to page elements. Selectors allow you to style a particular piece of content, or whole sections of content, depending on the original design. A selector can be an HTML element (such as p or div), or even custom words you create for the sole purpose of applying styles.

To put this in other terms, let's compare it to building a house. After you've completed the basic construction (with the HTML), it's time to decorate each room. You might specify your crew paint all walls blue, with white moldings. If you were using CSS to tell the painters what to do, the code might look like this:

```
walls {color:blue; molding:white;}
```

In this example, *walls* is my selector; it's what aspect of the page (or house) we want to style. To help solidify how selectors are used in style sheets, let's take a look at the most common types of selectors.

Type Selectors

Suppose you wanted to cause all your level one headings to display in the Century Gothic font and to be colored blue. The simplest way to accomplish this would be to add a style declaration using the h1 element as your selector, like this:

```
h1 {font-family:'century gothic';color:blue;}
```

You'll notice that although the opening tag itself looks like this: <h1> when it's in your HTML code, you remove the brackets when using it as a selector in CSS. Any element that falls within the body section of the HTML page can be a selector. So if you want to style all the paragraphs on your page, you could use p as your selector. Or, if you wanted to style *all* of the text on your page (regardless of whether it's contained in paragraphs, lists, tables, or whatever), you could use body as your selector.

NOTE   *The W3C officially calls these type selectors, but I like to refer to them as tag selectors to make them easier for students to understand.*

ID Selectors

We covered id selectors a bit in Chapter 4, because they directly relate to the structuring of your pages. The most common use of id selectors is to uniquely style sections of a page. I say "uniquely style" because no two id values can be the same. In other words, after you name one content area "header," you cannot reuse that id name for any other content area affected by the same style sheet.

TIP *The* `id` *attribute can be added to any existing opening tag in the code, so long as it is used just once in each page. Because of that limitation, it is commonly used with the* `div` *element to separate the page content.*

When you want to style an element that has an id, you reference that id with its name prefaced by a pound sign:

```
#header {border:1px;}
```

The pound sign is necessary to let the browser know the selector in question is not an element, but rather the value of an `id` attribute somewhere in the page.

Class Selectors

Similar to the id selector, a class selector is a custom selector you create specifically for your pages. The difference, though, is that class selectors can be applied multiple times throughout your pages. For example, a class might be used to apply a style called "highlight" that adds a yellow background color behind various important bits of text on multiple pages.

In the HTML code, the `class` attribute is used to specify the class's name. Just like the `id` attribute, the `class` attribute can be added to any existing opening tag in the body section of the code, or you can use a `span` tag with the `class` attribute to apply a class to a section of text not already affected by another tag.

```
<span class="highlight">This text is highlighted.</span>
```

In the style sheet, classes are preceded by periods. This tells the browser that the selector is not an HTML element or the value of an `id` attribute, but a custom name applied with the `class` attribute.

```
.highlight {background-color:yellow;}
```

Other Selectors

Aside from the basic type, id, and class selectors, there are a number of other ways to be more specific about which element is being styled.

Universal Selector

The asterisk (*) is the universal selector in CSS. Similar to running a wildcard search, using an asterisk as your selector causes all elements on the page to be styled with the declaration. This can be helpful to force all the text on your page to use the same font family:

```
* {font-family: verdana;}
```

Attribute Selectors

When you style content with type selectors, you sometimes need to be more specific about which elements to affect. Suppose you needed to style all links to a particular website differently so they stood out. An attribute selector is perfect for situations like this.

```
a[href="http://www.mycompany.com"] {font-weight:bold;}
```

With the syntax for attribute selectors, the attribute is enclosed within straight brackets after the element name. Then, if you want to look only for attributes with a certain value (like in the previous example), you include that value inside the straight brackets as I did. In this case, it causes the style to be applied to all instances of the following HTML code within the page:

```
<a href="http://www.mycompany.com">
```

Descendent Selectors

What if you want to style the paragraphs in the main content section of the page differently from those in the header or footer? There are actually a couple of ways to accomplish this, one of them being descendent selectors.

Here's the HTML code for the scenario I just set up:

```
<div id="mainContent"><p>Text here</p></div>
<div id="footer"><p>Text here</p></div>
```

As you can see, if I use p as my selector, I will affect the paragraphs in both sections. To style them differently with descendent selectors, my style sheet might look like this:

```
#mainContent p {font-size:12pt;}
#footer p {font-size:10pt;}
```

TIP   *These types of selectors are called* descendent selectors *because they match elements that are descendents of other elements in the document's family tree. When you separate two selectors with a space, you're telling the browser to look for the first selector and then find the second selector inside the first one within the code. So in this case, these style declarations only affect paragraphs within the mainContent and footer divisions.*

Child Selectors

Child selectors are similar to descendent selectors, in that they allow you to style very specific aspects of the page. To understand the difference between descendent and child selectors, we need to take a step back and recognize how the HTML hierarchy works.

HTML includes its own set of parent-child relationships. In fact, we can create an HTML page's "family tree" just like you might have done in elementary school for your own family. Only, in this case, we're using HTML elements in place of family members' names. Take a look at the following illustration to see what I mean.

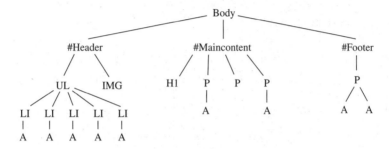

In this example, there is an unordered list (UL) in the header content division. That list contains five list items (LI). Each list item is therefore called a *child* of the ul element, as well as a *descendent* of the header content division and the body element. (All elements are descendents of the body element, so you might call him the granddaddy of them all…)

Each list item contains a link (A), and some of those links are bold. If we wanted to cause only the link colors inside those unbolded list items to be orange, we might use a child selector like this:

```
li > a {color: orange;}
```

If there were other lists on the page, though, things might get confusing. So to clarify, we could add a descendent selector to tell the browser to make only those links within a list item inside of the header content division orange:

```
#header li > a {color: orange;}
```

As you can see, child selectors are separated by a greater-than symbol in your style sheet, while descendent selectors are separated by a space.

Pseudo-Elements and Pseudo-Classes

What if you want to apply a style where no HTML element exists or is easily accessed? For example, a lot of designers are fond of creating drop caps for the first letter of key paragraphs. While this is easy to accomplish using print design software, there's no HTML element that lets you style the first letter of a paragraph. That's where pseudo-elements and pseudo-classes come in.

CSS provides several pseudo-elements and pseudo-classes to style aspects of HTML pages that are otherwise inaccessible. These are essentially "fake" elements and classes whose sole purpose is to apply styles. As of this writing, there aren't a whole lot of these pseudo-elements and pseudo-classes, but we can expect more to come with future revisions to the CSS specification. Tables 5-1 and 5-2 list those currently in use.

NOTE *Pseudo-elements and pseudo-classes are not supported by older browsers. So be sure to test pages that use these selectors in all target browsers.*

Each of these pseudo-classes and pseudo-elements are applied the same way, with a colon separating the real HTML element from the fake one, like this:

```
a:link {color:blue;}
a:visited {color:purple;}
a:hover {color:orange;}
a:active {color:yellow;}
```

In this case, the pseudo-classes are applied to the a element, because that's how links are created in HTML.

NOTE *The hover, active, and focus pseudo-classes aren't limited to links, and can be applied to other elements as well.*

TABLE 5-1   CSS Pseudo-Elements

Pseudo-Element	Description
:first-letter	Allows you to style the first letter of the first line of a text block
:first-line	Allows you to style the first line of a text block
:before	Allows you to insert content before other content, such as adding the word "New!" to the start of certain items in a list
:after	Allows you to insert content after other content, such as adding an asterisk after the text in certain table cells

TABLE 5-2 CSS Pseudo-Classes

Pseudo-Class	Description
:first-child	Allows you to style the first child element of another parent element
:link	Allows you to style elements that have not yet been visited
:visited	Allows you to style links that have already been visited
:hover	Allows you to style the way elements display as the mouse hovers over them
:active	Allows you to style the way elements display as they are being clicked
:focus	Allows you to style the way elements display when users are interacting with them, such as text fields currently being completed
:lang	Allows you to style the language of specific elements

Combining Selectors

You can also apply styles to multiple selectors quickly and efficiently by combining selectors. When you do this, you simply separate them with a comma. Here's an example in which I change the font size for all paragraphs and table cells at once:

```
p,td {font-size:12pt;}
```

Importance

One last thing to keep in mind about selectors is this: If you apply a particular style using the p element name as a selector, all paragraphs will carry that style. If you want to overwrite that style, there are a few things you can do.

I've already shown you a few ways to be specific as you apply styles, thereby overriding more general styles in the process. One of those options is to create a custom selector and apply it to whichever paragraph you want to display differently. Here's an example in which I specify that all paragraphs should use a certain size text, except for one paragraph styled with a more specific selector:

```
p {font-size:12pt;}
p.footer (font-size:10pt;}
```

Remember that you can apply styles in different locations—internal, external, inline—with varying results. Generally speaking, rules set in external style sheets can be overridden by internal style sheets, which can then be overridden by an inline style sheet. To clarify, suppose you have an external style sheet that applies to all the pages of a website, and then an internal style sheet applying to one page in particular. If both style sheets specify different font sizes for level one headings, the internal style sheet rule is the one that will ultimately be used.

NOTE   *This discussion on importance just scratches the surface, as the CSS specification offers detailed guidelines with regard to which rule takes precedence in the case of conflicts. Refer to www.eskimo.com/~bloo/indexdot/css/topics/ cascade.htm to learn more about the details of those guidelines.*

Inheritance

With all this talk of children and descendents, we certainly need to at least mention inheritance. While HTML children don't inherit riches from their parents, they do inherit certain style characteristics. For example, consider the following list item containing a bolded element:

```
<li>Please remind your child to bring his/her musical instruction
to school <strong>every Wednesday</strong> between now and the
end of the school year.</li>
```

If you apply a color to all list items on your page, the text inside the `strong` element will also inherit that color styling. That is, unless you specifically *override* that color with a style specifically applied to the `strong` element, as in:

```
li > strong {color: green;}
```

Still Struggling

Wondering which styling aspects are inherited and which are not? Check out an online style sheet properties library to learn exactly what is inherited in style sheet: http://webdesign.about.com/od/css/a/aastylelibrary.htm.

Every CSS property also includes the optional value "inherit." So, if you find out a certain style characteristic is not being inherited, you can force it to do so by using this value. Specifying `p {margin: inherit;}` in your style sheet will tell the browser that even though the margin property is not normally inherited, it should be in this case.

TIP   *The* `background-color` *property is another that is not inherited. How-ever, several modern browsers display some parent element's background colors through to their child elements because the default value of the* `background-color` *property is* transparent. *As a work-around, make sure to specify all back-ground colors instead of leaving them to chance.*

The !important Declaration

When all else fails, you can attempt to force a certain style declaration to over-ride all others with the use of the !important declaration. Here's how this might work:

```
footer p {font-family: verdana; !important}
```

In this case, even if another style declaration specifies paragraphs should use a different font, all paragraphs in the footer content division will display in Verdana because of the inclusion of this specific !important declaration.

 **PROBLEM 5-1**

I am using an external style sheet to drive the design of the entire website, but need to override a few styles for just one page. What is the best way to accomplish this?

SOLUTION

This is actually a common situation. I often create site-wide style sheets (which are usually located at styles.css) that contain the styles for every page on the site. Then, I use custom selectors to get more specific. For example, while all of the level two headings might normally be displayed in black, what if I needed to display one of those headings in orange?

There are a couple of different ways to approach this. First, I could create a custom class and add it to only that heading tag, like this: `<h2 class="highlight">`. Alternatively, I could create a custom class for that page and add it to the body tag, like this: `<body class="sales">`. Then, I would use `body.sales h2` as a descendent selector when declaring my style. This latter option of assigning classes to each page of the site allows me to get very specific about styles while still using a site-wide style sheet.

Font Styles

Now that you know how to specify which elements to style, let's move on to the properties used to actually style those elements. You can alter all sorts of aspects of your page through a long list of CSS properties. The first, and most commonly used, properties to discuss are the font properties. Table 5-3 lists the properties that affect aspects of fonts on webpages.

Here's an example of how these properties might be used to adjust the style of a paragraph:

```
p { font-style: italic;
    font-size: 1em;
    font-weight: bold;
    font-variant: small-caps;
    font-family: arial; }
```

After reading that, you may be wondering if there isn't a more efficient way to code all those font properties when several are used within a single rule. Thankfully, these can be grouped together using CSS shorthand, via the font property. In other words, you can adjust all five of the characteristics shown in the preceding code sample at once within a single property, like this:

```
p { font: italic 1em bold small-caps arial; }
```

Still Struggling

Check out www.w3.org/Style/Examples/007/fonts to see each of these font properties in action.

Font Sizes

Table 5-3 lists several different ways you can specify font sizes in CSS, including absolute keywords (small, medium, large), relative keywords (smaller or larger), or lengths (using numbers followed by units) or percentages.

The most common units used to specify fonts for screens are px (short for pixels) and em (refers to the width of the M in the current face and point size). Two less popular, but equally acceptable, units are pt (short for points) and % (percentage).

TABLE 5-3 CSS Font Properties

Property	Description	Possible Values	Default Value
font-family	Changes the font family in which text is displayed	*<family name>* *<generic family>*	*Varies*
font-size	Changes the font size in which the text is displayed	*<keyword>* *<relative size>* *<length>* *<percentage>*	*Varies*
font-size-adjust	Adjusts the font size up or down, relative to the current font size	*<number>* none	none
font-stretch	Changes the horizontal width of the font	normal wider narrower ultra-condensed extra-condensed condensed semi-condensed semi-expanded expanded extra-expanded ultra-expanded	normal
font-style	Adjusts whether text is italicized	normal italic oblique	normal
font-variant	Adjusts whether text is displayed in small caps	normal small-caps	normal
font-weight	Adjusts the heaviness of the text	normal bold bolder lighter 100 200 300 400 500 600 700 800 900	normal
font-effect*	Makes the letters look engraved or embossed	none emboss engrave outline	none

*Note: As of this writing, the `font-effect` property (which is part of a newer CSS specification) is not yet supported by many browsers.

Ems

Em is a scalable unit of measurement, which means it can increase or decrease depending on the user's browser settings. One em is equal to the current font size. So if you specify in your body element that a document's font size is 12 points, then for that document 1em = 12 pt. If you later specify that a headline should be 2 em, the headline would display at 24 pt.

TIP   *Dreamweaver uses ems when you specify your page layout should be* elastic, *because text sized with ems can vary depending on the fonts used.*

Pixels

Pixels are the common unit of measure for screens. Depending on your computer and monitor, webpages may display at 72 or 96 pixels per inch (ppi). Unfortunately, pixels are not scalable, which means users cannot increase the font size if you code a page using pixels for font measurements.

When you size your text with pixels, the text will remain the same size regardless of whether the browser window is resized. This is useful when you are trying to create a fixed layout where various items on the page need to be aligned with one another.

Points

Points are the common unit of measure for print. Seventy-two points make up one inch on the printed page. Just like pixels, points are fixed and not scalable.

Percentages

You can also specify font sizes by percentage. Like ems, percentages are scalable. In addition, they are dictated by the current font size (either in the page, or if that's not specified, then for the browser). So if the current font size is 12 pt, then 100 percent is equal to 12 pt, while 150 percent would be 18 pt.

TIP   *If you create a new page layout in Dreamweaver using a liquid layout, you'll notice Dreamweaver uses percentages as the preferred unit of measurement to allow text to grow and shrink as needed.*

Which to Use?

Ultimately, which unit of measure you use will depend on the goals of your site. If accessibility is a chief goal, you will want to steer clear of any unit of measure that doesn't allow your site's users to adjust the font sizes. So, you'll likely end up using ems and/or percentages.

The problem with adjustable units of measure is that you risk losing control over the layout. So if you're working with a layout that might break if a user increases the font size so much that your text can no longer fit in its allotted space… pixels and points are a more reasonable choice. Ultimately, you must consider your audience and how best to meet its needs.

Still Struggling

Check out A List Apart's Article entitled "How to Size Text in CSS": www.alistapart .com/articles/howtosizetextincss.

Font Families

Another important font characteristic is the font itself. In CSS, the font name is listed as the value of the `font-family` property.

For most browsers, the default font is something like Times New Roman, which is not exactly the easiest font to read on screens. Many designers choose to change the default font to something a bit more screen-friendly, using the `font-family` property:

```
body { font-family: verdana; }
```

TIP   *Table 2-2 in Chapter 2 lists the most popular and widely supported screen fonts.*

Font Stacks

Because it's common for some fonts not to be available on certain users' machines, you can include multiple fonts in your font specification. This process is referred to as defining font stacks, because the browser looks for the first font on the user's system and then moves on to the next if the first is not found. If none of the fonts are available, the text is displayed in the default font. Here's what this might look like in a style sheet:

```
body { font-family: verdana, arial, helvetica sans-serif; }
```

If you use a development tool like Dreamweaver, you may notice several font stacks built into the tool. But you shouldn't think these are the only font stacks available. You can create whatever list of fonts you'd like, so long as any of them would work in the space allowed. Ideally, you would pick three or more fonts of similar size, shape, and weight so the text looks similar regardless of which font is used.

Regardless of which fonts you use, here are a couple of points to remember:

- Some font names include two words, such as Century Gothic. Whenever a style sheet value includes a space, use single quotes to contain it.
- The capitalization of font names varies according to the operating system. Therefore, I recommend sticking with lowercase letters in font names.
- The actual font names may be a bit different across computer systems. To compensate, try including any possible names for a font commonly known by multiple names. For example, the font Comic Sans can sometimes be installed as Comic Sans MS. You might include both in your font stack, like this: 'comic sans', 'comic sans ms'.

Still Struggling

Smashing Magazine has a great guide to CSS font stacks: www.smashingmagazine .com/2009/09/22/complete-guide-to-css-font-stacks.

Color

I've already briefly mentioned several different ways to add color to webpages, but it's important to outline the proper methods of actually specifying colors in style sheets. Table 5-4 outlines the two most common properties used to change colors in style sheets.

Hexadecimal Color

The "normal" numbering system in the United States is decimal, meaning it is based on the number 10, where we have 10 units (0-9) to use before we have

TABLE 5-4 CSS Color Properties to Style Text

Property	Description	Possible Values	Default Value
background-color	Specifies the background color of the element by hexadecimal code (#FFCC66), RGB values (102 102 102), or keyword (red)	\<color\>	Varies
color	Specifies the color of the element by hexadecimal code, RGB values, or keyword	\<color\>	Varies

to repeat a unit. Because standard HTML couldn't handle decimal color values, the hexadecimal system was used to specify color when the Web was first developed.

The hexadecimal system uses the same concepts as the decimal system, except it is based on 16 units, as shown in Table 5-5.

There are many ways to convert from decimal to hexadecimal values and figure out a color's code. Modern web design tools also offer conversion tools. All that aside, we are no longer limited to hexadecimal values to specify color because CSS also permits us to use RGB values and color names.

RGB Values and Percentages

Computer monitors display color in RGB mode, where R = Red, G = Green, and B = Blue. Each letter (R, G, and B) is represented by a value between 0 and 255, with 0 being the darkest and 255 being the lightest. So white has an RGB value of 255, 255, 255, while black's RGB value is 0, 0, 0. (Note: If you decided to code those values using hexadecimal code instead, white would be FFFFFF and black 000000.)

TABLE 5-5 Hexadecimal and Decimal Numbering Systems

Decimal	0	1	2	3	4	5	6	7	8	9	10	11	12	13	14	15
Hex	0	1	2	3	4	5	6	7	8	9	A	B	C	D	E	F

You can use those RGB color values to define color like this:

```
<p style="color: rgb(0,0,0);">
```

Or, you could use the RGB percentages, like this:

```
<p style="color: rgb(0%,0%,0%);">
```

Notice that a comma separates each RGB value and the entire set of values is placed inside parentheses. A lowercase `rgb` precedes those parentheses.

Color Names

You can also specify a color name with the `color` property:

```
<p style="color: black;">
```

   HTML 3.2 and 4.0 defined a standard set of 16 colors, which could be referenced by names. The first version of CSS continued with those 16 colors, and orange was added in CSS 2.1. CSS3 finally gives us a larger set of acceptable colors. Refer to this online reference to see an updated list of supported color names: www.w3schools.com/css/css_colornames.asp.

TIP   *Wondering which method to use when defining color? Any of them! You can tailor your color presentation method to your particular site, using whichever method makes the most sense to you.*

Transparent Colors

The CSS3 specification defines a new way to specify color so as to make certain areas partially transparent. Using RGBA, you can adjust the *alpha value* (or transparency) of a color, using a value between 0.0 (completely transparent) and 1.0 (fully opaque). For example, you might use the following code to tell the browser to display a headline at 50 percent of its defined color:

```
h1 {color: rgba(255,50,125,0.5);}
```

As of this writing, the latest version of Safari, Firefox, and Chrome all support RGBA color specification. In addition, the Internet Explorer 9 preview promises support for this powerful feature. Be cautious in going crazy with RGBA until it is fully supported by the majority of browsers in your target audience. In the meantime, visit www.css-tricks.com/rgba-browser-support for tips and guidance on using RGBA.

Other Popular Properties to Style Text

Aside from those properties that begin with font-, a few more are available to customize text. Table 5-6 outlines each one. You can find out more about these properties at www.w3schools.com/css/css_text.asp and www.w3schools.com/css/css_background.asp.

> **NOTE** *The* `text-shadow` *property is relatively new to CSS and as such is not yet supported by all browsers. To see examples of how this can be used in a webpage, check out http://maettig.com/code/css/text-shadow.html.*

Keep in mind that whenever a length value is possible for these properties, you must also specify the unit of measurement being used. For example, if you

TABLE 5-6 Nonfont CSS Properties to Style Text

Property	Description	Possible Values	Default Value
direction	Specifies in which direction the text flows	ltr rtl	ltr (left to right)
letter-spacing	Adjusts the amount of space between letters	normal *<length>*	normal
line-height	Adjusts the amount of space between lines of text	*<length>* *<percentage>*	normal
text-decoration	Adds lines above, below, or through text	none underline overline line-through blink	none (for plain text) underline (for links)
text-indent	Specifies the amount text is indented	*<length>* *<percentage>*	0
text-transform	Changes the case of text	capitalize uppercase lowercase none	none
text-shadow	Adds a drop-shadow to the text	*<shadow offset>* *<blur radius> <color>*	none
word-spacing	Defines the amount of space displayed between words	normal *<length>*	normal

wanted to indent the first line of all paragraphs by 50 pixels, you could use the following style:

```
p { text-indent: 50px; }
```

The next chapter will also discuss two additional properties that have to do with the alignment of text on the page.

Link Styles

I mentioned that the `color` property can be used to change the color of text. But what about links? If you apply the `color` property to a paragraph containing a link, you'll notice the link does not inherit the color applied to the containing paragraph. Instead, if you do not specify otherwise, the links on your pages will display according to the browser settings.

As you might have deduced from the section about pseudo-classes, there are special ways to style links. The `a:link` selector allows you to specify the style of the links before they are clicked, while `a:visited` alters the links after they've been selected. The `a:hover` selector specifies the style of the link when the cursor is positioned over them. Finally, `a:active` states how the link should display as it's being clicked.

The order in which you define these is important. Some people use the LoVe/HAte mnemonic device to remember the proper order. Each of the capitalized letters stands for one of the four elements: Link, Visited, Hover, Active. It may help you remember to always style your links in the following order:

```
a:link {color: blue; font-weight: bold;}
a:visited {color: purple;}
a:hover {color: orange; text-decoration: none;}
a:active {color: green;}
```

As you can see from this example, you don't have to stop at changing the colors of your links. You can format links using any of the other properties already discussed. In this case, I styled the links as bold before they have been clicked and removed the underline for the hover state. But the possibilities are endless.

Having said that, I do have a few words of caution. Avoid using different size fonts in each link state, unless changing the font size in no way affects the surrounding content. (It can be very annoying to a reader to move his mouse across a page and then not be able to read the content because some links become

Still Struggling

For more on ways to style links, check out www.elated.com/articles/styling-links-with-css.

large enough to block the text around then.) Also, avoid making any changes that cause the text to move or jump around on the page (such as text size changes) when a link is activated. And be sure to choose colors that complement the rest of the page and don't distract the reader.

Multiple Link Styles

Whenever you have a page with lots of links, particularly when those links are on different colored backgrounds, it may be necessary to create multiple link styles. This is easily accomplished using some of the specific selectors discussed earlier in the chapter.

For example, you might create two sets of link styles, one for the links in the navigation content division, and another for those in the main text area, like this:

Notice you can use the general a selector without a pseudo-class to make a general style that applies to all link states.

```
#navigation a {text-transform: uppercase;}
#navigation a:link {color: white;}
#navigation a:visited {color: #ccc;}
#navigation a:hover {color: #f90; text-decoration: none;}
#navigation a:active {color: #fc3;}
#mainContent a:link {color: blue; font-weight: bold;}
#mainContent a:visited {color: purple;}
#mainContent a:hover {color: orange; text-decoration: none;}
#mainContent a:active {color: green;}
```

Button Links

So far, I've only styled links by changing their text characteristics. But did you know you can actually add borders, background colors, and even images to links? One of the beauties of CSS is its ability to easily customize almost any aspect of the HTML page. We'll cover the properties used to adjust borders and backgrounds in Chapter 6, but for now here's a glimpse at how this might be accomplished:

```
a { border-style: solid;
    border-width: 1px 4px 4px 1px;
    text-decoration: none;
    padding: 4px;
    border-color: #F90 #C60 #C60 #F90; }
```

Added to the page's style sheet, this would quickly turn a standard text link into a button link by turning off the default underline and adding a colored border. Additional style sheet declarations could be added to change the background color or border color when the user interacts with the link.

List Styles

You can style the text within a list using any of the CSS properties discussed thus far. In addition, there are three list-specific CSS properties, as outlined in Table 5-7. For additional help with each of these properties, refer to www .w3schools.com/css/css_list.asp.

You can also use the `list-style` CSS shorthand to reduce the amount of typing necessary when multiple list-style properties are styled, like this:

```
ul { list-style: inside circle; }
```

Navigation Lists

Every website has some sort of navigation method. Depending on the type of navigation you design for your site, you may be able to use a list to code and style it. The following illustration shows an example of a navigation created with a simple list.

To better understand how this works, let's first look at the HTML used to code the list:

```
<div id="nav">
   <ul><li><a href="about.html" title="Learn more about Merrie">About
Merrie</a></li>
      <li>|</li>
      <li><a href="news.html" title="News/Events">News/Events</a></li>
      <li>|</li>
```

TABLE 5-7 CSS Properties to Style Lists

Property	Description	Possible Values	Default Value
list–style–image	Uses an image before each item in a list	<URL> none	none
list–style–position	Specifies whether items in a list display inside or outside of the bullet	inside outside	outside
list–style–type	Specifies the type of bullet that precedes items in a bulleted or numbered list	disc circle square decimal decimal-leading-zero lower-roman upper-roman lower-greek lower-alpha upper-alpha upper-latin lower-latin Hebrew Armenian Georgian cjk-ideographic kiragana katakana hiragana-iroha katakana-iroha none	disc

```
      <li><a href="join.html" title="Find out about supporting Merrie's
campaign">Join the Campaign</a></li>
      <li>|</li>
      <li><a href="index.html" class="active">Home</a></li>
   </ul>
</div>
```

NOTE *The vertical line in between each menu item is created, in this case, by adding pipe characters as menu items. This is just one way to achieve this look; you could also use the `border` property to customize the left and/or right edges of each menu item.*

I added a special class called "active" to the Home link in the list. This helps set apart the page currently being viewed in the navigation. In this case, it means the home page link is styled a bit differently from the other links to help remind the user that this is the current page.

Without the CSS, this really is just a regular bulleted list. It's the style sheet that causes the list to go from looking like a list to looking like a navigation bar. The related styles for this particular navigation list look like this:

```
#nav {
        width:900px;
        height: 25px;
        background-color:#181858;
        }
#nav ul {
        list-style:none;        ◄──────────────  Here I turn off the bullets.
        font-size:11pt;
        color:#006daf;
        font-family:Arial, Helvetica, sans-serif;
        text-transform:uppercase;
        margin:0;                                 When specifying values for four sides,
        padding:0 0 0 20px;  ◄─────────────       they are always done in the following
        }                                         order: top, right, bottom, left.
#nav li {
        display:inline;  ◄─────────────          This causes the list items to display one
        padding:0 8px;                            after another, horizontally across the page.
        line-height:25px;
        font-size:11pt;
        }
#nav a,
#nav a:link,
#nav a:visited {
        color:#fff;
        text-decoration:none;
        }
#nav a:active,
#nav a:hover {
        color:#fff;
        text-decoration:underline;
        }
#nav a.active {
        color:#9bccea;
        font-weight:bold;
        text-decoration:none;
        }
```

NOTE *Some of the CSS properties used to style this list will be covered in more detail in Chapter 6.*

The first declaration sets the stage for the content division named *nav*. Then, I set some ground rules for the list in general by styling the ul element. Next, I style the individual list items with the li element as a selector, before finally styling the various link states.

Although you may not yet feel ready to code something like this, it's important to consider the many possibilities that exist with regard to coding and styling navigation. If a design calls for its navigation to be contained in boxes, you may not have realized those can be created with a basic list. I encourage you to delve deeper into HTML and CSS to discover the creative ways you can use code more efficiently and effectively.

Form Field Styles

The final section in this chapter seeks to cover form field styles. As with links and lists, you can use any of the CSS properties already mentioned to customize your forms, plus a few more we'll cover in Chapter 6. This means you can do away with those boring white and gray text boxes… and even make them purple if it suits your design. Most of your form elements can be styled using the input element as a selector, like this:

```
input { border: 1px solid #fc0; background-color: #fc3; }
```

TIP *If you want to customize individual form fields, you can add an id attribute to each field, and then reference the value of that id in your style sheet.*

This adds a yellow background and a 1-pixel red border to each aspect of the form inserted with an input element, but you could change those property values to completely alter the look of your form field elements.

Still Struggling

Here are a few online resources to inspire your form styling: www.1stwebdesigner .com/inspiration/91-trendy-contact-and-web-forms-for-creative-inspiration and www.noupe.com/css/form-elements-40-cssjs-styling-and-functionality-techniques.html.

You can also style select menus and text areas, using `select` and `textarea` as your selectors. Keep in mind, however, that the display of form fields does vary a bit from browser to browser, and operating system to operating system. For this reason, be sure to test your forms thoroughly while they are being styled.

Chapter Summary

Whereas Chapter 4 dug into the HTML, Chapter 5 focused more on the CSS. In web design, you use a healthy dose of both HTML and CSS to achieve the desired effect in translating mockups to code. In the next chapter, we'll circle back around to integrate HTML and CSS for page layout.

QUIZ

Choose the correct responses to each of the multiple-choice questions.

1. **Which is an example of a type selector?**

   A. p
   B. list
   C. #footer
   D. .highlight

2. **Which is an example of a class selector?**

   A. p
   B. list
   C. #footer
   D. .highlight

3. **What is the universal selector?**

   A. .
   B. !
   C. #
   D. *

4. **Which is an accurate use of an attribute selector?**

   A. a.href="http://www.mycompany.com"
   B. a[href="http://www.mycompany.com"]
   C. a(href="http://www.mycompany.com")
   D. a > href="http://www.mycompany.com"

5. **Which character separates child selectors from their parents in a style sheet rule?**

   A. a space
   B. a semicolon (;)
   C. a period (.)
   D. a less-than symbol (<)
   E. a greater-than symbol (>)

6. ***:hover* is an example of which type of style sheet selector?**

   A. id selector
   B. class selector
   C. child selector
   D. descendent selector
   E. pseudo-class selector

7. *#header* is an example of which type of style sheet selector?
   A. id selector
   B. class selector
   C. child selector
   D. descendent selector
   E. pseudo-class selector

8. Which style sheet property adjusts the heaviness of the text to which it applies?
   A. font-style
   B. font-effect
   C. font-family
   D. font-weight
   E. font-variant

9. Which style sheet property specifies whether text is italicized?
   A. font-style
   B. font-effect
   C. font-family
   D. font-weight
   E. font-variant

10. Which style sheet property can display text in the Verdana font?
    A. font-style
    B. font-effect
    C. font-family
    D. font-weight
    E. font-variant

Integrating HTML and CSS for Layout

Chapters 4 and 5 covered the basics of HTML and CSS separately. In this chapter, we'll move on to some of the more powerful (and complex) aspects of CSS that allow you to completely customize a page's layout. To get started, we need to talk about how HTML places elements on the page.

CHAPTER OBJECTIVES

In this chapter, you will

- Understand how content boxes are specified with CSS
- Differentiate between the four flavors of CSS positioning
- Identify the steps necessary to position page elements with CSS
- Style page and element backgrounds with CSS

Box Properties

Every element on a webpage—text, photographs, logos, drop-down menus, and so on—is contained within a box of sorts, or at least it's considered to be a box in coding terms. This is important to realize, because you must code each element on the page as if it had four corners and four sides, even if it doesn't look like that when it's displayed in the browser.

As mentioned in Chapter 4, two types of boxes are used in web development: block and inline. By default, each type of element falls into one of those two categories. However, the box type can also be changed as needed, using the `display` property:

```
div#nav {display:inline;}
```

Using a value of *inline* causes a normally block-level element to display as if it were an inline element. By contrast, an inline element can be made to display as a block-level element with a value of *block*. Or, you can use `display:none` to hide the content altogether.

TIP   *Refer to Table 4-1 in Chapter 4 for a reminder of the differences between block and inline elements.*

All block-level elements use five basic spacing properties that affect the area around the element's "box":

- Height
- Width
- Border
- Margin
- Padding

Height and Width

When the box in question is a block-level element, it will fill the available horizontal space by default. This means that unless you specify a smaller width, paragraphs (which are block-level elements) will always run all the way across the page.

The `height` and `width` properties are used to specify the amount of horizontal and vertical space a box will initially fill. I say "initially" because the margins, padding, and border you specify for any box are always added to the height and width dimensions. So if you define a paragraph to be 500 pixels in width and then add a 5-pixel border, your entire box will actually take up 510 pixels of horizontal space on the page (500 + 5 for the left border and 5 for the right border). Here's an illustration to help explain:

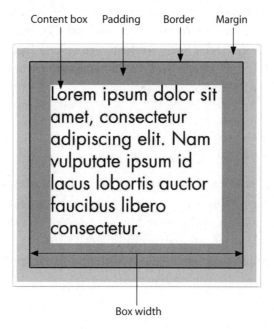

Box width

PROBLEM **6-1**

I'm having trouble with some of my content areas displaying properly in older versions of Internet Explorer. I've used your guidelines for specifying box widths, but the sizes are off in those older browsers. What's going on?

SOLUTION

The W3C box model as I have specified it has not always been supported uniformly by Internet Explorer. In particular, versions prior to version 6 supported a different methodology for determining box widths.

According to the W3C, the total width of a box is determined by adding the left margin, left border, left padding, content width, right padding, right border, and right margin. But in those nonconforming versions of IE, the padding and border sizes are considered to be inside the content width. This means if you specify that your content should be 100 pixels wide, with a 40-pixel padding and a 3-pixel border, older versions of IE will incorrectly subtract the padding and border to leave you just 14 pixels for the actual content. By contrast, browsers conforming to the W3C box model will leave 100 pixels for the content and add the padding and border to it for a total box width of 186 pixels.

If your target audience contains a large portion of users with older browsers, this could be an issue for you. To compensate, some designers create multiple style sheets and serve the correct one according to which browser is being used. Check out http://en.wikipedia.org/wiki/Internet_Explorer_box_model_bug and http://webdesign.about.com/od/css/a/aaboxmodelhack.htm for work-arounds.

Border

The `border` property identifies the color, size, and style of each element's outside edges. Sometimes those edges are not visible because they are the same color as the page background. Other times, you want to call attention to the edges to help set the element apart from others on the page. For example, the following bit of code would create a 1-pixel, solid black border on all sides of any paragraph assigned to the class named "note":

```
p.note {
    border-width: 1px;
    border-color: black;
    border-style: solid;
}
```

These and other border properties are outlined in Table 6-1.

TIP   *You could use CSS shorthand to combine all three border properties in the previous code example, like this:* `border: 1px solid black.`

Each of the border properties listed in Table 6-1 can also be specified individually for each side of the element. So, you could turn off the borders on the left and right while leaving them on for the top and bottom, like this:

```
p.note { border-width: 2px 0 2px 0; }
```

Remember, when using shorthand to style the different sides of a box, values are always assigned in a clockwise manner, starting with the top (as in top, right, bottom, left).

TABLE 6-1 CSS Properties to Style Borders

Property	Description	Possible Values	Default Value
border-color	Defines an element's border color	*<color>* transparent	Varies
border-style	Defines an element's border style	none hidden dotted dashed solid double groove ridge inset outset	none
border-width	Specifies the size of an element's border, either with keywords or a specific numeric value	thin thick medium *<length>*	medium

Margin and Padding

The `margin` and `padding` properties are used to specify the space in and around a box's edges. In the preceding illustration, did you notice how the padding was actually contained within the borders of the text box? This means you can use the `padding` property in a style sheet to give the content in the box a buffer zone of empty space on one, two, three, or four sides.

TIP *You might think of margins and padding in terms of a framed painting. The padding affects how far the paint is from the edge of the canvas, while the margin corresponds to how wide the matte and/or frame is.*

The total width of a box is determined by adding the width to the left padding, right padding, left border, right border, left margin, and right margin. Similarly, the total height of a box is determined by adding the height, top padding, bottom padding, top border, bottom border, top margin, and bottom margin.

With margins and padding (just like with borders), you can define the values for one, two, three, or all four sides of the box, such as in the following example:

```
p { margin-bottom: 25px;
    margin-top: 5px;
    margin-right: 15px;
    margin-left: 5px; }
```

Remember, there should never be a space between a value and its unit of measurement. You must always specify a unit of measure, unless the value is zero.

You can also use shorthand to specify the `margin` and `padding` properties very quickly. For example, `padding: 25px` adds a 25-pixel padding on all four sides. Alternatively, you can specify four different values within a single margin or padding value. So if we wanted to shorten the previous code example, we could style all four sides at once (starting with the top and moving clockwise around the box) like this:

```
p { margin: 5px 15px 25px 5px; }
```

Basic Alignment

In Chapters 4 and 5, I discussed adding images, links, text, and all sorts of other HTML elements. But as of yet we haven't really covered how to move them around on the page. That's because the movement is all achieved with a few powerful CSS properties. The most basic of these are two properties used to align text: `text-align` and `vertical-align`.

- The `text-align` property defines the horizontal alignment of text and block-level elements. Possible values include left, right, center, and justify. The default value is left for most elements.
- The `vertical-align` property specifies the vertical alignment of text and inline-level elements (including text within table cells). Possible values include baseline, sub, super, top, text-top, middle, bottom, and text-bottom. The default value is baseline.

Both affect the way text is aligned relative to the container object. If I wanted to justify all the paragraphs on my page, I could simply add the `text-align` property to my style sheet like this:

```
p { text-align: justify; }
```

Floats

Beyond the basic text alignments possible with the `text-align` and `vertical-align` properties, the `float` property allows you to "float" an element to the left or right edge of the container object. When an element is floated, it remains stationary while the rest of the content flows freely around the page.

The `float` property tells the browser to place the floated element nearest whichever container edge is specified (left or right) and then flow the rest of the page's content around it. To say it another way, content automatically flows along the right side of a left-floated element, and to the left side of a right-floated element.

TIP *Images are easy to float because they carry defined height and width values. If you try to float a block-level element, it will not work unless you specify a width that is smaller than the total width available so there is room to flow the remaining content around it.*

For example, if you wanted to place an image in the upper-right corner of several paragraphs of text, you could use the `float` property with a value of *right* to tell the browser to keep the image on the right side of the text. When coding floats, make sure your floated content is placed before any other content to wrap around it in the HTML:

```
img.portrait { float: right; }
```

Sometimes when you float an element, you need to prevent other content from wrapping around it. The `clear` property is used to tell the browser when to stop wrapping content around a floated object. For example, in the following code sample, the first paragraph wraps around the floated image, but the second one is forced to begin after the floated image ends:

```
<img src="photo.jpg" alt="Team Photo" style="float:right;">
<p>This paragraph of text will flow along the left side of the
floated image.</p>
<p style="clear:right;">There will be blank space in between the
two paragraphs. The clear property causes this paragraph to be
placed after the floated image, not around it.</p>
```

Possible values for the clear property are left (to clear items floated left), right (to clear items floated right), both (to clear all floated items), or none.

Still Struggling

Refer to www.brainjar.com/css/positioning for more information about positioning and floats.

CSS Positioning

So I've discussed basic text alignment and floats, but what about the more powerful positioning I mentioned? There are four basic types of positioning with CSS: static, relative, fixed, and absolute.

Static and Relative Positioning

Normal (also called *static*) is the default type of positioning that happens when no other type of positioning is specified. With normal positioning, items are placed one after another, starting at the upper-left corner of the page. By default, all elements are positioned normally unless you specify otherwise.

Relative positioning starts off using the normal positioning, but then allows for certain elements to be moved up, down, left, or right from the original position. In other words, boxes are moved relative to where they would normally be placed on the page. Here's an example of a level-two headline that is moved 100 pixels to the right of its normal position:

```
h2 { position: relative; left: 100px; }
```

When we use relative positioning, we're moving the box relative to its current location. So if we want to move a box to the right, we actually do that by asking the browser to look at the left edge and push it 100 pixels over to the right. To move it back toward the left edge, we'd instead specify a value of –100. With relative positioning, we have to think of this whole page as a big grid, with the zero point at wherever the box's edge would normally be placed.

Still Struggling

Visit www.w3schools.com/CSS/tryit.asp?filename=trycss_position_relative to learn more about relative positioning.

Fixed and Absolute Positioning

With normal and relative positioning, elements are free to move around on the page. Conversely, the final two types of positioning—*fixed* and *absolute*—both position elements in firm, concrete spots. The difference between the two is how that concrete spot is determined.

- When fixed positioning is used, the element is placed relative to the *viewable area within the browser window.*
- When absolute positioning is used, the element is placed relative to its *parent object.*

Okay… so what does that really mean? Have you ever visited a webpage and noticed that a certain page element stayed in the same place, even when you scrolled down the page? This element was placed in that exact spot using fixed positioning. The following code sample shows how that might be accomplished:

```
#nav { position: fixed;
       top: 10px;
       right: 10px;
       width: 100px; }
```

NOTE *Internet Explorer versions 6 and earlier do not support fixed positioning.*

By contrast, an element placed with absolute positioning will indeed move when the page is scrolled, but will move *with the rest of the page content.* In fact, absolutely positioned elements are removed entirely from the document flow, so they can be placed in a specific position regardless of what else is on the page.

Still Struggling

Visit http://dev.opera.com/articles/view/37-css-absolute-and-fixed-positioning for a great tutorial on fixed and absolute positioning.

How to Position Elements

When you need to position an element on the page, there are a few basic steps to follow.

Specify the Type of Positioning

First, you need to specify the type of positioning being used. This is done with the `position` property, using the value that corresponds to whichever method of positioning is being used. (Note: If you do not specify a method of positioning, the default "static" value is used.)

```
#header { position: absolute; }
```

Once you determine which method of positioning you'll use, you must figure out the lineage of the element. In other words, you need to identify the containing block that holds the element being positioned. When elements use absolute or fixed positioning, they are placed relative to their closest, positioned containing block. If there is no such containing block, the browser window is used.

TIP   *This means if you want to absolutely position an element, it's best to place it within a content division that is also positioned (using any method except the default static value).*

Set the Dimensions

After the type of positioning has been identified, it's time to specify where to position the element. The `top`, `right`, `bottom`, and `left` properties are used to tell the browser where each edge of the box should fall within the page:

```
#header { position: absolute;
          top: 20px;
          left: 20px; }
```

When an element is relatively positioned, you need only specify the locations of two perpendicular sides (such as top and left to tell the browser where to place the upper-left corner of the box) in relation to its current location.

NOTE   *Specifying two parallel sides can cause the browser to become confused because `left: -10px` and `right: 10px` essentially cancel each other out.*

But when you absolutely position an element, you can specify the locations of all four sides if needed. Or, you can set the position of just two sides of the box and then add the `height` and `width` properties to specify the size of the box (and ultimately the other two sides). Compare the following two code snippets to see how an element is affected by these different strategies.

First, here a box is positioned 20 pixels from the top edge and 20 pixels from the left edge of its containing block. The box is 800 pixels wide and 50 pixels tall.

```
#header { position: absolute;
          top: 20px;
          left: 20px;
          width: 800px;
          height: 50px;}
```

Now compare that to another strategy, where three sides of the box are positioned as well as the height, but the width varies according to the size of the browser window:

```
#header { position: absolute;
          top: 20px;
          left: 20px;
          right: 20px;
          height: 50px;}
```

In the second instance, the header content box will grow and shrink horizontally according to the size of the browser window as long as it is 20 pixels from the left and right sides of its containing block.

Adjust the Layering

When dealing with relative, fixed, or absolute positioning, CSS functions in three dimensions: width (along the x axis), height (along the y axis), and depth (along the z axis). The z-index property specifies the depth of an element, or more specifically, the layering of elements that overlap. If two elements overlap when they are positioned, the one with the higher z-index value is placed on top. This means you can actually use a negative z-index value to force a layer to drop behind others.

NOTE   *When multiple elements have the same z-index value (or when none have been set), the order in which the elements are listed in the HTML code generates the stacking order: Elements defined earlier are displayed behind those defined later.*

The following code sample creates two boxes that overlap on the page. Can you figure out which one comes out on top?

```
#hilite { position: absolute;
          top: 20px;
          left: 20px;
          width: 200px;
          height: 50px;
          padding: 10px;
```

```
              background-color: yellow;
              z-index: 2; }
#lolite { position: absolute;
          top: 30px;
          left: 30px;
          width: 200px;
          height: 50px;
          padding: 10px;
          background-color: gray;
          z-index: 1; }
```

The two elements in this sample overlap. However, the z-index value of the hilite content division is set to 2, which is higher than the value given to the `lolite` element. This placed the `hilite` element above the `lolite` element when viewed in a browser (as shown in the following illustration).

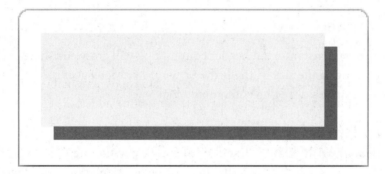

Set the Visibility

After you position an element, you may want to alter its visibility. Why? Sometimes it can be helpful to hide certain elements from view until they are needed. This can help you to create multiple layers of content within a single page and then bring the required layer forward as needed. It's easy to hide and display layers with the `visibility` property, like this:

```
#moreinfo { visibility: hidden; }
```

The possible values for the `visibility` property are *hidden, visible,* and *collapse.* By default, the visibility of elements is inherited from parent objects. Also, if you hide an element with relative or static positioning, its dimensions continue to affect the flow of the document's content. So if you don't want a hidden box to cause content to shift, set its display to *none* instead of *hidden.*

TIP   *The collapse value only works for table elements, but is quite useful in temporarily hiding a row or column without affecting the rest of the table's layout.*

Define the Overflow

Finally, when you position elements with defined sizes, you need to consider how to handle any content within those elements that doesn't fit.

Suppose you create a content division to hold your main body copy and give it an overall width of 500 pixels and a height of 600 pixels. What if the text for one of the pages doesn't fit within that size? By default, CSS sets all content to be visible, regardless of the size of the content box. This means you may end up with some not-so-readable results when the extra text flows out onto the rest of your page.

To prevent that from happening, you can define how the browser handles any content that doesn't fit—with the `overflow` property. The four possible values are *visible, hidden, scroll,* and *auto.* Visible and hidden are fairly obvious, and scroll is just what you'd expect: It adds a scroll bar to the box so users can access the overflow content.

Auto allows you to let the browser decide what is needed. This is particularly useful when a content division's styling is used on multiple pages—each with different amounts of content. If the content division is large enough to accommodate its content on one page, no scroll bar will be added. But if the content overflows on another page, a scroll bar will be added.

Adding Interactivity

The positioning of elements in a webpage can be a powerful way to add interactivity. In particular, this can occur when layers are hidden temporarily (using `visibility: hidden` in the style sheet) and then made visible based on user action. Here are just a few ways interactivity might be achieved through CSS positioning:

- **Advertising** Have you ever clicked on a link in a banner ad, only to have that ad appear to grow larger without the actual webpage changing? Very likely, the larger version of the ad was a hidden layer set to appear when you clicked the link.

- **Entertainment** While many online games use Flash for interactivity, many newer versions are switching to a combination of HTML and CSS, thanks to the additional interactivity offered in the forthcoming HTML5. These games often place different elements on layers so that they can easily be moved around on the page, independently of each other.

- **Navigation** We all have visited websites with drop-down navigation menus. These types of navigation systems can easily be accomplished by placing the submenu content into a layer that is made visible when the user clicks a particular link.
- **Rollovers** Adding interactivity to links is a useful way of letting website visitors know which aspects of the page are clickable. When someone interacts with the link by moving the mouse over the top of it or clicking on it, the style of the link can change.

Positioning Properties

In summary, Table 6-2 lists the CSS positioning properties I just covered (and any others that relate to positioning) to give you an easy reference.

TABLE 6-2 CSS Properties to Position Elements

Property	Description	Possible Values	Default Value
position	Specifies how an element is positioned on the page	static relative absolute fixed	static
top	Defines the location of the top edge of a positioned element	*<length>* *<percentage>* auto	auto
left	Specifies the location of the left edge of a positioned element	*<length>* *<percentage>* auto	auto
right	Defines the location of the right edge of a positioned element	*<length>* *<percentage>* auto	auto
bottom	Specifies the location of the bottom edge of a positioned element	*<length>* *<percentage>* auto	auto
height	Defines how much vertical space an element consumes	*<length>* *<percentage>* auto	auto
width	Defines how much horizontal space an element consumes	*<length>* *<percentage>* auto	auto
z-index	Specifies the stacking order of the positioned element	*<integer>* auto	auto

TABLE 6-2 CSS Properties to Position Elements (*continued*)

Property	Description	Possible Values	Default Value
visibility	Specifies whether/how an element is displayed on the page when it first loads	visible hidden collapse	inherit
display	Specifies how the item should be displayed within the page flow	inline block list-item run-in compact marker table inline-table table-row-group table-header-group table-footer-group table-row table-column-group table-column table-cell table-caption none	inline
float	Pushes an element to the left or right of other page elements; can be applied to any element that is not absolutely or relatively positioned	left right none	none
clear	Specifies whether content flows around a floated element	none left right both	none
overflow	Defines how to handle content that doesn't fit within a particular block-level box	visible hidden scroll auto	visible

Backgrounds

Another aspect of the page that can be styled is the background. For most designers who work in graphics programs such as Photoshop, layering is a very important tool. Photoshop allows you to place images, colors, and textures below other elements through the use of semitransparent layers.

You just reviewed how the z-index property can be used to layer elements in a webpage. Other tools available to help with this task are the five background properties identified in Table 6-3.

Each of these properties can be used to customize the background for an entire page or for specific page elements. For example, you could add a colored background to a paragraph and a repeating image to the background of a table cell. Here are two code samples to show how these backgrounds might be added:

```
p { background-color: #012345; }
td.textured { background-image: url(images/pattern.jpg); }
```

TIP *When you want to use more than one background property for a single element, use CSS shorthand to avoid coding them all longhand:*
P {BACKGROUND: URL(STAR-BG.GIF) NO-REPEAT;}.

TABLE 6-3 CSS Properties to Style Backgrounds

Property	Description	Possible Values	Default Value
background–attachment	Defines whether a background image scrolls when the page is scrolled or remains fixed in its original location	scroll fixed	scroll
background–color	Defines the background color of an element	*<color>* transparent	transparent
background–image	Defines an image to be used as the background pattern	*<URL>* none	none
background–position	Defines the starting position of the background color or image with *x* and *y* positions (if you specify only one keyword, the second will automatically be 'center')	*<percentage>* *<length>* top center bottom left center right	0% 0%
background–repeat	Specifies how a background image repeats	repeat no-repeat repeat-x repeat-y	repeat

Use Backgrounds to Create Columns

You can quickly and easily give the appearance of different colored and/or textured columns with a single background image containing each of the faux columns. Consider the following illustration to see what such an image might look like when viewed in Photoshop.

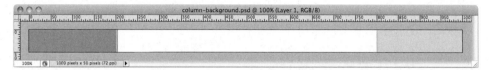

When this image is used as the background of the page and repeated along the vertical axis, we get the appearance of columns that can be used to contain various content divisions on the page (as shown in Figure 6-1). For example,

FIGURE 6-1 · Faux columns using a single background image

the left column might house the page's navigation, while the center area is reserved for the bulk of the body copy. The right column can be used for supplemental information, advertisements, or related links.

To accomplish this, my style sheet is coded as follows:

```
body { background-image: url(column-background.gif);
     background-repeat: repeat-y; }
```

Still Struggling

Refer to www.alistapart.com/articles/fauxcolumns for another explanation of how to achieve faux columns with background images.

Use Backgrounds to Customize Bullets

The default bullets typically used for unordered lists sometimes don't fit a site's design scheme. An easy way to replace them with custom images is to turn off the default bullets and add the images to the list's background.

Take a look at this illustration to see this type of background customization in action, and then look at the code sample to understand how this was achieved.

> ⊙ First list item
> ⊙ Second list item
> ⊙ Third list item
> ⊙ Fourth list item
> ⊙ Fifth list item

```
<!DOCTYPE html PUBLIC "-//W3C//DTD XHTML 1.0 Transitional//EN"
"http://www.w3.org/TR/xhtml1/DTD/xhtml1-transitional.dtd"> <html
xmlns="http://www.w3.org/1999/xhtml">
<head>
<style type="text/css">
#navlist {
          margin-left: 0;
          padding-left: 0;
          list-style: none;
          color: #7b98b6;
          font-family: Arial, Helvetica, sans-serif;
          font-size: 14px;
          }
#navlist li {
          padding-left: 20px;
          padding-bottom: 6px;
          background-image: url(arrow.gif);
          background-repeat: no-repeat;
```

```
                background-position: 0 0;
                }
</style>
<title>List Backgrounds</title>
</head>
<body>
<div id="navcontainer">
<ul id="navlist">
<li>First list item</li>
<li>Second list item</li>
<li>Third list item</li>
<li>Fourth list item</li>
<li>Fifth list item</li>
</ul>
</div>
</body>
</html>
```

NOTE *You may remember there is a `list-style-image` property specifically geared toward replacing traditional list bullets with images, and wonder why I suggest a different strategy. The reason for using background images is that it provides greater consistency in terms of spacing when replacing bullets with images. But I encourage you to do your own testing to determine which works best in your situation.*

Use Backgrounds to Add Shadows

Designers frequently like to add drop-shadows to various page elements, if for no other reason than to add a little depth to an otherwise flat page. Many sites use partially transparent images in an element's background to achieve a drop-shadow effect in web design. Take a look at Figure 6-2 to see several different background effects in action, including a partially transparent image used to create a shadow effect.

 Still Struggling

Refer to http://nontroppo.org/test/shadow.html and http://www.projectseven .com/tutorials/images/gradient_tiles2/index.htm for two different online examples.

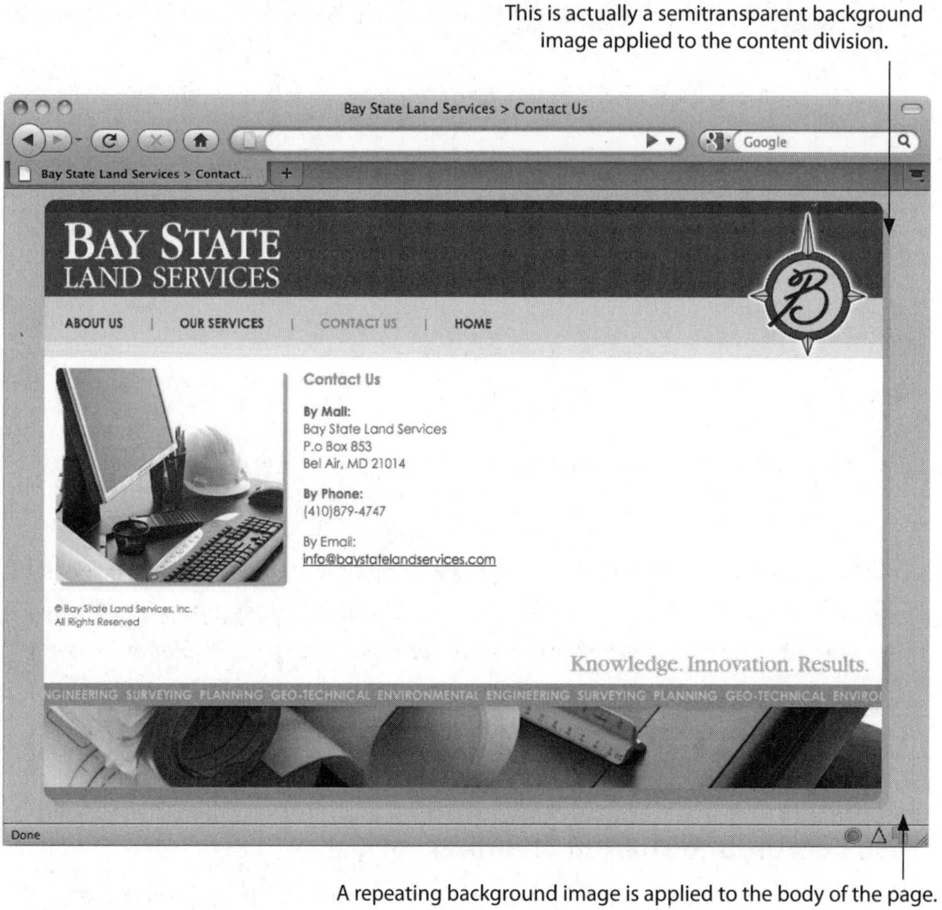

This is actually a semitransparent background
image applied to the content division.

A repeating background image is applied to the body of the page.

FIGURE 6-2 · Using semitransparent background images to create shadow effects

In this example, the faint texture of the background is accomplished through a tiny (it's only 56 pixels by 32 pixels) repeating background image. The shadow effect behind the main page content is a semitransparent image saved in the PNG file format. When it is placed on top of the textured background, behind the content area, it gives the appearance of a shadow while still allowing the background texture to show through.

Use Backgrounds to Customize Links

You can also use the same concept to style image-based links by adding different images to the background of text links. Suppose you wanted to create a navigation bar with a series of images, and you wanted those images to change when the user's mouse rolled over them. Before the advent of CSS, designers had to use complicated JavaScript to code image-based rollover effects. Thankfully, it is now possible to achieve the same results with some background images and a few simple CSS instructions.

The following illustration shows the background image you might use to create such a rollover effect. Notice there are three different versions (normal state, rollover state, and active state) contained within a single image. We'll use some of the CSS properties from Table 6-2 to specify which version of the image is visible at any given time.

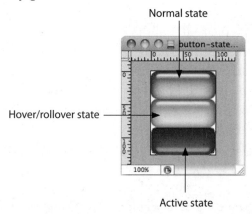

First, take a look at the HTML used to create the image-based link:

```
<a href="home.html" class="imageRollover" title="Home">Home</a>
```

Then, consider the CSS capable of switching the image view as needed:

```
a.imageRollover {
    display:block;
    width: 100px;
    padding: 12.5px 0;
    font-family: verdana;
    font-size: 10pt;
    color: #003;
    background: url("button-states.jpg") 0 0 no-repeat;
    text-align: center;
    text-decoration: none;
    text-transform: uppercase;
    }
a.imageRollover:hover {
    background-position: 0 -42px;
    }
a.imageRollover:active {
    background-position: 0 -84px;
    color: #fff;
    }
```

The `display` property tells the browser to fill the available space with this link, which, in this case, should be 100 pixels wide because of the width of the image. The padding is set next, to prevent the top of the text from sitting along the edges of the button. I've set a 12.5-pixel padding along the top and bottom edges, but no padding along the left and right edges.

Next I specify the font settings and colors, before finally adding the background image. I set the initial position of the image to 0 0, which essentially makes the first button visible in the box I've created.

I use the `text-decoration` property to turn off the underline for the text link, align the text to the center of the button, and then force each text link to display in uppercase with the `text-transform` property. For the hover and active states, I then move the background image down a bit each time. Because each button is 42 pixels tall, I position the background for the hover state at −42px to move it up by 42 pixels. (The hover or rollover state is the second button in my background image.)

For the active state, the background is moved up 84 pixels to display the bottom button in my background image. Whenever we move "up" the page in positioning, we use a negative number. So the vertical position of the image changes to −84px. Take a look at Figure 6-3 to see the different states as they appear in the browser:

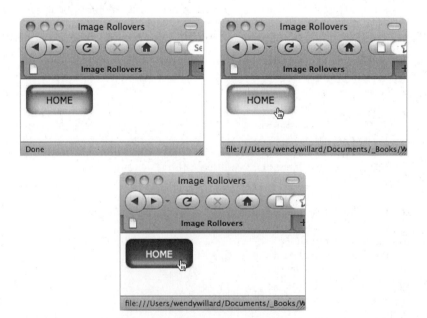

FIGURE 6-3 · Using image backgrounds to customize text links

Still Struggling

Check out http://monkeyflash.com/tutorials/css-image-rollover-navbar to see another example.

Chapter Summary

By the end of this chapter, you should have a good understanding as to how CSS can transform basic page elements through positioning and backgrounds. As with the rest of the coding outlined in this book, these techniques will require some practice to further clarify how they work. I encourage you to practice moving elements around on a page, not by shifting the HTML code, but by merely adjusting the positioning with CSS.

In the next chapter, we'll move beyond HTML and CSS to touch on a few additional technologies you are likely to encounter as a web designer.

QUIZ

Choose the correct responses to each of the multiple-choice questions.

1. **True or False: Block and inline are two types of boxes used in web development.**
   A. True
   B. False

2. **Which property has possible values that include solid, dashed, and dotted?**
   A. border-color
   B. border-style
   C. border-width
   D. border-format

3. **Which property is used to specify the buffer space inside the border of a box?**
   A. float
   B. border
   C. margin
   D. padding
   E. whitespace

4. **Which property defines the vertical alignment of text and inline-level elements?**
   A. text-align
   B. font-align
   C. text-vertical
   D. vertical-align

5. **Which is not a possible value of the position property?**
   A. float
   B. static
   C. fixed
   D. relative
   E. absolute

6. **When absolute positioning is used, how is the element placed?**
   A. relative to its child object
   B. relative to its current location
   C. relative to the browser window
   D. relative to its positioned parent object
   E. relative to where they would normally be on the page

7. **True or False: Absolutely positioned items are removed from the normal document flow.**

    A. True

    B. False

8. **What is the purpose of the z-index property?**

    A. It specifies the depth of an element.

    B. It specifies the width of an element.

    C. It specifies the height of an element.

    D. It specifies the visibility of an element.

9. **Which property is used to define how the browser handles any content that doesn't fit within the box area?**

    A. scroll

    B. display

    C. position

    D. visibility

    E. overflow

10. **Which property controls the starting position of the background color or image?**

    A. background-color

    B. background-scroll

    C. background-image

    D. background-position

    E. background-attachment

Beyond HTML and CSS

Just about any website today uses some type of technology beyond HTML and CSS. Thankfully, you don't have to be a skilled programmer to achieve a basic understanding of technologies like JavaScript, Hypertext Preprocessor (PHP), Extensible Markup Language (XML), and Really Simple Syndication (RSS). I've included an introductory-level primer on each of these tools here in the hopes it will inspire you to try your hand at each one. Perhaps you'll even find a particular technology you'd like to focus on as you expand your skills.

CHAPTER OBJECTIVES

In this chapter, you will

- Understand how JavaScript is used to add interactivity to webpages
- Understand how PHP is used to extend the capabilities of HTML
- Understand how XML is used to move and store data

JavaScript

JavaScript is referred to as an object-oriented scripting language used to perform actions in webpages. JavaScript is extremely popular among developers, due in part to the fact that it enjoys widespread support among web browsers.

JavaScript is an interpreted language, which means it is not compiled, or translated into machine-language (1's and 0's) before use. Like HTML, you can use any text or web development editor to write JavaScript.

When you use JavaScript, it's often placed in the HTML of your page. This means you can learn JavaScript from visiting your favorite websites, just as you can with HTML, and viewing the page source from within the browser.

NOTE *It is a common misconception that JavaScript is part of Java. While JavaScript was originally created with Java's syntax and terminology in mind, the two are quite different.*

Terminology and Syntax

JavaScript can either be included within your HTML pages or left alone in .js files that are then linked to the HTML pages of your site. When included within the header content of your HTML page, JavaScript is placed in between opening and closing `script` tags:

```
<script language="JavaScript" type="text/javascript">
... script goes here ...
</script>
```

You should learn several new terms before you use any JavaScript. Given that scripts are essentially a set of instructions to the browser, you can often read them as a series of commands, made up of statements and expressions. One type of statement is an *if… else* control statement, also called a *conditional*, which tells the browser to do one thing if x is true and to do something else if x is false.

While HTML entities are contained within angle brackets, JavaScript *if* statements are surrounded by curly brackets. In addition, all statements (instructions) end with semicolons, similar to CSS. Here's a simple example of the layout you'd use when creating a set of JavaScript instructions:

```
if (something) {
    do this;
}
else {
    do this;
}
```

You must write *if* and *else* in lowercase letters to avoid generating an error.

One of the most important aspects of JavaScript is the *object*. Quite simply, an object is anything that can be manipulated or changed by the script. In the following example, *document* is acting as a JavaScript object. It's telling the document within the browser to write "I can write JavaScript!":

```
document.write ("I can write JavaScript!");
```

This line of code is referred to as a JavaScript *statement*.

Objects can have *methods*, which indicate what happens to the objects, just as real-world objects can perform actions. (A car can drive or stop, for example.) In the case of the previous code snippet, the document is *written to*. Methods are followed by a set of parentheses containing specific instructions on how to accomplish the task. That's why the text to be written to the document was contained within parentheses in the previous example.

Just as an object, such as a car, has features (make, model, color, and so forth) in the real world, JavaScript objects can also have properties. Objects and properties are separated by periods. For example, HTML documents can have names, images, forms, backgrounds, and so on. When you want to specify the value of a property, such as the color of the background, you add the value after the property, as in this example:

```
window.name="popup";
```

In JavaScript, a *variable* is something you specify for your own needs, similar to custom selectors in CSS. You might think of variables as labels for changeable values used within a single script. To define a variable, type **var**, followed by the one-word name of your choice. Remember that JavaScript is case-sensitive. If you capitalize a letter when you first define a variable, you must also capitalize the letter every time you refer to it. Also, variables must begin with a letter or an underscore (_), and never a number.

```
var DrivingAge;
```

Likewise, a *function* is a group of statements to which you give a name so you can refer to the group later in the script. To create a function, type **function**, followed by the function name and a set of parentheses. Then, type the statements that are part of the function below the name enclosed in curly brackets, like this:

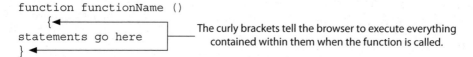

```
function functionName ()
    {
statements go here
}
```

The curly brackets tell the browser to execute everything contained within them when the function is called.

Different from the other terms discussed here, *event handlers* aren't typically run when the page loads. Instead, event handlers allow you to run code independently from the page loading, as they are embedded within your HTML to respond to a user's interaction. For example, placing the onclick event handler within the opening a tag causes the event to occur when the user clicks the link. So if I wanted to change the page's background color when a link is clicked, I could use the following code:

This prevents the link from taking the user to another page when it is clicked. Instead, only the page background color is changed.

```
<a href="#" onclick="document.body.style.backgroundColor='#006699';return
false;">Change color</a>
```

Still Struggling

Check out www.w3schools.com/js for plenty of easy-to-understand information on JavaScript.

Usage: Creating a Drop-Down Navigation Bar

In Chapter 6, I discussed how you could have hidden layers of content within your webpage. While the layers can be created and hidden with CSS and HTML, you can use JavaScript to easily make them visible when a user interacts with the page. The most common use of this in webpages is for drop-down navigation bars, in which a submenu appears after you click a link or mouse-over a button. The drop-down menu provides additional link choices without refreshing the HTML page itself.

These drop-down navigation bars can become extremely complex, but the core concept is relatively simple, and that's what this section discusses: a bare-bones method for invoking submenus. For more on how to make your navigation bar bigger and better, refer to the online resources listed at the end of this section.

To try this out, place this JavaScript into the header of your page. The boldface text indicates pieces of the script you should customize.

```
<script language="JavaScript" type="text/javascript">
  function showLayer(layerName) {
      document.getElementById(layerName).style.visibility='visible';
  }
  function hideLayer (layerName) {
      document.getElementById(layerName).style.visibility='hidden';
  }
</script>
```

Next, adjust your style sheet to format the visible navigation button/link and the hidden submenu. Be sure to set the positioning so that the submenu displays below the top menu. What follows is the style sheet I used to create the menus shown in Figures 7-1 and 7-2.

```
body {
    font-family: verdana;
}
#aboutus {
    position: absolute;
    top: 20px;
    left: 20px;
    width: 100px;
    padding: 10px;
    text-align: center;
    background-color: #ccc;
    border:1px solid black;
    cursor: pointer;          ←——————— This changes the cursor to a pointer, to
}                                     help indicate that the content is linked.
#aboutus-sub {
    position: absolute;
    visibility: hidden;       ←——————— I set the visibility to hidden so the sub-
    top: 60px;                          menu is not shown when the page first loads.
    left: 20px;
    width: 100px;
    padding: 0px 10px;
    text-align: center;
    background-color: #333;
```

```
    color: #fff;
    border: 1px solid #999;
    cursor: pointer;
}
ul {
    padding: 0px;
    margin: 0px;
}
li {
    list-style: none;
    padding: 5px 0px;
    border-bottom: 1px dashed white;
}
li a {
    color: #fff;
    text-decoration: none;
}
.last {
    border: 0px;
}
```

The final piece is the actual HTML code for the content, which is placed between the opening and closing body tags:

The onclick JavaScript event handler tells the browser to display the "aboutus-sub" layer when the user clicks anywhere within the "aboutus" content area.

```
<div id="aboutus" onclick="showLayer('aboutus-sub');">ABOUT US</div>
<div id="aboutus-sub">
<ul><li><a href="history.html">History</a></li>
    <li><a href="location.html">Location</a></li>
     <li class="last"><a href="team.html">Team</a></li>
</ul>
</div>
```

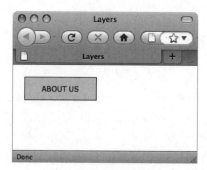

FIGURE 7-1 · This shows the navigation button before it's been clicked.

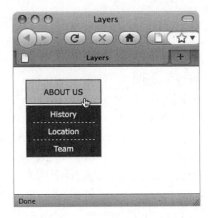

FIGURE 7-2 • This shows the navigation button after it's been clicked.

Learning More

If you'd like to learn more about JavaScript, check out some of the following resources:

- **SitePoint.com**   This site contains DHTML and JavaScript articles (www .sitepoint.com/subcat/javascript), as well as a whole blog about this stuff (www.sitepoint.com/blogs/category/dhtml-css).
- **Web Reference JavaScript Articles**   This website (www.webreference.com/ programming/javascript) includes tutorials, tips, and reviews of tools.
- **jQuery**   Why reinvent the wheel? A JavaScript reference library like jQuery provides users with predefined functionality, such as the ability to rotate sets of images or easily manage FAQ pages.
- *JavaScript: The Missing Manual* by David McFarland (McGraw-Hill, 2008)
- *JavaScript: A Beginner's Guide, Third Edition* by John Pollock (McGraw-Hill/Professional, 2009)

NOTE   *Always look for the most recent references you can find when working with JavaScript. Older scripts were written for older browsers and may or may not be valid today. Often, those older browsers required web developers to use special workarounds, called hacks, in their scripts. Many of those hacks are no longer necessary, and in some cases they can even "break" in modern browsers.*

PHP

The second scripting language I'd like to introduce you to is PHP, which is sort of an all-purpose scripting language well suited for web development. It is open-source, which means any developer can customize and deploy it on any web server without paying a license fee. Open-source technologies survive and grow because of the community of people using them, and PHP is no exception. PHP is likely the most widely used web scripting language today.

PHP runs on many different computer systems (Windows, Unix, Linux, and so on) and is compatible with just about any web server in use today. The official PHP specification is maintained at www.php.net.

NOTE   *PHP must be installed on the host system in order for you to use it in your webpages. Not to worry, though—because PHP is free, most host companies keep PHP updated on all their servers (although many don't offer PHP on Windows servers, because those systems use Active Server Page [ASP] instead). Here's a tutorial that walks you through the process of installing PHP, should you find it necessary to do so: www.php.net/manual/en/install.php.*

Terminology and Syntax

In PHP, the code is surrounded by the PHP tags: `<?php` and `?>`. Each line of code within the PHP tags usually ends with a semicolon, similar to JavaScript. However, unlike JavaScript, when an HTML file contains PHP, it usually must be saved with a .php file extension. If you include PHP code inside of an .html file, the PHP code might be ignored. The required extension varies from server to server, so check with your hosting provider for more information. Files saved as .php let the web server know to execute the PHP code within them when the content is sent to the web browser.

PHP has its own way of declaring *variables*, just like JavaScript. Variable values can include text strings, numbers, and many other types of data. In PHP, variables are preceded by a dollar sign, like this:

```
$variable_name = value;
```

There are a few guidelines you should consider when naming variables:

- Variable names must begin with a letter or underscore (_).
- Variable names can only contain letters, numbers, and underscores.
- Variable names cannot contain any spaces.

If your variable's value needs to contain spaces, as a line of text might, you can use a *string*, whereby the value is enclosed within quotes:

```
$text = "This is my first line of PHP";
```

PHP also uses the basic *if... else* statement I showed you in the JavaScript section. As with most scripting languages, the real meat is found in the *functions* being performed when the page is loaded. PHP has more than 700 built-in functions—plus an unlimited number of custom functions—which means there's a whole lot you can do with it!

Even though there are so many options, the same basic process is used. First you tell the system you're starting a function, then you give it a name and specify the instructions it contains, like this:

```
function functionName ()
{
//instructions go here;
}
```

Prefacing a line of code with // tells the browser this is a comment from the author and should be read, not run.

Notice the syntax of a function is the same in JavaScript and PHP.

Another important aspect of most scripting languages is the *operator*. These characters are used to specify how two different values are compared. There are many different types of operators, but the most basic operators are probably quite familiar to you already. Take a look at Table 7-1 to see what I mean.

TABLE 7-1 Basic Scripting Operators

Operator	Description	Example
+	Addition	x+2
−	Subtraction	x−2
*	Multiplication	x*2
/	Division	x/2
++	Increment	x++
−−	Decrement	x−−
=	Assignment	x=2
==	Is equal to	x==2
!=	Is not equal to	x!=2

Now that you've had a chance to become familiar with some of the terminology and syntax of PHP, let's take a look at an example of how it might be used in web design.

Usage: Process a Form

A common use of PHP is to process a web form. Three built-in PHP variables are perfectly suited for this purpose: $_GET, $_REQUEST, and $_POST. In Chapter 4, I outlined how to create a form using HTML. I do not, however, provide you with a way to process that form because HTML does not include such a method. For that, you must use some other language, such as PHP.

The first thing you need to do is create your HTML form and then reference the new PHP file from the opening form tag. What follows is a basic contact form that asks for the user's name, e-mail address, and comments:

```
<form action="processform.php" method="post">
Name: <input type="text" name="name" /><br />
Email: <input type="text" name="email" /><br />
Comments:<br />
<textarea name="comments" rows="10" cols="50"></textarea>
<br />
<input type="submit" />
</form>
```

Next, create the processform.php file. The contents of that file are included here:

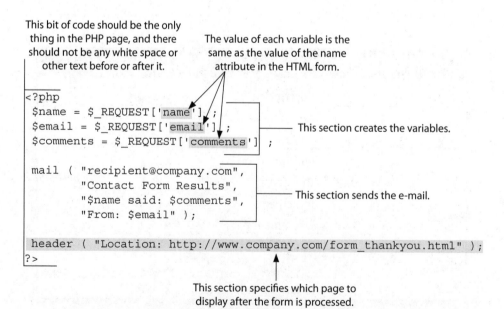

This bit of code should be the only thing in the PHP page, and there should not be any white space or other text before or after it.

The value of each variable is the same as the value of the name attribute in the HTML form.

```
<?php
$name = $_REQUEST['name'] ;
$email = $_REQUEST['email'] ;
$comments = $_REQUEST['comments'] ;
```
— This section creates the variables.

```
mail ( "recipient@company.com",
       "Contact Form Results",
       "$name said: $comments",
       "From: $email" );
```
— This section sends the e-mail.

```
header ( "Location: http://www.company.com/form_thankyou.html" );
?>
```

This section specifies which page to display after the form is processed.

PHP has a special function called *mail* that is able to send e-mail using the data sent through the file. In this case, the data being sent is the person's name, e-mail address, and comments (as defined in the original HTML form).

This PHP file has three distinct sections: one to create the variables, one to send the e-mail, and one to identify the next webpage to be displayed. Within the section that sends the e-mail, there are four arguments.

- The first one defines the e-mail address to which the message should be sent.
- The second argument identifies the subject line.
- The third one defines the contents of the e-mail message.
- The fourth argument specifies the e-mail address to be listed in the *From* field.

The final section should list the page to be shown after the form is processed. This is a different HTML page from the one that housed the form. It should contain text that lets the website visitors know the form has been processed. I also like to include contact information in case the visitor wants to reach a live person before he receives an e-mail response.

After you become comfortable with this most basic method of form processing (which does not include any way to prevent spam), you may want to tackle more complex forms, perhaps including form validation (making sure the fields are completed correctly) and spam prevention. Check out www .digital-web.com/articles/bulletproof_contact_form_with_php for a great PHP form-processing resource.

Learning More

If you'd like to learn more about PHP, check out some of the following resources:

- **PHP Junkyard**   This site contains free, downloadable PHP scripts, as well as lists of books and tutorials (www.phpjunkyard.com).
- **PHP Freaks**   This website (www.phpfreaks.com) bills itself as "your number one PHP resource," mostly because it boasts an online community of more than 90,000 members. Here you'll find tutorials, free scripts, and tons of folks willing to help you learn and use PHP.
- **PHP Builder**   This section of Internet.com (www.phpbuilder.com) is specifically geared toward web developers using PHP.

- **PHP.net**   As I mentioned, PHP.net is run by the people who maintain and update the language. As such, it is a great resource for all information about PHP.
- *Beginning PHP and MySQL* by W. J. Gilmore (Apress, 2006)
- *Wicked Cool PHP: Real-World Scripts That Solve Difficult Problems* by William Steinmetz (No Starch Press, 2008)

XML

XML stands for Extensible Markup Language. It is similar to HTML, in that the two languages share the same basic structure and formatting. The key difference is that XML holds the data while HTML structures it. Plus, you can create your own XML elements, according to the type of data being contained.

XML was developed to move and store data, but not to replace HTML, which was developed to display data. This means you can use the two complementary languages together to store and display data.

Let's look at a few code samples to clarify the difference between the two markup languages. First, consider this simple HTML sample from a calendar of events:

```
<h1>New York Bus Trip</h1>
<h2>Saturday, May 8, 9:00am - Sunday, May 9, 8:00pm</h2>
<p>Bus departs from Fallston Park and Ride promptly at 9:00am on
Saturday. Contact Pam Trell for more information.</p>
```

As web designers, we can read this code snippet and understand that the level one heading contains the event title, the level two heading contains the event date, and the paragraph includes event details. But what if a database needed to evaluate this data? The database might not understand the various HTML elements, or be able to associate their content with the data they contain. Here's where XML excels. That same calendar of events could be coded with XML to clarify the purpose of each bit of data:

```
<calendar>
   <eventTitle>New York Bus Trip</eventTitle>
   <eventDate>Saturday, May 1, 9:00am - Sunday, May 2, 8:00pm</eventDate>
   <eventDetails>Bus departs from Fallston Park and Ride promptly at 9:00am
on Saturday. Contact Pam Trell for more information.</eventDetails>
</calendar>
```

TIP *The W3C maintains the XML standards. Visit www.w3.org/standards/xml to learn more.*

When I tell you that XML is meant to store data, you might wonder why I'm not calling it a database. The reason is traditional databases are tied to specific software and/or computer systems, but XML is platform- and software-independent. Databases require that software in order to be interpreted properly, whereas XML is referred to as "self-describing" because it contains both the data and the element and attribute names to describe it. Having said that, many databases allow importing of XML data and exporting as XML files.

Terminology and Syntax

XML has elements and attributes, just like HTML. The syntax is pretty much the same as in HTML. In HTML, we use the `!DOCTYPE` statement at the top of all HTML files to let the browser know which version of HTML the page follows. Likewise, the first line of an XML document includes the XML declaration, like this:

```
<?xml version="1.0"?>
```

NOTE *XML is case-sensitive, which means <eventTitle> and <EVENTtitle> are two different elements.*

I've already mentioned that you create your own XML elements. While this means XML is quite powerful, it has the potential to get confusing. To counteract that, the W3C has set up a few guidelines for developers. A *well-formed* XML document must follow each of the following rules:

- The document must have a single root element that contains all other elements.
- All elements must be properly nested.
- All elements must be closed.
- All attributes must be included in the opening tags with values enclosed between quotes.

In addition, here are a few more guidelines to keep in mind when naming elements:

- Names cannot begin with any of the following: numbers, punctuation, or "xml."

- Aside from the first letter, the rest of the name can include any letter or number.

- Names must not contain any spaces.

So if we return to our calendar of events, here's what a more complete example might look like:

```
<?xml version="1.0"?>
<calendar>
  <event id="0501">
    <eventTitle>New York Bus Trip</eventTitle>
    <eventDate>Saturday, May 1, 9:00am - Sunday, May 2, 8:00pm</eventDate>
    <eventDetails>Bus departs from Fallston Park and Ride promptly at
9:00am on Saturday. Contact Pam Trell for more information.</eventDetails>
  </event>
  <event id="0508">
    <eventTitle>Mother's Day Tea</eventTitle>
    <eventDate>Saturday, May 8, 2:00pm - 4:00pm</eventDate>
    <eventDetails>Tea is open to all moms and those who love them. Contact
Lois Burt for more information.</eventDetails>
  </event>
</calendar>
```

After your data is organized with XML, you can use other coding methods to display it. An XSL (Extensible Stylesheet Language) document contains the presentation instructions for an XML document, in much the same way a CSS file specifies how to style HTML content.

Still Struggling

Check out the XML tutorial on W3 Schools: www.w3schools.com/xml.

Usage: Exchange Data with RSS

The primary use of XML today is in the exchange of data between sources. In fact, a ton of information is exchanged every day through the use of RSS feeds. RSS (Really Simple Syndication) has grown so quickly in recent years that even though you might not have known what it means, you've likely seen it referenced at one website or another.

Many news sites and web blogs include little orange or blue rectangular buttons near a story that is available for syndication by the general public. For example, visit www.foxnews.com/rss to see a list of the Fox News content available for syndication. Another example comes from Netflix, who provides everything with a feed, from new DVD releases to personalized feeds of your movie queue: www.netflix.com/RSSFeeds.

Here's an example that shows the structure of an XML document used to hold an RSS feed:

```
<?xml version="1.0"?>
<rss version="1.0">
   <channel>
      <title>WendyWillard.com</title>
      <link>http://www.wendywillard.com</link>
      <description>a healthy mix of creativity and code</description>
      <language>en-us</language>
      <item>
         <title>Adding Third-Party Content</title>
         <link>http://wendywillard.com/blog/2010/04/20/adding-third-party-
content</link>
         <description>When you create websites, you often need to integrate
content from other sources. Suppose you wanted to load the current weather
forecast into a page on your site...</description>
      </item>
      <item>
         <title>Web Design Links</title>
         <link>http://wendywillard.com/blog/2010/04/20/web-design-links</
link>
         <description>Here's an ever-growing compilation of links from my
web design books that are useful to web designers.</description>
      </item>
   </channel>
</rss>
```

As you can see, a feed includes a *channel* element, which has title, link, description, and language (optional) elements, followed by one or more *item* elements, each of which has its own title, link, and description elements. This file is saved as an .xml or .rss file and stored on your web server.

The next step to creating an RSS feed is to validate it using Feed Validator (www.feedvalidator.org). If a problem is found, the tool will let you know so it can be corrected.

TIP   *To "read" such syndicated content, you need to open the RSS feed in a news reader (also called an aggregator). Check out http://blogspace.com/rss/readers for a list of some popular news readers.*

The final step is to add the feed to your page. There are two places you can link the feed. First, you can provide a clickable link within the body of your page, which users can click to access the feed:

```
<a href="feed.rss">RSS Feed</a>
```

In addition, you can add the reference to the header content of your page. When you do so, you're telling the browser where to find the RSS feed for the page, even if there is no clickable link. That way, if a user attempts to view the feed for the page through any RSS reader, the correct content will be shown.

```
<link rel="alternate" type="application/rss+xml" title="RSS Feed"
href="http://www.cnn.com/feed.xml" />
```

Using an RSS Service

Plenty of tools will create a standard XML RSS feed out of the content on your site (or anyone else's, for that matter), so you don't have to. Here are a few tools you can use to easily create, edit, and publish RSS feeds:

- FeedFire (www.feedfire.com)
- FeedForAll (www.feedforall.com)
- Feed43 (www.feed43.com)
- Feedity (www.feedity.com)

Also, if you use a content management system or a blog to build and maintain your site, you probably can take advantage of built-in RSS tools.

Learning More

If you'd like to learn more about XML, check out some of the following resources:

- **XML Standards**   This site (www.w3.org/standards/xml) is worth mentioning a second time, because it contains the XML standards, as well as all sorts of additional information for beginning and advanced users alike.
- **About.com's XML Resources**   This website (webdesign.about.com/od/xml/XML.htm) is full of links to everything XML, including information about XSLT and a complete XML glossary.
- **Internet.com's XML Resources**   This section of Internet.com (www.xmlfiles.com) is specifically geared toward web developers using XML.
- *XML: Visual QuickStart Guide* by Kevin Howard Goldberg (Peachpit Press, 2008)

Chapter Summary

While web design coding might begin with HTML, it certainly doesn't end there. Many other tools and technologies are used to extend the capabilities of HTML on webpages. This chapter provided an overview of three of those technologies: JavaScript, PHP, and XML.

As with most web technologies, things can get rather complex with more comprehensive projects. When that happens, don't be afraid to call in some backup and engage the skills of a developer more experienced in whichever technology is being used. Word of mouth is the best way to find a reputable developer, so contact your local web developer networking group if you have one. Alternatively, try visiting the computer sciences department of a local college for people who can help.

Chapter 8 explains templates and media types in web design, and how each one can greatly increase the usability and maintainability of your webpages.

QUIZ

Choose the correct responses to each of the multiple-choice questions.

1. When included within the header content of your HTML page, JavaScript is placed in between which tags?
   A. <link></link>
   B. <script></script>
   C. <object></object>
   D.
   E.

2. Which JavaScript event handler is used to cause something to occur when the user activates a link?
   A. onblur
   B. onlink
   C. onclick
   D. onload
   E. onchange

3. True or False: JavaScript is a subset of the Java programming language.
   A. True
   B. False

4. What term is used to refer to custom values defined in JavaScript in much the same way classes are in CSS?
   A. object
   B. method
   C. variable
   D. function
   E. operator

5. Which is *not* true about the guidelines you must follow when naming PHP variables?
   A. Variable names can contain spaces.
   B. Variable names must begin with a letter or an underscore.
   C. Variable names can only contain letters, numbers, and underscores.
   D. Variable names are preceded by dollar signs when they are declared.

6. **+ and – are examples of what aspect of JavaScript and PHP?**
   A. objects
   B. methods
   C. variables
   D. functions
   E. operators

7. **Which is most like HTML in terms of structure and formatting?**
   A. Java
   B. CSS
   C. PHP
   D. XML
   E. JavaScript

8. **True or False: XML is case-sensitive.**
   A. True
   B. False

9. **Which is *not* true about the guidelines you must follow when naming XML elements?**
   A. XML element names cannot contain any spaces.
   B. XML element names can include any letter or number (aside from the first letter).
   C. XML element names are preceded by question marks when they are declared.
   D. XML element names cannot begin with any of the following: numbers, punctuation, or "xml."

10. **Which type of document contains the presentation instructions for an XML document?**
    A. JSS
    B. CSS
    C. PHP
    D. XSL
    E. XSS

Templates and Media Types

When you are designing for the Web, at some point you will face the question of when to use a web template. In web terms, a template is an empty layout waiting for your content. Throughout the course of this chapter, we'll look at ways you can use templates to save time both during development and maintenance of a site, as well as to make your pages more accessible to users.

CHAPTER OBJECTIVES

In this chapter, you will

- Recognize the benefits of using templates in web design
- Differentiate between hosted and downloadable blogging options
- Understand how Dreamweaver templates can help nontechnical users maintain webpages
- Identify ways to customize style sheets for printing and mobile users

There are pros and cons to using templates. On the positive side, templates can save you a lot of time (and money!) in developing a layout. In addition, if you're new to web design, using a template can help you learn more about webpage layout as you work with existing files.

The drawbacks include a potential lack of originality and flexibility. While some templates are easily customized, others can require so much work to move elements around on the page that you'd be better off writing your own code.

Stock templates are available for all sorts of sites, from very basic marketing sites to corporate blogs and even shopping sites. The first half of this chapter helps you identify the right type of template for your needs and then use it to get started on the right foot.

In the second half of the chapter, we move on to another sort of template: one that specifies how your pages will display in alternative viewing conditions, such as the printed page or a mobile device. Because these types of conditions can cause a page to appear completely differently from the way they do in traditional desktop-based web browsers, it's important to create special instructions for the browser.

Finding Stock Templates

Thousands of sites offer templates for free or for sale. Because of the sheer number of templates available, it's easy to get distracted by the many flashy options. While searching for a web template, it's important to focus on the goals of your site and what your users need to accomplish through it.

With the large number of templates available, it can be difficult to find quality products. Here are a few guidelines to consider as you search:

- Files should be editable using your favorite web editor
- Coding should be up to W3C standards, and ideally the files should validate (http://validator.w3.org)
- Files should come with instructions regarding how to edit and upload
- Pages created should display in any modern web browser without generating errors

TIP   *As mobile users make up a growing part of web audiences, many templates also include mobile versions. If you are interested in developing a mobile version of your site, be sure to look for templates with mobile options.*

Template Options

The first step is to identify the type of template you need. Many different options exist, so I outlined the basic types of templates in Table 8-1.

Basic website templates are fairly easy to download and use. Shopping cart and CMS templates, however, require you to have some knowledge of the site's host environment. For example, before you can even start searching through CMS templates, you must know which CMS is being used.

The most popular content management systems include WordPress, Joomla!, and Drupal, each of which is freely distributed as open-source software. Once you have that piece of information, it's much easier to sort through the various options for your specific tool.

TABLE 8-1 Types of Web Templates

Type	Description	Included Files
Single-page template	Includes code and graphics to create a website that uses one design for all its pages. (Some single-page templates also include editable Photoshop files.)	.html .css .psd (sometimes)
Full site template	Includes all code and graphics needed to create a home page and interior pages for the site. (Some website templates also include editable Photoshop files and Flash animations.)	.html .css .psd (sometimes) .fla (sometimes)
Flash template	Includes Flash files to create a website built entirely in Flash, and the HTML file to reference the Flash movies.	.html .fla .swf
Shopping cart template	Includes all code and graphics to create an online store. Many also include the shopping cart software, or work with existing software on your host computer.	*varies according to the technologies used* .psd (sometimes) .fla (sometimes)
Content Management System (CMS) template	Includes all code and graphics to integrate the theme with an existing CMS on your host computer.	*varies according to the CMS used* .psd (sometimes) .fla (sometimes)

Still Struggling

Having trouble wrapping your head around exactly what a content management system is? Check out Wikipedia's definition to learn more: http://en .wikipedia.org/wiki/Content_management_system.

Software Requirements

When you're building a site that uses a shopping cart or content management system, you will end up with pages built with something other than basic HTML and CSS. As such, there are additional requirements for the site's host computer. A shopping cart template, for example, might require certain versions of tools like PHP and MySQL. Be sure to check with your site's host company before purchasing any templates with additional software requirements.

Page Size

Another aspect of the template to consider is the page size. Throughout this book, I've discussed how important it is to build pages that work for the intended audience. To that end, be aware of the size of any template you consider. Reputable companies advise users as to a template's page width, which is typically anywhere from 800 px to 1200 px. If you find a template that fits your project but is the wrong size, check to see if the template company offers customization. Many offer customizations, such as page width changes, for an additional fee.

Template Themes

Templates are organized by category or theme. When a designer uploads a template to an online repository, she adds keywords to help associate the template with a few categories or themes. This can be helpful if you're looking for a specific theme, such as one featuring animals or one that highlights certain holidays.

However, I caution you against feeling pigeon-holed into the "education" category, for example, just because you're creating a site for an educational organization. Instead, check out multiple themes to be sure the template you identify is the best one for your site, regardless of which category it is housed in.

Template Sites

There really are thousands of template sites out there—some better than others. Most work under one of three financial models:

- Pay per template
- Subscription
- Free

Obviously, we'd all love to use the free templates, if possible. But usually those either aren't as high quality or don't offer as much flexibility. Having said that, free templates can work quite well for some projects. Just be sure to check the license details to verify your project fits within the license guidelines.

The other two options—pay per use and subscription—each involve payment for services. Subscription-based sites allow you to download and use a certain number of templates each month without paying any additional fees. These types of sites typically cater to web designers who frequently use templates for multiple projects each month.

If that doesn't sound like you, consider simply paying a "per template" fee when you find the template you'd like to use. The *regular price* is typically lower, but doesn't limit others from also using the same template. If you'd like to purchase the template and take it off the market, ask for the *unique price*. While the unique price is typically up to ten times the cost of the regular price, it means no one else will be able to use that template for another website.

Here are just a few template sites you might try to get started:

- **Template Monster**   www.templatemonster.com
- **DreamTemplate**   www.dreamtemplate.com
- **Templates.com**   www.templates.com
- **Ice Templates**   www.icetemplates.com
- **Template World**   www.templateworld.com
- **Pixel Mill**   www.pixelmill.com
- **Theme Vault**   www.themesvault.com
- **Web Design Library**   www.webdesign.org
- **Studio Press**   www.studiopress.com

Blogging

You know a technology has gone mainstream when your mom tells you she started a blog to journal online about her gardening techniques. Yup, blogs have officially "arrived."

In fact, they've gone so mainstream that many companies are taking advantage of blogging tools to manage corporate websites. This is happening because blogging tools are powerful enough to allow any non-technical author to write, edit, and publish web content quickly, without using any HTML code. For cash-strapped businesses, this translates into a real financial benefit.

Blogging software can be used as content management systems, which means sites built upon them can be managed without ever coding a single HTML tag. If you decide to use a blog, you're not limited to creating a site that looks like a personal journal. Blogging tools are flexible enough that you can use them for all sorts of business websites. And the best part is that some really great blogging tools are free!

Two popular blogging tools are Google's Blogger (www.blogspot.com) and WordPress (www.wordpress.com). Both are available as free *hosted* blogging tools for anyone wanting to use them. The hosted part refers to the fact that someone else (Google or WordPress) maintains the server on which the blog is housed.

However, of the two, only WordPress also offers a version that can be downloaded, installed, and completely customized on the web server of your choice. This means you (or your system administrator) can download all the source files necessary to run the blogging software and install them on your own server without incurring any additional cost. This downloadable version of WordPress is found at www.wordpress.org instead of wordpress.com.

NOTE *If you want to research other downloadable blogging tools, check out http://en.wikipedia.org/wiki/Blog_software#Examples.*

Hosted Blogging

If you don't need control over or access to the web server, a hosted option from Blogger or WordPress is probably a good choice. Table 8-2 compares the most basic features of each tool.

TABLE 8-2 Blog Features

Feature	WordPress	Blogger
Ability to import content from another source	Yes (from a variety of formats)	Yes (only from another blogger.com blog)
Ability to use different themes (designs)	Yes, but you can't edit the style sheet for a theme without a paid subscription	Yes (you can also edit the style sheet for each template)
Ability to add static pages that are not part of the blog system	Yes (unlimited)	Yes (up to 10)
Ability to add a built-in contact form	Yes	No, but you could create your own and host it elsewhere
Ability to make the blog content private	Yes, but you are limited to 35 readers of private pages, unless you upgrade to a paid subscription	Yes, but you can restrict access only to those with Google accounts
Ability to allow others to author content	Yes (four levels of access: Administrators, Editors, Authors, and Contributors)	Yes (two levels of access: Administrators and Non-Administrators)
Ability to upload and add images	Yes, 3GB of storage with free account	Yes (1GB of storage with free account—uses Picassa Web Albums)
Ability to moderate comments	Yes	Yes, but you can't edit comments
Ability to use custom domain name (www.myblog.com)	Yes (only with paid subscription)	Yes

Beyond those basic features, both tools offer thousands of additional features called plug-ins (or gadgets). (Do a search in Google for "WordPress plug-ins" to see tons of options.) Most of these have been created by individuals throughout the world who then upload and share them with the rest of the blogging community.

You can do just about anything with blog plug-ins. You know those iPhone commercials claiming "there's an app for that"? The same commercials could be used for blog plug-ins. If you have an idea for a way to extend the capabilities of your blog, there's probably a plug-in to accomplish it. For example, if you want to earn money with ads on your blog, there's a plug-in for that. Need a slideshow or poll? There are plug-ins for those, too. Want to include a searchable database of audio files? There's a plug-in for that.

The one caveat to plug-ins is that you can only use official Blogger or Word-Press plug-ins on hosted blogs. Therefore, if you find another plug-in on the Web and want to install it on your hosted blog, you're out of luck unless it's supported by Blogger or WordPress. So if you want to take advantage of the wealth of nonofficial plug-ins and themes available for download, it's time to consider hosting your own blog.

Custom Blogging

When you encounter a project that needs a custom blog hosted on a server you (or your administrator) can manage, you can still take advantage of a free blog-ging tool. As I mentioned, WordPress also offers a downloadable version you can install (free of charge) on any server that meets the basic requirements (www.wordpress.org/about/requirements).

Most hosting providers actually make the installation process quite painless. In fact, several (which are promoted at www.wordpress.org/hosting) offer one-click installations of WordPress for any sites they host. Using a hosting company that offers this type of quick installation is well worth it, and makes WordPress accessible to even beginning designers.

After the installation is complete, you'll want to focus your efforts on the template files. As of this writing, those are located in the wp-content/themes folder. You can download additional theme templates from developers all over the Web (as described in the section on finding stock templates in the beginning of this chapter) and paste them into this directory as well.

TIP   *Themes are a collection of files and styles that work together to create the look of your site. When you download a theme, it will contain various page templates as well as one or more style sheets to carry the theme through the entire site.*

Each theme comes with multiple templates to handle different types of pages displayed through the blogging tool. For example, here are a few of the template files contained within the default theme:

- archives.php
- comments.php
- footer.php
- header.php
- index.php

- page.php
- sidebar.php
- style.css

If you want to change the theme's layout, or even create your own custom theme, you'll want to check out each of these files to see what needs to be edited. Or, you could just edit the style sheet to change elements such as backgrounds and font characteristics.

Templates in Dreamweaver

Even if you don't use a stock template, you will likely use some sort of template when you build websites. For example, you might create a master page with the site's layout and navigation and then copy it each time you need to create a new page. While this can definitely save you a ton of development time, there is a drawback. If you later need to make a change to the navigation or layout that cannot be achieved by changing the style sheet, you may have to edit each and every HTML page based on the initial page.

Adobe Dreamweaver, a popular development tool among web designers, has its own type of template files that can help prevent this problem. These templates are special master files containing certain editable regions. Any pages created based on these master templates allow parts of the pages to be edited without affecting other areas blocked from edits. Those areas that are locked can only be edited by changing the original master template. When you edit the master template, all changes propagate to any pages using that template, which means you only have to make the change once.

This can also be a huge benefit to a web designer who needs to develop a website she will then turn over to someone else to maintain. Many times, the person maintaining the website has little experience with HTML or other scripting languages. When such maintainers are faced with the challenges of editing text mixed with HTML, they can often lose interest in the site maintenance or, worse yet, make changes that cause problems with the site display.

As the template creator, you can specify which parts of the templated pages can be edited by maintainers and which can only be edited by a template administrator. The templates and any pages built off these templates can then be edited in Dreamweaver or its counterpart, Contribute. (I'll cover more about Contribute shortly.)

Working with Dreamweaver Templates

A common way to create a template in Dreamweaver is to first start with an existing webpage you've designed. This might be the first of a series of interior-level pages for a large website being developed. Suppose you create the initial page according to the original design mockups and get it approved from the client. Now you need to build the rest of the pages that follow the same style and layout as the first page. Here's where Dreamweaver's template feature comes in.

Creating a template depends on whether you're starting from scratch or an existing page:

- **To create a template from an existing page**, choose File | Save As Template, give it a unique name, and specify the site in which to save the file. Then click Save.
- **To create a template from scratch**, choose File | New and select HTML Template as the page style before clicking Create.

When you create a new template in Dreamweaver, it is given a .dwt file extension. All templates must be stored in the site's Templates folder (if the folder doesn't already exist, Dreamweaver will create it for you).

TIP *If you're new to Dreamweaver, check out this helpful three-part series about building websites in Dreamweaver from Adobe's Developer Connection: www.adobe.com/devnet/dreamweaver/articles/first_website_pt1.html.*

Template Regions

After you've identified the file as a template, it's time to specify the types of regions in the document. Dreamweaver allows for four types of template regions:

- **Editable regions** can be edited and changed by any user. All templates need to have at least one editable region. An example of an editable region might be the page headline or its main text area.
- **Locked regions** cannot be edited or changed by any user unless the user is a template administrator or when the template is edited in Dreamweaver. An example of a locked region might be the navigation bar of the page. This is the default type of region for a template.

- **Optional regions** can be hidden or shown by any user. Depending on the parameters you set, optional regions can contain editable regions. An example of an optional region might be a box containing links to related content.

- **Repeating regions** can be duplicated, edited, and changed by any user. An example of a repeating region might be a row of data within a table.

To create a new region, select the area that contains the content to be included in the region and choose Insert | Template Objects. Then select the type of region you'd like to insert (editable, optional, or repeating).

TIP *Any content that is not inside an editable, optional, or repeating region is automatically considered locked.*

When you create a region, Dreamweaver adds some comments around the section in your HTML code. Here's an example of those comments, as they create an editable region to contain the page title:

```
<!-- TemplateBeginEditable name="doctitle" -->
<title>FREE Delivery</title>
<!-- TemplateEndEditable -->
```

You shouldn't remove those comments, unless you want to get rid of that region.

In addition, you can create editable *attributes*. This lets you unlock an HTML tag attribute in a template so that attribute can be edited within a template-based page. For example, you can lock which image appears in a webpage, but allow the alignment of that image to be editable.

Still Struggling

Refer to the Template section of Adobe's Dreamweaver Developer Connection: www.adobe.com/devnet/dreamweaver/templates.html.

Using Library Items

One of the great benefits of templates in Dreamweaver is that you can reuse layouts for multiple pages. Dreamweaver also lets you reuse smaller chunks of code throughout multiple pages on a website by storing them inside of a site library.

In fact, you can put anything that would be in the body of the document into a library item.

These chunks of code are referred to as *library items.* These files are saved with an .lbi extension and housed in a folder called Library in the main directory of the website. To create a library item, try one of the following actions:

- Select File | New, then choose the Blank Page (or Basic Page) category, and select Library Item.
- Highlight a part of a file and select Modify | Library | Add Object To Library.
- Highlight a part of a file within the body of the document, and click the New Library Item button at the bottom of the Assets panel.

After a code selection is saved as a library item, it can easily be used throughout the entire site as many times you feel is necessary. To use a library item, first make sure the library is visible in the Assets panel (click the book icon on the left side of the Assets panel to open the library). Then, drag the item into any open page to insert it.

If you switch to Code view in Dreamweaver, you can see the code that was added when you dragged the item into the page. Here's an example of a library item I use to add fine print to HTML e-mails for a client:

```
<!-- #BeginLibraryItem "/Library/LD-Fine-Print.lbi" -->
<p style="font-family:Verdana, Arial, Helvetica, sans-serif;font-size:10
px;color:#666666;margin:20px;width:660px;">Let's Dish! is the region's
leading meal-assembly chain, where customers stock up on homemade,
freezer-ready meals that take the stress out of dinnertime. For more
details visit letsdish.com.</p>
<!-- #EndLibraryItem -->
```

Whenever you need to edit a library item, you simply double-click the item in the library category of the Assets panel and make any necessary changes. Then, all pages using that library item will be automatically updated.

NOTE   *You will still need to upload all changed pages to the live web server after edits have been made to any corresponding library items.*

Still Struggling

Refer to this online tutorial for more information about using library items in Dreamweaver: http://webdesign.about.com/od/dreamweaverhowtos/a/aa090406.htm.

Using Server-Side Includes

At the end of the previous section, I mentioned that pages using library items will need to be reuploaded to the live web server after any changes are made to embedded library items. This is required because Dreamweaver's library items are stored locally on your personal computer.

What if you stored those code selections on the live web server instead and allowed the web server to assemble the pages on the fly? This would mean you only had to update a code snippet and then all the other pages using that snippet would automatically be updated (without you needing to reupload them). This can be accomplished through the use of *server-side includes* (SSIs).

NOTE *If you try to use SSIs without success, it may be because they have not been enabled on your web server. Contact your site's system administrator for help in configuring your account to use SSIs.*

To create an SSI, you simply start with a blank page in Dreamweaver or any other HTML editor. Add the code to be reused on multiple pages and save the file with an .ssi, .inc, or .txt extension. (Note: Check with your server administrator to confirm the correct SSI extension for your server.) Be sure the only code included in the SSI is the code to be added to other pages (in other words, there is no need to add html, head, or body elements unless those are part of your code selection).

After the SSI is ready, you use a #include directive to add the SSI to your HTML pages:

This single slash at the beginning of the link tells the browser to start looking for the file at the root, or main, level of the website.

```
<!--#include virtual="/includes/footer.ssi"-->
```

SSIs must be stored on the same web server as the pages containing them. To make maintenance easier, it's a good idea to keep them all in the same folder (such as one named *includes*, like I used in the previous example).

TIP   *If you're using Dreamweaver to build your pages, you can also add an SSI to a webpage by choosing Insert | Server-Side Include. The contents of the SSI display in Dreamweaver's Design view, but only the #include directive is shown in Code view. Dreamweaver uses "file" instead of "virtual" in the SSI directive, which just means the file parameter is defined relative to the document path instead of the document root.*

After an SSI has been added to a webpage, that HTML file must be saved with a different extension. Instead of .html, you can use .shtml to tell the server it must compile the page with its SSIs before displaying it in the browser. (Note: If you're building dynamic pages, such as those created with PHP or ASP, there's no need to change the file extension because the server already knows to check those pages before displaying them in the browser.) But to be sure, always check with your server administrator to ask about the proper extensions when coding SSIs.

To edit an SSI, simply open the file in your favorite web editor and make the necessary changes. When you save the file to the live web server, all pages using that SSI will display the updated content.

Still Struggling

Find plenty of online resources about SSIs here: http://websitetips.com/ssi.

PROBLEM 8-1

I've made changes to my SSI file, but am not seeing those changes in the live webpages. Why not?

SOLUTION

Most likely, you have not reuploaded the edited file to the web server. First, check to be sure you have indeed made the changes to the SSI file, and then save it. After that, use FTP to upload the file to its final destination on the live web server, making sure to overwrite the old version of the SSI. Then, use your browser to view the page using the updated SSI, making sure to click Refresh if you've recently viewed the file. If you still cannot see

the changes, you might have the old file cached on your computer, which means you might have an old copy stored locally. Follow these directions to clear your browser's cache and try again: www.wikihow.com/Clear-Your-Browser%27s-Cache.

Maintaining Pages with Adobe Contribute

After you've created templates and built pages off those templates, you've created a site that can easily be maintained by nontechnical editors. In particular, there is one piece of software nontechnical editors can use to easily update pages created with Dreamweaver templates.

Adobe Contribute is a website management tool built to work with Dreamweaver files. Some people refer to Contribute as a scaled-down version of Dreamweaver, geared toward nontechnical website managers.

TIP *Visit www.adobe.com/contribute to learn more about this website management tool.*

When a user opens a template-based page in Contribute, the tool recognizes which regions are editable and which are locked. If someone tries to edit a noneditable region in Contribute, he is prevented from doing so. Furthermore, while a Dreamweaver user can override a noneditable region by disconnecting the page from its template, Contribute users are not able to do so. This gives website developers powerful control over which aspects of their pages can be edited by nontechnical website maintainers.

Media Types

So far in this chapter, I've mostly discussed using templates to speed up web development and maintenance. But there is another important reason templates are used in web design: to target different users or display methods.

For example, creating a main style sheet for your website means that all the pages will carry the same look and feel when viewed in a web browser. But what about how the pages display when they are printed or viewed on a mobile device? You can create additional templates, or in this case style sheets, to specify how your pages are displayed in different types of media.

By default, style sheets apply to all media types. But it is easy to create and link additional style sheets for different media types. The following code sample shows how three different style sheets might be used to target three different display methods:

```
<link rel="stylesheet" media="screen" href="screen.css" type="text/css">
<link rel="stylesheet" media="print" href="print.css" type="text/css">
<link rel="stylesheet" media="handheld" href="screen-small.css"
type="text/css">
```

This method works well when you need to set up completely different style sheets for each different media type. If, instead, you only want to change a few styles within your main site style sheet, you can use the @media rule in your style sheet, like this:

```
@media print {
    body { font-size: 10pt; }
}
@media screen {
    body { font-size: 12px; }
```

Possible media types (whose names are case-sensitive) include:

- all
- braille
- embossed (used for paged Braille readers)
- handheld
- print
- projection
- screen
- speed
- tty (used for teletypes, terminals, and portable devices with limited display capabilities)
- tv

Printer-Specific Style Sheets

Ever visited a webpage and seen a button labeled "click for printer version" or something similar? While that may have led to a PDF or Microsoft Word version of the page, it more likely led to the same page displayed with a printer-specific style sheet referenced in one of the two methods I just outlined. When creating printer-specific style sheets, here are a few things to keep in mind.

Color

First, always set your background color to white and remove any background images you might have already assigned to the page. This ensures the user doesn't waste ink printing a black background with white text for no real reason. What may have looked attractive on screen might only be a big bleed of ink on the printed page.

Also, consider the color of text-based content to make sure it will be readable even if the page is printed in black and white.

Links

If you turned your link underlines off, be sure to turn them back on. Likewise, consider making them bold or otherwise emphasized so they'll stand out even more if printed in black and white. CSS even allows you to specify that link URLs should be displayed after the linked text. This would be quite useful if someone prints your page and then wants to access its links at a later date.

The following code specifies that the URL should be printed after both visited and unvisited links:

```
a:link:after, a:visited:after {
    content: " (" attr(href) ") ";
}
```

If you have a lot of internal links on your pages, you may need to add your domain name to this code. Without it, users might see only a portion of the URLs printed, such as index.html or aboutus/contact.html. Here's how to add the domain:

```
a:link:after, a:visited:after {
    content: " (http://www.company.com" attr(href) ") ";
}
```

TIP *If you have a combination of internal and external links on your pages, you could create a custom class to attach to only those links you want to affect with this type of style sheet declaration.*

Fonts

The standard font measurement for printed pages is points. Therefore, if you used another measurement for your screen pages, such as pixels, be sure to change that for your printer-specific style sheet.

Page Size

Whereas webpages are designed for screen format (landscape, 800 × 600 pixels, and so forth), printed pages should be designed for the paper on which they will be printed. Most users in the United States will probably print in portrait format on standard letter-size paper (8.5 × 11 inches). Be sure to leave at least a half-inch margin on all sides.

Positioning

If you styled any aspects of your page to be absolutely positioned, consider removing that declaration and allowing the content to flow freely on the printed page.

Image Resolution

Images created for the Web are low in screen resolution (72 dpi) because that makes them quicker to download. It does not, however, make them pretty when printed. In fact, printed web graphics often look quite bad. Therefore, when creating alternate versions of webpages that will be printed, avoid graphics whenever possible. If that's not an option, it's probably best to instead offer the page as a downloadable PDF. I prefer turning off the images and navigation whenever possible to allow users to save on ink they might otherwise waste printing images they don't need.

Mobile-Specific Style Sheets

Due to the large number of people accessing the Web from handheld devices, it's common for modern websites to also offer custom versions geared toward those users. In particular, you want to restructure the content so it can be easily viewed on smaller screens.

Before I list the areas of concern for mobile-specific style sheets, I need to mention a few caveats. First, there are some handheld devices that do not support enough CSS to recognize different media types. Those devices, unfortunately, will continue to display the screen media styles.

Second, there is a handheld device that (as of this writing) will display webpages with mobile-specific style sheets even though its screen is quite a bit larger than most phones and personal digital assistants (PDAs). Apple's iPad, launched in 2010, contains the word "mobile" in its user agent string, which means it should follow styles specified in the handheld category. You could use a detection script to identify iPad users and deliver a more appropriately styled page.

Refer to http://davidwalsh.name/detect-ipad and http://detectmobilebrowsers .mobi for some examples.

Links

If you've ever tried to click a link on a small, handheld screen, you can appreciate how difficult it can be. With that in mind, take steps in your mobile style sheet to make your links as easy as possible to click. You might consider using `display:block` to cause text links to span the entire width of the content area (thereby making the clickable area larger), and add a background color to make them highly visible.

Images

Many mobile users pay according to the amount of data transferred in a given month. This means your hefty images can cost users money, in addition to extra download time. Consider greatly reducing image sizes to make them quicker to download and allow the text to take center stage. Certainly any images that aren't crucial to the content delivery could be removed entirely.

Because many mobile users access webpages via text-only browsers, it's all the more important to include alternative text for every image in your site.

Page Size

Whenever possible, avoid absolute widths. There are just so many different screen sizes in the mobile market that you'll end up pleasing very few people with a page width of 150 pixels, for example. Stick with relative widths, such as 100 percent, to reach the widest possible audience.

Positioning

Designs based on absolute or fixed positioning, as well as those with floats, rarely translate well on a handheld device. Consider that a fluid, single-column layout is much easier to navigate and read on small screens.

To take advantage of every square pixel of space, try removing the extra margins and padding you might have added when creating your default style sheet. You rarely need more than three to five pixels of buffer space between the edge of the mobile browser and your page's content.

When reviewing the positioning of your content divisions, take a critical look and decide whether a few of those content divisions could be hidden from display on mobile browsers. The advertisements might be necessary on the desktop-based version of the site, but if they block the actual content from being accessible on smaller screens, your mobile readers will go elsewhere.

Special Effects

Some handheld devices do not support multimedia files, specifically those created with Flash. If you're creating a mobile-specific style sheet, consider hiding Flash files and offering other ways of accessing that content.

In addition, disable any rollovers, pop-up windows, or other scripted features that could cause your pages to render incorrectly (or even to not render at all) when displayed on mobile devices.

Still Struggling

Refer to www.alistapart.com/articles/pocket and http://perishablepress.com/press/2009/08/02/the-5-minute-css-mobile-makeover for excellent overviews of how to write mobile-specific style sheets.

Chapter Summary

Templates can be amazing time-saving devices in web design, both for the original design and the person who ends up maintaining the site. This chapter provided a broad overview of how you can use templates to your benefit for almost any web project.

In addition, we covered the use of media-based style sheets to create customized versions of a site, specifically for printing and mobile users. Both templates and media-based style sheets can significantly increase the usability and maintainability of your website.

In the next chapter, we'll look at the final pieces of the puzzle as you make your webpages live.

QUIZ

Choose the correct responses to each of the multiple-choice questions.

1. **Which is not true about blogs available from WordPress.org?**
   A. They are free.
   B. They can be used as Content Management Systems.
   C. They don't require any special setup on the host computer.
   D. They can be downloaded and installed on your own server.

2. **Which file extension is used for Dreamweaver template files?**
   A. .txt
   B. .ssi
   C. .dtf
   D. .dwt
   E. .html

3. **Where are Dreamweaver templates stored?**
   A. In the Source directory at the root level of your website
   B. In the Templates directory at the root level of your website
   C. In the Templates directory in the Dreamweaver folder on your local computer
   D. In the Source directory in the Dreamweaver folder on your local computer

4. **All Dreamweaver templates should have at least one of which type of region?**
   A. locked region
   B. editable region
   C. optional region
   D. repeating region

5. **When editing a page based on a template, which type of Dreamweaver template region cannot be changed?**
   A. locked region
   B. editable region
   C. optional region
   D. repeating region

6. **Which type of template region can be duplicated by any user?**
   A. locked region
   B. editable region
   C. optional region
   D. repeating region

7. **Chunks of code stored in .lbi files and used in multiple places throughout a website are referred to as what in Dreamweaver?**
   A. assets
   B. library items
   C. local includes
   D. server-side includes

8. **Which directive is used to add a server-side include to an HTML file?**
   A. #ssi
   B. #file
   C. #virtual
   D. #include

9. **Which file extension is not capable of handling SSIs by default?**
   A. .asp
   B. .php
   C. .html
   D. .shtml

10. **What is the value of the media attribute when linking to a mobile-specific style sheet?**
    A. phone
    B. screen
    C. mobile
    D. handheld

chapter 9

Going Live

The last few chapters have covered how to code your webpages to allow them to display as expected for as many people as possible. When you've completed that process, it's time to perform a final browser check before publishing your content. This chapter discusses that testing process, as well as the tools used to make your pages live for the world to see! Finally, the chapter closes with a look at site maintenance and getting your pages listed in popular search engines.

CHAPTER OBJECTIVES

In this chapter, you will

- Identify the purpose of testing webpages and the methods by which is it accomplished

- Differentiate between desktop and browser-based FTP

- Recognize how to effectively document a web development project

- Identify ways to improve a site's search engine ranking

Testing

In the beginning of the book, I discussed various aspects of a user's computer setup that affect how he or she views a website. During the testing process, you should try to replicate as many of those situations as possible. Obviously it is impossible to test your site using every setup method, but there are ways you can get a pretty good idea of how the site will come across in a wide variety of situations.

Testing the Code

One of the first tests most developers run is to validate the code. The process of validating your code checks it against the coding standards used by browsers during page display. Even though most modern web browsers do a pretty good job of displaying pages with minor code errors, there are certain errors that don't fare so well. This means pages containing those errors will display differently from browser to browser and platform to platform.

A great way to avoid putting up a page with such errors is to check it first, using a validation tool. To do so, visit http://validator.w3.org in your web browser. From there, you have a couple of options:

- **Validate by URI** This method allows you to validate a page that is already uploaded to a web server. Simply enter the address of the page and click the Check button.

- **Validate by file upload** This method works well for a page stored on your personal computer that hasn't yet been uploaded to a web server. Click the Validate By File Upload tab and then click the Browse button to locate the file in question before clicking the Check button.

- **Validate by direct input** This method is well suited to pages currently under construction, or even for smaller sections of code that seem to be causing a problem. Click the Validate By Direct Input tab, then enter the code you want to validate, and click the Check button.

NOTE *The W3C validator mentioned here only checks HTML, XHTML, XML, and Standard Generalized Markup Language (SGML) files. If you want to validate a CSS file, use http://jigsaw.w3.org/css-validator. Dreamweaver also offers built-in validation tools, located under the File | Validate menu.*

After the validator checks your file, you'll be presented with a page specifying whether or not your code checked out. If it passes, congratulations are in order. But if it doesn't, fear not, because plenty of us write code that doesn't initially pass inspection.

Thankfully, the W3C offers suggestions on how to improve the code so it can pass inspection. From time to time, you may encounter errors that are unavoidable. For example, you may recall that the original method of embedding video into a webpage was by using the embed element. However, the embed element is not recognized by the W3C as proper markup. So, if you include the embed element in an effort to reach users of older browsers, your pages won't validate.

PROBLEM **9-1**

I embedded a YouTube video on my site, using the HTML provided by You-Tube, but now my page won't validate!

SOLUTION

When adding YouTube videos to your site, you will likely be given code that contains the embed element, which will cause your pages to throw errors upon validation. There are several online sources that offer fixes for this problem. Check out www.tools4noobs.com/online_tools/youtube_xhtml or www.alistapart.com/articles/flashsatay.

Here are a few other common reasons why a page won't validate:

- **A missing end tag**   Probably the number one reason why a page doesn't validate is that a tag isn't closed. In my experience, that tag is frequently the div tag. I might open it (using `<div>`) and then code all of the content, but forget to close it (using `</div>`). Any of the table tags are also common culprits for missing end tags. You might start a new row (using `<tr>`) but then forget to close it after adding the row's cells. Also, empty tags like br require a trailing slash: `<br />` and won't validate as XHTML without them.

- **Incorrect DOCTYPE declaration**   If you forget to include the DOCTYPE tag at the beginning of your code, the validator won't know which document type against which to check it. Or, if you specify one document type but then code to a different one, your page won't validate.

- **Using deprecated (or phased-out) code**   If you have been around the HTML scene for a few years, you may have picked up a few bad habits along the way. One of those could include using the `align` attribute, for example, to quickly align an image within a paragraph of text. While this use of the `align` attribute used to be acceptable, it will cause errors if you use it on a page validated against the Strict XHTML validation. Instead, you have two options. You could change your DOCTYPE to transitional (which will allow for older attributes like `align`), or use the CSS properties `float` or `text-align` to properly align text and images on the page.

- **Missing alt attributes**   Images always need alternative text specified to help nonvisual browsers and search engines understand the content of the image. If you don't specify this text using the `alt` attribute in your `img` tag, your page will not validate.

- **Incorrectly nested tags**   When discussing proper HTML structure, I mentioned a structure used to code multiple tags in a row. For example, if you want to apply two sets of tags to the same bit of content, you need to open and close them like this so that the first to be opened is the last to be closed: `<p><strong>Red hat</strong><p>`

- **Random machine characters**   If you copy and paste code from Microsoft Word or another similar program, you frequently bring along extraneous characters and Microsoft markup that are not important to the HTML. In fact, those machine characters may not be visible to you, but they may break your code. If you suspect this might be the problem, try removing the copied text and then retyping it without using copy and paste.

After you've identified the errors, fix them one at a time, validating the page again after each attempt. It can be a daunting process to troubleshoot your code, as you go line-by-line looking for problems. Take breaks, and don't be afraid to ask a friend or colleague to give it a try. A fresh set of eyes can quickly scout out problem areas that tired eyes can't see.

TIP   *You can also validate your HTML and CSS from within the Web Developer toolbar for the Firefox browser. As an added bonus, the toolbar includes additional features to help you debug your pages right within the browser. Visit http:// chrispederick.com/work/web-developer to learn more.*

Testing the Display

After you've completed your code testing, it's time to verify that the page displays as you expect in all your target browsers and operating systems. Throughout this book, I stress the importance of checking your pages in multiple browsers and on multiple computer systems to make sure they appear correctly.

Even if you don't have more than one type of computer or browser, after your pages are live (uploaded to a web server), you can ask friends to test them for you. You can also visit local libraries, schools, and sometimes even shopping malls to see how the site fares in different environments.

Each time you visit the site on a different computer, record the browser, monitor size, screen resolution, and operating system used. This way, when you see errors or bugs, you can get help in determining the problem. Table 9-1 provides a sample testing checklist to help you record your results.

Alternatively, you can use an online tool like Adobe's Browser Lab (www .browserlab.adobe.com), Browsershots (www.browsershots.org), or Litmus (www.litmusapp.com), which will take screen captures of your page on a variety of different computer systems and browsers.

Testing the Usability

A key aspect of a website's success is how well it functions with users. Many designers fail to perform usability testing on sites before taking them live, leaving everyone to wonder whether the site will work. Instead, I encourage you to perform some simple, yet effective, usability tests on any site you build before it goes live.

People often think usability tests are expensive and time-consuming, when in fact they can be much more of a cost-saver when you consider how much time you might spend on a redesign to fix an unusable site. You don't need any fancy equipment or specialized training to test for usability.

In its most basic form, a usability test requires only three things: a website, a tester, and a facilitator. In fact, those three things don't even need to be in the same room (although that is preferable). I have even performed usability tests over the phone while watching the user's screen through a conferencing tool such as WebEx (www.webex.com).

TABLE 9-1 Sample Testing Checklist

Test Question	Results				Action Items
	B: ____ P: ____ R: ____	B: ____ P: ____ R: ____	B: ____ P: ____ R: ____	B: ____ P: ____ R: ____	
1. Do all pages load?					Confirm code is correct. Confirm pages exist.
2. Are all the links working properly?					Confirm code is correct. Confirm linked pages exist.
3. Is the overall flow of the navigation consistent?					Confirm page follows section template. Confirm section follows site template.
4. Is the appropriate content on each page and in each section?					Review content list. Verify nothing is missing.
5. Does the site map correctly reflect the structure of the site?					Review content list and site map.
6. Do all page elements load (including any multimedia)?					Confirm code is correct. Confirm links are correct. Confirm files are in correct place. Check plug-ins available.
7. Do page elements load in the appropriate order?					Verify all element sizes are specified in HTML. Review page structure.

TABLE 9-1 Sample Testing Checklist *(continued)*

Test Question	Results				Action Items
	B: ___ P: ___ R: ___	B: ___ P: ___ R: ___	B: ___ P: ___ R: ___	B: ___ P: ___ R: ___	
8. Do the height and width of all pages fit as intended into the specified resolution?					Confirm page size in table widths or CSS. Confirm image sizes are appropriate for page size.
9. Does resizing the browser window adversely affect the page, its images, or other individual elements?					Confirm page size in table widths or CSS. Confirm image sizes are appropriate for page size.
10. Are the most important elements on each page visible before scrolling?					Confirm page size in table widths or CSS. Review layout of elements on page.
11. Are the alt attributes for each element working?					Disable images and view page to confirm code is present and correct.
12. Is the meta data complete?					Confirm code is present. Confirm code is correct.

TABLE 9-1 Sample Testing Checklist *(continued)*

	Results							Action Items
Test Question	B: ___ P: ___ R: ___		B: ___ P: ___ R: ___		B: ___ P: ___ R: ___		B: ___ P: ___ R: ___	
13. Is the background color/style consistent?								Confirm code is present. Confirm code is correct.
14. Are the colors consistent and appropriate?								Check monitor settings. Confirm color palettes of page elements match the company's standard.
15. Is the text content readable?								Check monitor settings. Check browser's font settings. Confirm specified font settings in page.
16. Do any extraneous characters exist (such as □ or Ü) that might indicate some Microsoft markup is still hanging out or special characters have not been coded properly?								Confirm character entities are present. Confirm character entities are correct. Confirm all Microsoft markup is removed.

TABLE 9-1 Sample Testing Checklist *(continued)*

	Results						Action Items
Test Question	B: ___ P: ___ R: ___	B: ___ P: ___ R: ___	B: ___ P: ___ R: ___	B: ___ P: ___ R: ___	B: ___ P: ___ R: ___	B: ___ P: ___ R: ___	
17. Do all scripts work (i.e., JavaScript, scripts to process forms, etc.)?							Check browser settings. Confirm script is present. Confirm script location. Confirm script is correct.
18. Is the source code well commented in preparation for maintenance?							Confirm comments are present. Confirm comments are correct.
19. Is documentation up to date?							Confirm documentation exists. Confirm documentation is correct.

Key: B = Browser, R = Resolution, P = Platform (Operating System)

Technically, you may wonder why "a computer" wasn't included on my list of required items for a usability test. Suppose you wanted to test a site before it was built. You could do so by printing the mockups of the website and asking testers to explain how they might perform certain tasks using the sample screens. This process is referred to as *testing with paper prototypes* and can be a great way check the usability of a website well before extensive resources are used to actually build it.

Locate the Testers

So you have the website to be tested. How do you find the users? In my experience, you need only ask. Let's face it: lots of us like to be the center of attention… if only for a few minutes. You don't need a large number of testers either. As long as the testers you have are a good representation of the target audience, four to six people should be sufficient.

To locate potential users, first check with the client or site owner to identify current customers who might be able to help. If the business doesn't yet have an existing customer base, check out the competition. Look for people who currently patronize a competitor and ask if they might be willing to participate. You could offer a discount coupon as an incentive, or even a small payment to compensate them for their time.

It's a good idea to make sure the tester has not been involved in the design or development process at all, is completely new to the website, and is not working for the client or website owner. Beyond that, you can ask anyone who fits the site's target audience.

Create the Test

When planning your usability tests, refer back to the process you went through to identify the site's target audience. What goals did you have for the user? What did you expect they'd want to accomplish on the site? Use the answers to questions like these to write the test scenarios for your users.

You want to be prepared before the usability test so as not to waste anyone's time. It's best to limit the actual test to about 10 or 15 minutes so you have time to debrief the tester afterward and she still is finished in under 30 minutes.

With each test, try to determine whether the user understands the page being tested and can successfully use the site's navigation to locate information. General usability tests might evaluate whether a page is difficult to read, where users tend to get lost, and how easily accessible the information is. More detailed tests might seek to know whether a user can perform a specific task or locate a certain piece of information.

Consider running a trial test with a colleague prior to facilitating the test with actual users. This can tell you whether your testing procedure is too long, too short, confusing, and so on.

Facilitate the Test

When you've found the users and created the test, you can set up some time to run the test. At that point, you'll need a facilitator to guide the users through the test and record the results. Because you might have a tendency to correct the tester or defend the design, it is best to find someone else to facilitate the test.

At the start of the test, have the facilitator remind the user that he is not being tested—the website is. Also, ask him to think out loud so his thoughts about the site can be recorded. For example, when evaluating a site for a bank, the facilitator might ask, "What would you do if you were looking for information about a used car loan?" Then the facilitator should not direct the tester in any way. Instead, she should simply record where the user clicks and what he does to accomplish the task.

Avoid asking the tester to make suggestions about how to fix the site. This is your job. Do have the facilitator take notes and (if the budget allows) record the test to video. While obviously an additional cost, recording usability tests can save money down the road because you always have the video to refer back to if questions arise.

After the test is completed and the user has been debriefed, the facilitator needs only to thank the tester and offer any payment or gift promised before compiling the results. The best part of usability tests is they provide instant access to how real users are interacting with the site.

Uploading to a Web Server

When the site is ready to go live (where it is accessible to visitors on the Web), it's time to transfer the pages to the host web server. You use File Transfer Protocol (FTP) programs to make this transfer.

The concept of using an FTP program is similar to moving things around on your own personal computer. But instead of moving files from one folder to another on your computer, you're moving them from one folder on your computer to another folder on a different computer.

Depending on what type of computer you have and who is hosting the site, you may use one of many different types of desktop or web-based FTP programs. Or you might use an FTP tool that comes with your HTML editor, such as the built-in FTP capabilities with Adobe Dreamweaver.

Desktop FTP

While there are hundreds of FTP programs available, they all function in the same basic way. To begin, you must choose which computer you want to access. If you want to upload your files to a web server, enter that computer's information in the space provided for "remote" computer.

NOTE *You should receive all the necessary login information (username, password, etc.) when you sign up for a hosting service. If you're unsure, check your host company's website or call its customer support line for assistance.*

Then, in the space provided for the "local" computer, navigate to the folder on your computer containing the file you want to transfer. After you select the file to be transferred, you can use the upload button to copy the file to the destination location on your host web server. For example, in Dreamweaver, the local computer is usually shown on the right, while the remote system displays on the left. After clicking a file to upload on the local computer, I can click the Put button (it's a blue "up" arrow) to upload the file to the remote system (Figure 9-1).

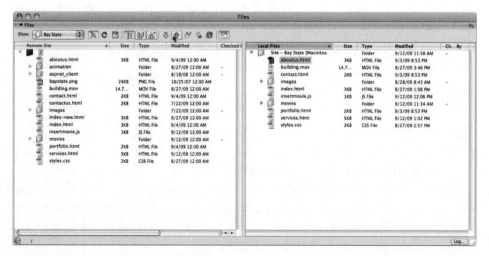

FIGURE 9-1 · Screenshot of Dreamweaver's FTP

You can also navigate through the host computer's directory structure by clicking the folder names to expand or condense them. Most FTP tools also allow you to create new folders on the remote computer and to adjust the settings of those folders.

This is the most basic method of FTP, where you are simply copying files from one computer to another. There will likely be additional options and settings, depending on which FTP tool you decide to use.

Here are a few desktop FTP programs you might check out if you're using a Windows operating system:

- **CoffeeCup Free FTP**   www.coffeecup.com/free-ftp
- **SmartFTP**   www.smartftp.com
- **FTP Voyager**   www.ftpvoyager.com
- **WS_FTP**   www.ipswitch.com

And for Mac users…

- **YummyFTP**   www.yummyftp.com
- **Fetch**   www.fetchsoftworks.com
- **VicomsoftFTP**   www.vicomsoft.com
- **Transmit**   www.panic.com

Web-based FTP

If you're using a free service to host your website, you probably have FTP capabilities through that company's website. This is called web-based FTP because you don't need any additional software to transmit the files—in fact, you perform the file transfer directly within your web browser.

Even if your host company doesn't offer web-based FTP, if you use the Firefox web browser, you have an even better option. While I typically use the built-in FTP capabilities in Dreamweaver, since that's my preferred HTML development tool, I sometimes have a need for file transfer outside of Dreamweaver. In those cases, I use a Firefox add-on called FireFTP.

To install FireFTP (or another web-based FTP tool for Firefox), open Firefox and visit https://addons.mozilla.org. Search for FTP. Locate the app you want to add, and click the corresponding Download or Add To Firefox button.

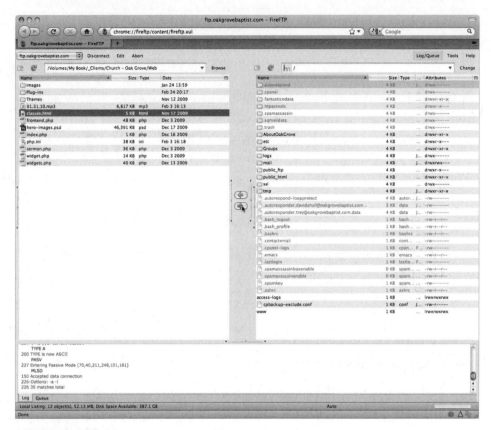

FIGURE 9-2 · Screenshot of FireFTP for Firefox

After the FTP app has been installed, you can locate it under the Tools menu in Firefox. Similarly to how the previously discussed FTP tool functions, FireFTP displays your local files on one side and the remote files on the other. You then use the arrows in the middle to transfer files back and forth. Figure 9-2 provides a screenshot of this tool in action.

NOTE *You can also perform basic FTP functions using Internet Explorer on Windows without any additional software or plug-ins. To do so, enter the server name with the FTP protocol into the address bar, like this: ftp://servername.com. The browser will prompt you for your username and password (if the server requires it). You can then upload files by dragging them into a window.*

Documentation

The most successful web projects are thoroughly documented throughout the design and development phases. In addition, effective and efficient sites are continually redocumented after the site's launch and during any updates. While this may seem like the least enjoyable aspect of the project, it can often save immense amounts of time and money while the site is being maintained.

In the beginning of the book, I outlined some common types of documentation for web projects. At the end of any project, it is important to confirm that all appropriate documentation has been updated according to the final outcome. Let's review those documents briefly to determine which need updating.

- **Proposal (used to sell the project to the client)**   This does not need to be updated.

- **Statement of Work/Design and Architecture Specification (used to detail the exact course of action to be taken during development)**   Addendums may be added to document any changes, regardless of how small, and to avoid questions later.

- **Mockups/comps (used to give visual descriptions of how the site will be implemented)**   Mockups should be updated to show any changes required during the development process.

- **Site maps, wireframes, and storyboards (used to outline the site's structure and flow)**   Notes and addendums should be added to document any changes that occurred during production.

Style Guides

There is one additional piece of documentation that needs to be created, if it hasn't been already. The style guide is a document that spells out the decisions made in designing the site. For example, what fonts were used? It's important to specify not only the font name, but also the sizes used, as well as any other typographical details needed to reproduce all graphical and web-based text.

Style guides don't have to be fancy or long. Rather, they just need to effectively transfer the style information from the original designer to whoever might need to maintain or edit the site. In fact, because you—the original designer—might not even know who will make changes to the site in the future,

TABLE 9-2 Sample Details from a Style Guide

Element/Selector	Specifications		Color			Styling
	Font family	Size	Name	RGB	Hex	
Level 1 headlines (h1)	Trebuchet	16pt	orange	255,153,0	#FF9900	bold
Level 2 headlines (h2)	Trebuchet	14pt	yellow	255,255,204	#FFFFCC	bold
Paragraph text (p) and block quotes (blockquote)	Trebuchet	10pt	black	0,0,0	#000000	n/a

it is best to err on the site of caution and record as much information about the site's creation as possible. (And if you do end up maintaining the site at some point, I can promise even you will find the style guide handy when you attempt to figure out what font you used months or even years before.) Table 9-2 gives a brief example of some of the information you might include.

Helping Users Find the Site

After the website is designed, coded, tested, uploaded, and documented your job is finished, right? Not necessarily. You may also be asked to help get the site listed in popular search engines, or even to help the site owner market the site with online advertising or targeted e-mails (which we'll cover in the final chapter). For now, let's take a look at the first area: getting listed. But before we do that, you need to understand how search engines work.

Search Engine Methodology

Traditional search engines rank pages according to the number of times a key word or search term appears on the page. In the past, this has caused some less-than-honorable people to repeat key words over and over again in an effort to increase their ranking. The search engines caught wind of that practice, however, and started banning sites that repeated key words in an unreasonable manner.

Google, the most popular search engine, takes a slightly different approach. According to its website, their process works like this:

> We use more than 200 signals, including our patented PageRank™ algorithm, to examine the entire link structure of the web and

determine which pages are most important. We then conduct hypertext-matching analysis to determine which pages are relevant to the specific search being conducted. By combining overall importance and query-specific relevance, we're able to put the most relevant and reliable results first.

In essence, Google examines not just the page, but the whole website (and even linked social media sites), to evaluate the relationships between the pages and, therefore, the importance of the content within them. This means a key word used in a headline could indicate that it is of greater importance than a key word used only within the body copy.

Google is often referred to as a "crawler-based" search engine because its systems "crawl" or "spider" the Web to find relevant data. By contrast, some search engines are directory based and merely provide an index of sites, but they don't necessarily seek out related data. Each search engine has its own way of indexing data in an effort to increase speed and efficiency.

As of July 2010, the top three search engines garnered a whopping 93.9 percent of the United States market share, according to comScore (www.comscore.com). Google comes in first with just over 65 percent, followed by Yahoo! at just over 17 percent, and Microsoft (Bing) with 11 percent. Why is this important? Simple: You really only need to be listed in these three search engines to reach the vast majority of search engine users. With that in mind, let's focus on these three for the rest of this discussion.

Search Engines Look for Key Words

When someone starts a web search, the popular search engines evaluate key words and phrases found throughout webpages to find the best matches. Of course, content is king, so the best way to ensure users find your site in search engines is to include the content they are looking for. But, it's also important to repeat your site's key words in specific places.

- **The address**   A site whose address is www.marylandflorist.com will probably rank higher than the same site with an address like www.flowersbywendy.com, simply because "Maryland" and "florist" are key search terms. For this reason, many companies register multiple domains: one with the business name and at least one other that describes what the business does.

- **Headlines**   Many designers don't use the heading elements (h1, h2, and so on) because they don't see the need. These elements are actually quite valuable, because the words contained within them signify importance to search engines as well as users. Using relevant headlines can go a long way toward increasing the usability and searchability of your site.

- **Body copy**   This one can't be emphasized enough. If you are building a website for a florist, the site surely needs to include content about flowers as well as the products and services offered. Avoid "getting off on a tangent" because it not only dilutes your message but also lowers the page's importance in search engines.

- **Images**   No, search engines can't "see" your images, but they can read the alternate text (`alt` attribute) associated with them. This alternative text offers a really great opportunity to enhance the searchability of your site. Here's an example: `<img src="image.jpg" alt="Photo of ABC Company CEO, James Rile" />`.

- **Links**   Don't forget about your links. HTML provides for the `title` attribute to be included within opening a tags as a way to attach a readable, searchable title to each link. Here's an example: `<a href="link.html" title="Click to find about more about ABC Company's swimming pool products and services">`.

- **Page title**   The title at the top of the page may seem insignificant, but it's typically the first thing a search engine user sees from your site, so make it count. A title like "Company Home Page" isn't nearly as effective as something like "Flowers by Wendy – Your Source for High Quality Floral Arrangements in Northeastern Maryland."

Finally, use meta data to aid those search engines that support them in identifying your content. Meta data is hidden instructions about your webpage, such as a description and keywords.

To incorporate meta data, the meta element should be added to each page on your site in between the opening and closing `head` tags. Here is an example of how meta elements might be used on a page listing events at a local restaurant:

```
<head>
<title>Half Pints Pub | Entertainment Calendar</title>
<meta name="description" content="With dozens of huge HD TV's at
Half Pints, you can catch all your favorite games and sporting
events while enjoying live entertainment, spirited competition,
and good old-fashioned camaraderie." />
```

```
<meta name="keywords" content="sports bar, pub, English, concert,
band, music, live entertainment, football, sports, Baltimore
Ravens, restaurant, family dining, take-out, delivery" />
</head>
```

Customize the content of these tags to identify a description that properly explains the purpose of your site in a sentence or two (20 to 50 words is a good place to start) and key words that parallel what users might search for. Because most users search for words in lowercase, you can avoid capital letters in your key words. The number of key words you use varies somewhat according to the search engine; make sure your most important key words are listed first because some limit the contents of your key words to about 900 characters.

One additional note about meta elements: I've listed these last as a way to identify their importance when it comes to search engine optimization. While it's true these specific meta elements can transfer the description and key words to search engines, the other places I listed previously garner greater importance among modern search engines. So it's still good to include relevant meta data, but you shouldn't rely on it as the only way to get the information to search engines. (Remember that the content of meta elements isn't displayed on your pages, but is only visible to search engines and browsers.)

 Still Struggling

Visit Search Engine Watch (www.searchenginewatch.com) for more tips on using meta elements.

Search Engines Favor the Popular Crowd

In junior high, I was not a fan of popularity contests, but when it comes to search engines it is a different story. Search engines like Google consider how many related sites link to a particular page and increase the rankings of those pages. It determines which pages are popular by evaluating both the incoming links and user input.

When complementary websites link to yours, Google considers that to be an indication of your site's value or worth. Similarly, those pages that other searchers have "promoted" rise to the top of the search results faster than those not promoted. Users can click the "promote" button next to a link in Google's search results to let Google know this particular page is relevant to the search terms.

Even search engines that don't allow users to promote certain links do consider user input. When you search for a phrase, the search engine tracks which links are actually clicked within the results. It records that information and adjusts the results as needed to ensure the most likely (that is, most popular) links display before those that are rarely clicked.

This means we end up with a bit of the "chicken and egg" syndrome. I often hear, "How can I increase my ranking if I'm showing up on page 30 of the results and no one gets the opportunity to click my link?" Keep reading…

Submit Your Site

All three of the top search engines provide free online forms used to recommend new or updated sites.

- **Google** http://www.google.com/addurl
- **Yahoo!** http://siteexplorer.search.yahoo.com/submit
- **Bing** http://www.bing.com/docs/submit.aspx

Usually, submitting your site using these free tools is enough to get your site listed, but it's not enough to get you anywhere near the top of the search results. That, I'm afraid, is not free.

Increase Your Ranking

As a web designer, one of the most common questions I hear from site owners is this: How can I increase my ranking in Google? Search engine optimization (SEO) involves not only preparing the site to be indexed by the search engines, but also being proactive about bringing new customers to the site through those same search engines (often in the form of sponsored search advertising).

While SEO should be a key part of any modern website project, many people are of the mindset that "if you build it, they will come." Because of that, SEO is often left by the wayside, with companies not really understanding its importance until they realize no one is visiting their site.

It's your job, as a web professional, to educate clients about the importance of SEO. If a site is built with SEO in mind from the beginning (using the concepts I mentioned previously), it will be easier to increase the site's presence in the major search engines.

After the site has been built with SEO in mind, the best way to increase your site's visibility, popularity, and ultimately its ranking in the search engines is to take advantage of pay-per-click (PPC) advertising. All of the major search engines offer it, and if you've done any amount of searching you've already seen it. I'm referring to those "sponsored links" or "sponsored sites" that display on search results pages.

Here's how it works:

1. **Identify the key words or phrases you want to sponsor.** Certain words and phrases are more popular than others and therefore cost more to sponsor.

2. **Create the ad.** All sponsored ads are text-based, with a limited number of characters.

3. **Place a bid, which is the amount of money you're willing to pay each time someone clicks your ad.** For example, if you bid $0.10 per click and 100 people click your ad, you will be charged $10.

4. **Set a daily, weekly, and/or monthly spending limit for your advertising campaign.** If you specify not to spend more than $100/day, your ad won't be shown after that budget is reached each day of the campaign.

That's it! PPC advertising on the major search engines is easy to set up, but be warned that it can quickly become a full-time job. The most successful search engine advertisers sponsor a variety of different search terms, using multiple ads and campaigns to see what works. Here are links to each of the top three search engine PPC advertising tools:

- **Google AdWords**   http://adwords.google.com
- **Yahoo! Advertising**   http://advertising.yahoo.com/smallbusiness/ysm
- **Microsoft Search Advertising**   http://advertising.microsoft.com/search-advertising

Still Struggling

PPC advertising and SEO are huge industries, with plenty of resources to help you navigate through. Here are few reputable places to help get you started:

Google Webmaster Central (www.google.com/webmasters)
Search Engine Watch (www.searchenginewatch.com)
SEO Logic (www.seologic.com/guide)
Website Grader (www.websitegrader.com)

Track Your Progress

Anyone investing in a website needs some method of measuring the success of those efforts. In the search engine optimization world, there are a few key things you want to monitor:

- **Site visits and page views**   The amount of traffic on your site is obviously an important part of your site's success. Measuring the number of people accessing your site each day, week, and month can help you plan when and where to advertise for additional customers.

- **Incoming links**   When other sites link to yours, the popularity of your site increases. (As I mentioned, Google considers a site with lots of incoming links to be more important than a similar one without any incoming links.) You can help increase your chances of acquiring more incoming links by performing such tasks as reviewing relevant products on Amazon and other online stores, creating a page about your business on Wikipedia, and commenting on relevant blogs.

- **Conversion rate**   Any web site owner obviously wants to meet the goals set for the site or for a particular advertising campaign. Whether the goal is to increase sales of a particular product or get more people to sign up for your newsletter, you can track that progress by monitoring goal conversion data. In other words, the data tells you how many site visitors actually purchased a product or signed up for a newsletter.

- **Bounce rate**   Monitoring the number of people who view only one page of your site or who leave the site quickly can help identify how engaging the site's content is. If a particular page on the site has a high bounce rate, it's probably time to reevaluate the content on that page.

The most widely used method of monitoring these and other aspects of websites is a tool called Google Analytics (www.google.com/analytics). To use Google Analytics (GA), website owners add a bit of GA code to each page they want to monitor. Then, GA tracks how people find the site, how they use it, and how you can help them use it more efficiently and effectively.

Because Google Analytics is a free tool, you really have no excuse not to track how your site is performing. You simply add a bit of custom code to your pages and then watch the results with Google's browser-based tool (see Figure 9-3). Better yet, take advantage of Google's other webmaster tools (found at www.google.com/webmasters) to really boost your site's online presence.

FIGURE 9-3 · Screenshot of Google Analytics

Chapter Summary

Chapter 9 sought to close the loop in the web design process. What started as merely a design concept is now a living, breathing website. This chapter covered testing your site and then uploading it to its permanent home on the web server, where it is accessible by members of your target audience.

The later part of the chapter touched on search engines and their impact on your site's success. In Chapter 10, we'll take a look at another way to increase the success of your site: e-mail marketing.

Choose the correct responses to each of the multiple-choice questions.

1. **Which term refers to the process of checking your code against the W3C standards?**
   A. testing
   B. procuring
   C. validating
   D. confirming
   E. compromising

2. **Which will not cause an error when a page is checked against the latest W3C standards?**
   A. missing end tag
   B. incorrectly nested tags
   C. missing alt attributes
   D. missing image captions
   E. incorrect DOCTYPE declaration

3. **True or False: Web page colors can appear differently according to the user's environment.**
   A. True
   B. False

4. **Which is not required for a basic web usability test?**
   A. a tester
   B. a website
   C. a facilitator
   D. a computer

5. **What is considered an acceptable minimum test sample when conducting a website usability test?**
   A. one to two people
   B. four to six people
   C. eight to ten people
   D. twelve to fifteen people

6. **What is the purpose of an FTP program?**
   A. to transfer files from one computer to another
   B. to automate the process of coding HTML files
   C. to check webpages against the W3C specifications
   D. to tabulate facts and figures in preparation for web use

7. **Which type of website documentation does not need updating at the end of a project in preparation for maintenance?**
   A. proposal
   B. site maps
   C. mockups/comps
   D. design and architecture specification

8. **Which piece of project documentation outlines the design decisions made during the site's development to ease maintenance of the site?**
   A. mockup
   B. site map
   C. style guide
   D. design plan

9. **Which is the most popular search engine (as of this writing)?**
   A. Ask
   B. AOL
   C. Bing
   D. Yahoo!
   E. Google

10. **What does the web acronym SEO stand for?**
   A. systems evaluation office
   B. search engine optimization
   C. security engineering officer
   D. social extension opportunity
   E. synchronous enhancement organization

chapter **10**

E-mail Design

The final aspect of web design I'd like to cover is an area that has grown tremendously over the past decade: E-mail design. In fact, you've probably watched it grow as your inbox has become a lot more colorful (and a lot busier!).

In this chapter, you will

- Identify the pros and cons of e-mail marketing
- Recognize how designing for e-mail readers is different from designing for browsers
- Understand the use of e-mail service providers

Ten years ago, e-mail programs weren't capable of interpreting HTML within e-mails. But now, widespread support of HTML and CSS by e-mail readers has significantly changed the face of business e-mail. While most companies still provide plain-text e-mails to customers who request them, the vast bulk of business marketing and advertising e-mail is now sent with embedded HTML.

For the web designer, this brings a whole new avenue of work opportunities, as well as new headaches. Why? Because an e-mail embedded with HTML is essentially just a webpage (like those you've learned to create in the rest of this book). So if you can design and code webpages, you can design and code HTML e-mail.

The reason for the headaches is this: Support for HTML and CSS is growing among e-mail readers, but it still lags behind on many fronts. In fact, coding HTML for e-mail now is a lot like coding HTML for web browsers was a decade ago—which means you'll spend a lot of time testing, and testing, and testing, and revising and testing some more.

E-mail Standards

The first thing we need to discuss about e-mail design is its standards. Earlier in the book, I discussed how the W3C maintains standards for various web coding languages. Those standards are then used by browser developers to ensure that webpages viewed in their browsers display as expected.

The same concept holds true for e-mail coding… to a point. The problem is that e-mail application developers don't currently follow one particular set of standards for e-mail display. In November 2007, a group of people got together to form the Email Standards Project. This organization works with e-mail application developers and the design community to improve web standards support and accessibility in e-mail.

While this is undoubtedly going to be a slow process, there is great hope among the design community that this organization will help bring the same level of consensus that the W3C brought on the web browser front.

You can download the Email Standards Project's "Acid Test" to see exactly how they tested each e-mail client. You can also view the results of their test, and learn more about the movement, at www.email-standards.org/acid-test.

Planning for E-mail Design

Much of the beginning of this book was devoted to helping you plan a website design project. E-mail design requires the same amount of planning to ensure the e-mail is sent, received, and viewed successfully. When planning a website, it's important to determine which technologies best meet the site goals. Likewise, with e-mail design, you must take a step back before designing to determine what type of e-mail will best serve the target audience: plain-text or HTML.

Pros and Cons of HTML E-mail

The most basic e-mail is referred to as plain-text, in that it contains only text characters and no additional formatting or coding. This is the type of e-mail most of us have been sending and receiving for years. HTML e-mail, by contrast, is actually an HTML page displayed in an e-mail reader. While there are some great benefits to sending webpages through e-mail, there are also many drawbacks.

Con: HTML E-mail Sometimes Dilutes the Message

First, let's consider the purpose of e-mail. At the end of the day, we use e-mail to communicate with each other. While there certainly are many forms of communication, e-mail has traditionally used written language to communicate. All e-mail readers allow users to read written text.

When you start styling that text with color and other formatting, you stop relying on the written word to communicate your message. Before you make the decision to send HTML e-mails, you need to determine the specific message of the e-mails being sent, and whether any extra formatting will affect that message.

Con: You Can't Control the Display Method

Unlike web browsers, which have become much more uniform in their display and support of HTML, e-mail readers are plentiful and vastly different from one another. Consider all the ways you read e-mail. If you have a Yahoo!, Hotmail/Live Mail, or Gmail account, you probably read your e-mail in a web browser.

But you still have the option to read your e-mail in a stand-alone e-mail program like Outlook or Apple Mail. And if you are like a growing number of people, you might also check your e-mail on a smart phone like a Blackberry or iPhone. I just named seven different ways to read an e-mail, and I'm only getting started!

It is virtually impossible to know how your HTML e-mails will display when read by the end user. Testing in as many of the popular e-mail readers as possible is certainly important, but ultimately you must make smart design decisions that ensure the widest possible audience can still glean the message being communicated. Keep this in mind when deciding whether HTML is the best delivery method for a particular e-mail.

Con: Readers May Not Even Receive Your Message

Due to the proliferation of HTML e-mail spam, the simple truth is that plain-text e-mail is more likely to actually get to the reader. This may mean that the most important e-mail communication with a customer—such as receipts—should be kept in plain text.

Many e-mail readers block images and attachments from unknown senders or suspected spammers. One reason this happens is that anything attached to an e-mail is capable of harboring viruses and other malicious code. Also, when you send HTML e-mail with images stored on a web server, you can tell whether the e-mail was opened by simply reviewing the site's access logs to see if the images were displayed. This allows spammers to differentiate between active e-mail addresses and those that are bad.

In fact, HTML e-mails are more likely to be tagged as spam simply for having embedded images. That means your beautifully designed HTML e-mail may end up in a customer's spam bucket and eventually in the trash without the customer even knowing it.

Con: HTML E-mail Takes Longer to Download

Another reason HTML e-mail might not make it to the reader is size. If you get a little crazy with large images and hefty attachments, you can cause someone's e-mail system to slow down or even crash. E-mail readers on mobile devices often only download the first 100k or so of an e-mail, so it's important to create web graphics that are small in file size and quick to download.

Okay, now that we've moved through a few of the drawbacks, let's switch gears and consider the reasons you might want to use HTML e-mail.

Pro: HTML E-mail Is More Visually Appealing

Let's face it: Most of us react more quickly to an image of a double-dip choco-late ice cream cone on a hot summer day than we might to those words mixed in with other text in a crowded paragraph. As the saying goes, "a picture is worth a thousand words." When it comes to marketing, those pictures can mean the difference between closing a sale and losing a customer.

Pro: HTML E-mail Is Cost Effective

Advertisers who used to rely on expensive print-mail campaigns are largely embracing HTML e-mail as an efficient way to get their messages in front of customers more quickly and less expensively. While design costs are about the same, the cost of sending a thousand e-mails is significantly less than the cost to print and snail-mail a thousand postcards to customers.

Pro: HTML E-mail Is Targeted

While most companies do target certain ZIP codes when sending snail-mail ads, e-mail advertising allows you to target specific demographics and behaviors. For example, suppose you are a customer of a certain grocery store that has recently started offering delivery services. Being interested in this service, you viewed a page on the company's website describing this new feature, but you never actually purchased it. Because you were logged into your account with this company at the time you viewed the delivery page, they decide to send you a targeted e-mail ad offering free delivery on your next order. Such targeted e-mails tend to be highly successful.

Know Your Audience

From a legal standpoint, the most important thing to know about your audience is whether you have permission to contact them in this manner and for this purpose. In short, spam is any e-mail sent without the permission of the recipient.

Here are a few guidelines to help you e-mail the right people (at least legally):

- **Send e-mail to current customers.** Most people consider anyone who has purchased from you within the last two years to be a "current" customer.
- **Send e-mail to people who request information from you,** either in person or online, but only about relevant topics. In other words, if someone responds to a job posting on a company's website but isn't hired, it's not okay for that company to start sending him marketing e-mail about its products.

This means it's not okay to send marketing messages to e-mail addresses you've found on other messages that have been forwarded to you or those found on the Internet. Just because I post my e-mail address on my personal website doesn't mean I want to receive marketing e-mail from any business who visits my website.

While it may be tempting to send mass e-mails to strangers in the hopes they might one day become a new customer, it is much more effective to target people who have already expressed an interest in your business or product. If you regularly message people who didn't ask to receive your e-mail, you risk being put on "blacklists" held by the various e-mail service providers. Once your site has been identified as one that sends spam, it can be difficult to get any of your messages through, regardless of whether they are being sent to legitimate recipients.

As a web designer, it's often up to you to educate others about the dangers of spam. If you're working with a business that is unsure whether its marketing list is legal, consider passing along a free "Permission Guidelines Handout" from Campaign Monitor: www.campaignmonitor.com/downloads/permission-guidelines-handout.

Follow Federal Trade Commission Guidelines

Federal law requires you to always provide a way for a recipient to specify that he no longer wishes to receive your messages. At a bare minimum, this means you must provide a valid return address to which users can send a "please remove me" e-mail. Most reputable e-mail systems offer efficient unsubscribe mechanisms allowing recipients to opt out through an online form linked from all e-mails.

Federal law further requires you to keep such unsubscribe methods available for at least 30 days after e-mails are sent. After receiving an unsubscribe request, companies have 30 days to stop sending the recipient e-mail.

To avoid your e-mail being blocked as spam, you also must use legitimate headers and subject lines. In other words, you can't send an e-mail with a subject of "Free delivery on your next order" unless the offer is valid and indeed available to recipients. The from and reply-to address fields must also contain valid, active e-mail addresses. Finally, the company's business name and physical mailing address must also be visible on the message.

TIP *Check out www.ftc.gov/bcp/edu/pubs/business/ecommerce/bus61.shtm for more information about the CAN-SPAM Act.*

Know the Available Tools

The tools used to develop and send HTML e-mails depend somewhat on the purpose of the messages being sent and the company that is sending them. As I mentioned, an HTML e-mail is really just a webpage. So first, let's consider the tools used to design and develop HTML e-mail.

Design and Development Tools

I don't have a lot of new tools to tell you about in this section, because the tools used to design and develop HTML e-mails are, for the most part, the same as those used to develop standard webpages. This means you can continue to use Photoshop (or another favorite design tool) to design your e-mails, and Dreamweaver (or another favorite development tool) to code them. The real difference comes when you want to *publish* the e-mails.

Publishing Tools

In the previous chapter, I talked about using FTP software to publish your webpages—thereby making them live and accessible by anyone with Internet access. HTML e-mail has a completely different publishing process.

The best way to publish, or send, bulk HTML e-mail is to use an e-mail service provider (ESP). Similar to an Internet service provider, an ESP handles all aspects of bulk e-mail delivery, from managing the recipient lists (both subscribe and unsubscribe features) to tracking the number of times each e-mail is opened and clicked.

Just as there are hundreds of ISPs out there, you also have your choice of quite a few ESPs. While web designers typically get to choose the design and development tools used for a project, we don't often get to select the ESP. More commonly, it is the company sending the e-mail who chooses the e-mail service providers.

As a freelancer, I have used a fair number of ESPs, depending on the company sending the messages. Each of the tools I've used has its own list of pros and cons, depending on the business and its audience. Sometimes I am asked to make suggestions to companies selecting a new ESP. Here are a few features I suggest you look for when researching ESPs:

- Contact management tools to handle the subscriber list
- E-mail creation tools to help format and lay out the content
- E-mail sending tools to help you test your e-mails

- Design services to help with graphic design and creative support
- E-mail reporting tools to help track things like click-throughs, opens, and conversions
- Ease of use
- Support

Many e-mail service providers include e-mail creation tools to help you format and lay out the content before the message is sent. These tools allow you to select a design template and then use "fill in the blank" forms to enter the e-mail content. Tools like this can be great for companies with little budget to send custom-designed e-mails each and every time a message is sent. But they often offer little flexibility and don't do much to keep a company's branding consistent.

A great way to take advantage of the e-mail creation tools without compromising design and flexibility is to design a custom template. I frequently am hired to create customized templates (which include the client's branding) that are then imported into the ESP's software. The custom templates then allow anyone within the client's business to easily create and send a branded e-mail.

As with any software, it's important to try before you buy. ESPs typically charge either a monthly fee or per-e-mail/per-recipient fees (or a combination of both). Many also offer rebranding tools to allow designers to create their clients' e-mails, and then give the clients the tools to send and manage them. A few of the most popular ESPs include:

- **Blue Hornet**   www.bluehornet.com
- **Campaign Monitor**   www.campaignmonitor.com
- **Constant Contact**   www.constantcontact.com
- **Emma**   www.myemma.com
- **iContact**   www.icontact.com
- **Lyris**   www.lyris.com
- **MailChimp**   www.mailchimp.com
- **Vertical Response**   www.verticalresponse.com

Coding for E-mail Design

Throughout this book, I've provided instruction on using HTML to code webpages. For the most part, all of the elements and attributes discussed thus far will also work for HTML e-mail. But because of the inconsistency of support for CSS among e-mail readers, there are certain differences you need to be aware of.

Recommendations

When you are coding a webpage that will ultimately be viewed in an e-mail reader, there are certain steps you must take to ensure the page displays properly. A few of the following recommendations may go directly against something I told you in previous chapters, but that's okay. As I mentioned, coding for e-mail has some unique challenges that sometimes cause us to change our standard coding methods.

TIP *Campaign Monitor, a fabulous ESP and wonderful resource for all things HTML e-mail, is part of the Email Standards Project. As such, they have a ton of information about CSS support among the most popular e-mail readers. You can find this information at www.campaignmonitor.com/css and www.email-standards.org/clients.*

Keep It Simple

Remember the purpose of your e-mail and stick to it. You don't need to include the entire website's navigation or layout in an e-mail design. Usually, a header and footer, in addition to the main body content, are sufficient.

While we're talking about keeping it simple, I should mention that background images aren't supported by all the browsers. As such, stick to solid-color backgrounds that can be applied with HTML, as opposed to gradients or patterns that require image-based backgrounds.

Figure 10-1 shows an example of a typical HTML e-mail I create for my clients. Notice that this e-mail is not text heavy, but instead gets the message across in just a few sentences. The rest of the e-mail is photographic in nature, to be visually appealing and attention-getting. There is a link at the top of the page for readers who can't see the images in their e-mail readers. That link takes users to view the same e-mail in their web browser (which generally does a better job of displaying HTML e-mail). I've marked a few other aspects of the design to point out other ways e-mail design is different from that of a traditional webpage.

Use Absolute Paths

Whenever you add a link or an image to a webpage, you have the option of using either absolute or relative path names. Relative path names are shorter

Here's my teaser text, telling readers what they can expect to find when this e-mail is displayed in its entirety.

This is not the same navigation used on this company's website, but rather a customized set of links specific to this e-mail.

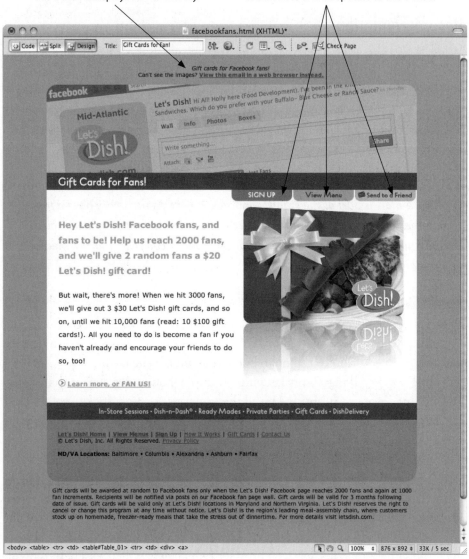

FIGURE 10-1 • Sample HTML e-mail

than absolute path names, because they don't include the full URL, but rather a URL that is relative to the current file. For example: "images/header.jpg" is a relative path, while "http://www.company.com/images/header.jpg" is an absolute path.

Because your e-mail is downloaded and displayed on the reader's system, you need to make sure all images are stored on a web server and referenced with complete, absolute URLs (i.e., those that start with http://). Likewise, all links to other webpages or content need to be absolute.

Store Images on a Live Web Server

I just mentioned this, but I can't stress how important it is. In order for images referenced in an HTML e-mail to display once the e-mail is downloaded by the recipient, they must be stored on a live web server and referenced with an absolute URL. So, your images will not display if your code looks like this:

```
<img src="header.jpg" />
```

When it comes to image storage for e-mail design, you essentially have two choices:

- Create a folder on the company's web server to house all e-mail-related files and images. In this case, your image URLs might look like: `<img src="http://www.company.com/email/images/header.jpg" />`.
- Store the images on your ESP's web server. If you go this route, your image references might look like this: `<img src="http://files.myesp .com/989543789/6785436574.jpg" />`.

Use Tables for Layout

So far, I've not discussed any other layout method except for that which is accomplished with style sheets. That is because CSS is the preferred layout method for webpages that are viewed in web browsers. Unfortunately, e-mail readers haven't yet caught up to web browsers in the display of HTML and CSS. So web designers are forced to turn to "old school" layout methods when designing for e-mail.

In particular, Microsoft Outlook does a poor job at rendering CSS. As of this writing, it does not support the float or position properties in CSS and has very little support for padding, margins, and background colors.

So what do you do if you need to create columns in pages designed to be viewed in Microsoft Outlook or other e-mail readers? Although it's a bit archaic and somewhat complex to maintain, you can use HTML tables for page layout. Compare Figures 10-1 and 10-2 to see how a table-based layout might work for an HTML e-mail. Figure 10-2 shows the layout in "Expanded Tables mode"

in Dreamweaver, which allows you to see which pieces of the design are in which cells.

While Chapter 4 outlined the basic concepts behind tables, there are a few additional things to consider when using tables for page layout. First, there are two attributes that can be added to the opening `table` tag to define the space in and around the cells:

- **cellpadding** Defines the space between the content in the cell and the edges of that cell
- **cellspacing** Defines the space in between each of the individual cells

It is common for designers to split apart e-mail designs and then put them back together using tables (as I did with the design shown in Figures 10-1 and 10-2). When doing so, you need to eliminate all the space in between the cells to make them display seamlessly. The easiest way to accomplish seamless tables in e-mail design is to set the table element's `cellpadding`, `cellspacing`, and `border` attributes to zero, like this:

```
<table cellpadding="0" cellspacing="0" border="0">
```

Here are a few other guidelines to keep in mind:

- Always define the width of your table cells (with the `width` attribute added to the opening `td` tag) to ensure your layout stays as you intend it to.
- If your table cells contain images, use absolute sizes when defining the width or height those cells. In other words, stick to pixel widths instead of percentages.
- Start with the border set to 1 (`border="1"`) to help you visualize the table during development. Then switch it to zero for testing and the final delivery.
- Use the `align` attribute inside the opening cell (`td`) and row (`tr`) tags to specify the horizontal alignment of the content.
- Use the `valign` attribute inside the opening cell (`td`) and row (`tr`) tags to specify the vertical alignment of the content.

Still Struggling

Here's a great resource that includes lots of tips and tricks for coding HTML e-mail with tables: www.reachcustomersonline.com/2010/01/23/09.27.00.

Use Inline Styles

In previous chapters, I discussed three different methods of including CSS in your pages: inline, internal, and external. Unfortunately, as of this writing, some e-mail readers ignore internal and external styles, which means we are left only with the inline option. This means all styling information must be included within the elements it affects, like this:

```
<p style="font-family:verdana;font-size:12pt;color:blue;">
```

While you're steering clear of internal and external style sheets to reach the widest possible audience, you should also avoid all CSS shorthand. Instead, write out every complete style declaration like I did in the previous code example (instead of grouping all the font styles like this: `font: verdana 12pt`).

TIP   *Check www.campaignmonitor.com/css to see an updated list of which e-mail readers support CSS.*

Add Alt Text and Teaser Text

Yes, I've mentioned this one before as well, but it is worth revisiting. When designing for e-mail, you must expect that your images will not always be visible to the user for a variety of reasons. Some e-mail readers, like Gmail, do not load the images in an e-mail unless the user has given the okay. If your e-mail is composed completely of text, this means your users will initially see a big empty space with a broken image link.

Gmail leaves it up to the user to decide whether to display the message's images. (Users can choose to display images for a single e-mail, or always display images from this sender.) There are two ways you can help your users make that decision: with alt text and teaser text. Figure 10-3 shows an example of teaser text and alt text displaying when an e-mail is displayed in Gmail.

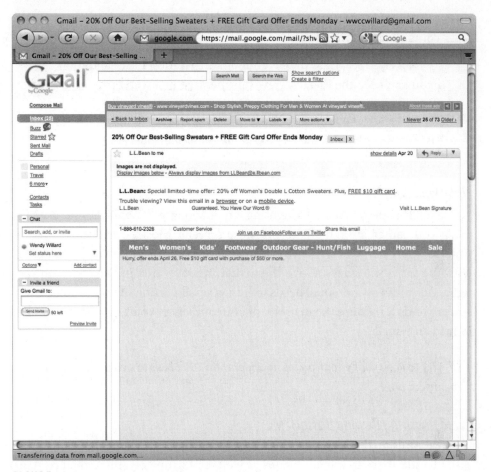

FIGURE 10-3 · Alt and teaser text displayed in Gmail

Alt text is the alternate text that is displayed when an image doesn't, and is added with the `alt` attribute to the img element. Make sure to use descriptive words that explain what users will find when the image is viewed. For example, if the image contains a coupon for $20 off, you might code your image like this:

```
<img src="http://mycompany.com/email/images/coupon.jpg" alt="Use
this coupon to get $20 OFF your next purchase" />
```

Another way to help users understand the e-mail content is to include teaser text at the top of the page. When an e-mail is initially displayed in an e-mail reader, the bottom half can easily be hidden depending on the user's monitor size and screen resolution. And as you just read, the images may be turned off as well. To combat that, many designers add one or two lines to the top of the page, containing text like this:

IN THIS ISSUE: $20 OFF coupon, Stay-cation ideas, and more!
If you can't see the images, <u>view this message in a web browser instead</u>.

NOTE   *Teaser text should be included on the first line after the opening body tag to ensure it is displayed at the very top of the e-mail message.*

Limit Page Widths

While it's true people seem to be using larger and larger monitors, that doesn't mean you can create e-mails to fill those screens. Most e-mail readers use a paneled approach, where the list of mailboxes might run down the left side, with the list of messages above the actual message area in the space on the right. This means your e-mail needs to fit in a small portion of the overall e-mail reader window because the majority of your audience won't scroll horizontally to read an e-mail.

TIP   *Try to keep your e-mail pages no wider than 700 pixels to avoid the right side being cut off.*

Avoid Anything Beyond Basic HTML

Because multimedia is so prevalent in web design, it's not uncommon to be asked to add them to e-mail designs as well. Unfortunately, the e-mail readers aren't able to handle multimedia the way web browsers do.

As of this writing, the only reliable way to include any sort of video in an e-mail is with an animated GIF. And there is no support for sound at all in any e-mail reader. So in short, you cannot realistically add audio or video to any HTML e-mail.

And the recommendation isn't any better for Flash lovers, because Apple's Mail program is the only e-mail client to offer native support for video and Flash files. While you can include a "fallback" image when embedding Flash files in normal webpages for browsers to display when the Flash player isn't available, most e-mail clients won't even let you do that. So at this point it is best to avoid Flash when designing HTML e-mail.

Finally, avoid any sort of client-side scripting like JavaScript, as it won't work and will likely cause your page to be marked as spam.

Still Struggling

MailChimp provides a great list of the top HTML e-mail design mistakes. Check it out to make sure your e-mails have a good shot at being read by your target audience: www.mailchimp.com/articles/top-html-email-coding-mistakes.

Testing

After you've coded your HTML e-mail is when the fun begins. While we've come to the point where webpages that work in Firefox and Internet Explorer are considered "safe" for the Web as a whole, HTML e-mail still requires extensive testing in multiple clients.

Thankfully, many ESPs offer services to make this process a bit easier. For example, Campaign Monitor provides screenshots to show how your e-mail will look in more than 15 of the most popular clients, including Outlook 2007, Yahoo!, Gmail, and Lotus Notes (including mobile devices). Visit www.campaignmonitor.com/testing to learn more. Figures 10-4, 10-5, and 10-6 show how the same test e-mail displays differently depending on the e-mail client. These screenshots show samples taken using Campaign Monitor's testing tool.

Another great option is a stand-alone testing tool like Litmus. Billing itself as the "advanced testing tool for web professionals," Litmus offers testing for both standard webpages and HTML e-mail. Litmus' basic account offers unlimited e-mail previews in all major e-mail clients (including mobile devices) for about $50 per month. Additional fee-based options allow spam testing and analytics. Visit www.litmusapp.com for details.

Spam Test

One of the unique aspects you can test is the likelihood of your e-mail being flagged as spam. Most of the popular ESPs offer this testing along with their e-mail messaging services. (If yours does not, there are other tools you can download to test HTML e-mail locally. MailingCheck, available from www.mailingcheck.com, is a free Windows-based spam checker.)

SpamAssassin is the most widely used spam filter processing e-mail received by ISPs. If your e-mail address gets blacklisted by SpamAssassin, you'll have

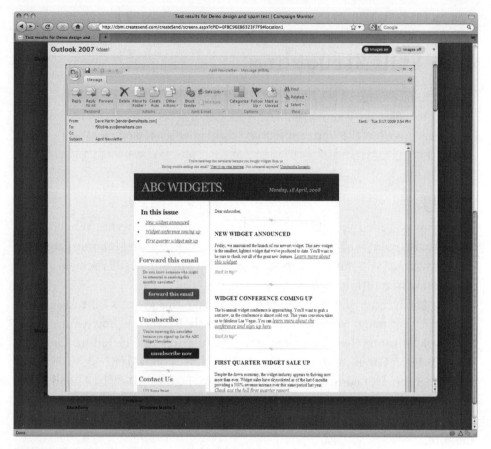

FIGURE 10-4 · Sample e-mail as it displays in Outlook 2007 with images turned on

a hard time getting your content in front of any of your subscribers. Refer to http://spamassassin.apache.org to learn more.

Wondering what might cause an e-mail to be flagged as spam? Here are just a few of the many reasons SpamAssassin might give you a higher "spam score." (And in this case, higher is not better.)

- HTML link text says "click here"
- A WHOLE LINE OF YELLING DETECTED
- Message includes "Dear Friend" or "Dear (Name)"
- Message contains "call" or "dial" or "toll free" followed by 800, 888, 877, 866, 855, 844, 833, or 822 (for example, "Call 877-555-5555 for your offer now!")

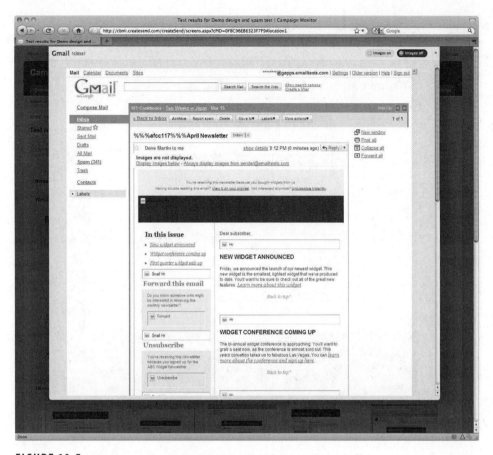

FIGURE 10-5 · Sample e-mail as it displays in Gmail with images turned off

- Message includes the phrase "risk free"
- HTML title contains "Untitled" (always title your webpages, even if they are being e-mailed)

Still Struggling

Visit www.mailchimp.com/resources/how_spam_filters_think.phtml to find out more about how spam filters work.

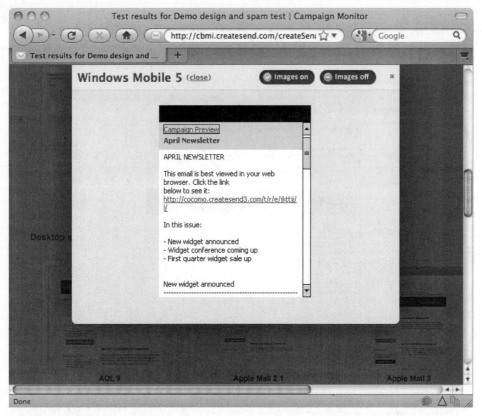

FIGURE 10-6 • Sample e-mail as it displays in Windows Mobile 5 (running on a mobile device)

Chapter Summary

In the final chapter of the book, I outlined the pros and cons of using e-mail marketing to drive traffic to your website, and also drew attention to the many ways in which e-mail design is different from traditional web design. I hope this chapter inspires you to add e-mail marketing to your toolbox. Be sure to visit the various online resources mentioned in this chapter to grow your skills and stay up-to-date on this ever-changing subject.

QUIZ

Choose the correct responses to each of the multiple-choice questions.

1. **True or False: It is acceptable to use CSS shorthand in HTML e-mail.**
   A. True
   B. False

2. **Which methods of adding interactivity to HTML e-mail are widely supported by e-mail readers? (Select all that apply.)**
   A. Flash
   B. audio
   C. video
   D. none of the above

3. **What is the best definition of spam?**
   A. any e-mail sent with a malicious intent
   B. any e-mail sent by a business for sales purposes
   C. any e-mail sent by a business for marketing purposes
   D. any e-mail sent without the permission of the recipient

4. **What does ESP stand for in terms of web design?**
   A. e-mail service provider
   B. e-mail systems preparer
   C. electronic service provider
   D. electronic systems participant

5. **True or False: The W3C maintains a special specification for HTML e-mail.**
   A. True
   B. False

6. **Which is the most widely supported layout method among e-mail readers?**
   A. CSS
   B. divs
   C. floats
   D. tables

7. **Which will *not* increase an e-mail's spam score in SpamAssassin?**
   A. changing the link colors
   B. a whole line of capital letters
   C. HTML link text that reads "click here"
   D. salutation that reads "Dear Friend" or "Dear (Name)"

8. Which is the most widely supported method of styling text in HTML e-mail?
   A. any CSS
   B. inline CSS
   C. internal CSS
   D. external CSS

9. Which attribute is added to the opening table tag to adjust the space in between each of the individual cells when coding tables for HTML e-mail?
   A. spacing
   B. margin
   C. padding
   D. cellspacing
   E. cellmargin
   F. cellpadding

10. Which link tag will accurately display an image in an HTML e-mail?
    A. <img src="image.jpg" alt="Image" />
    B. <img src="/images/image.jpg" alt="Image" />
    C. <img src="www.company.com/images/image.jpg" alt="Image" />
    D. <img src="http://www.company.com/images/image.jpg" alt="Image" />

Final Exam

Choose the correct responses to each of the multiple-choice questions.

1. Which task is considered part of the *project management* role within a web development team?

    A. labeling the site's content areas

    B. scheduling the project and its milestones

    C. coding the designs to display in web browsers

    D. creating mockups for key sections/pages/screens

    E. completing every web form to check the functionality

2. Which task is most commonly considered part of the *design* role within a web development team?

    A. labeling the site's content areas

    B. scheduling the project and its milestones

    C. coding the designs to display in web browsers

    D. creating mockups for key sections/pages/screens

    E. completing every web form to check the functionality

3. Reviewing and editing the site's content to add relevant keywords and phrases ideally falls under which role within a web development team?

    A. design

    B. coding

    C. animation

255

D. quality assurance

E. search engine optimization

4. **What technology is used to add style to webpages when they are coded?**

   A. SSL

   B. PHP

   C. CSS

   D. XHTML

   E. JavaScript

5. **Which characters surround all HTML tags?**

   A. quotes

   B. brackets

   C. parentheses

   D. curly brackets

   E. forward slashes

6. **ColdFusion is an example of which type of scripting language?**

   A. host-side

   B. client-side

   C. server-side

   D. browser-side

   E. database-side

7. **Which is *not* typically affected by a site's target audience?**

   A. design software

   B. design mockups

   C. target browsers

   D. target platforms

   E. target screen area/resolutions

8. **Which type of information architecture might be called "strict hierarchy"?**

   A. All pages are at the same level, where each is accessible from every other one.

   B. Pages are grouped into sections and each one follows a linear structure.

C. Pages are grouped into sections, and within each section the various pages are always accessible; a user must return to the home page to jump to a different section.

D. Pages are grouped into sections, and within each section the various pages are always accessible; a user can access other sections without returning to the home page.

9. **How is the structure of a website typically documented during the planning phase of the project?**

A. with a mockup

B. with a site map

C. with a wireframe

D. with a storyboard

E. with a technical specification

10. **How is the style of a website typically documented during the planning phase of a project?**

A. with a mockup

B. with a site map

C. with a wireframe

D. with a storyboard

E. with a technical specification

11. **Which color palette is used for screen-based designs?**

A. BMP

B. RGB

C. PNG

D. CMYK

E. Grayscale

12. **Which statement best describes how breadcrumb navigation might be used on a website?**

A. It provides access to content customized for each user.

B. It offers one-click access to essential functions of the site.

C. It provides related content typically pulled from a database behind the scenes.

D. It helps orient users and provides easy access to pages along their path in the site.

13. **At which dpi are web design mockups typically created?**

A. 24

B. 72

C. 96

D. 150

E. 300

14. **What does it mean when an image is royalty-free?**

A. It does not cost money.

B. It cannot be used for web design.

C. You must pay a fee each time the image is used.

D. You don't have to pay a fee each time the image is used.

15. **Which file format supports alpha transparency?**

A. GIF

B. BMP

C. JPEG

D. PNG-8

E. PNG-24

16. **Which is *not* true about dithering in web graphics?**

A. Dithering adds file size.

B. Dithering is available for JPEG files.

C. You can specify the amount of dithering between 0 and 100 percent.

D. Dithering can be useful in providing the appearance of gradations or subtle color shifts.

17. **Which file compression method requires data to be removed permanently from the image?**

A. lossy

B. lossless

C. inflated

D. deflated

18. **Which element is used to tell the browser what to display in the title bar?**

    A. \<title>\</title>

    B. \<head>\</head>

    C. \<html>\</html>

    D. \<body>\</body>

    E. \<header>\</header>

19. **Which tag could be used to tell the browser about the author of the webpage?**

    A. \<link>

    B. \<title>

    C. \<meta>

    D. \<style>

    E. \<author>

20. **In the following style declaration, which one is the property value?**
    h2 {font-family:verdana;}

    A. h2

    B. verdana

    C. font-family

    D. font-family:verdana

    E. h2 {font-family:verdana;}

21. **In the following style declaration, which is the rule?**
    h2 {font-family:verdana;}

    A. h2

    B. verdana

    C. font-family

    D. font-family:verdana

    E. h2 {font-family:verdana;}

22. **Which type of style sheet is embedded within the HTML element it affects?**

    A. inline

    B. internal

    C. external

    D. embedded

23. **Which is *not* true about current HTML specifications?**

    A. All tags must be closed.

    B. All tags should be lowercase.

    C. All tags must be nested properly.

    D. All tag values should be placed within straight quotation marks.

    E. All tags must be indented according to their location within the file structure.

24. **In the following style declaration, which is the selector?**
    h2 {font-family:verdana;}

    A. h2

    B. verdana

    C. font-family

    D. font-family:verdana

    E. h2 {font-family:verdana;}

25. **True or False: There are eight levels of heading elements, from <h1> down to <h8>.**

    A. True

    B. False

26. **Which is used to create the individual items in an ordered list?**

    A. <li>

    B. <ol>

    C. <ul>

    D. <dl>

    E. <dt>

27. **What must be added before an e-mail address when you're creating an e-mail link?**

    A. mms:

    B. mttp:

    C. email:

    D. mailto:

    E. message:

28. **Which creates a single-line text field in an HTML form?**

    A. `<input type="text" />`

    B. `<input type="radio" />`

    C. `<input type="single" />`

    D. `<input type="multiple" />`

    E. `<input type="textarea" />`

29. **Which element is properly formatted to include an image in a webpage?**

    A. `<object src="banner.jpg" name="image" width="400" height="20" />`

    B. `<img src="banner.jpg" width="400" height="20" alt="Products Banner" />`

    C. `<image src="banner.jpg" width="400" height="20" alt="Products Banner" />`

    D. `<img id="banner.jpg" width="400" height="20" title="Products Banner" />`

    E. `<object type="image" src="banner.jpg" width="400" height="20" title="Products Banner" />`

30. **Which is an example of an id selector?**

    A. p

    B. list

    C. #footer

    D. .highlight

31. **Which character separates descendent selectors in a style sheet rule?**

    A. a space

    B. a colon

    C. a period

    D. a less-than symbol

    E. a greater-than symbol

32. Which character precedes pseudo-classes in a style sheet rule?

    A. a space

    B. a colon

    C. a period

    D. a less-than symbol

    E. a greater-than symbol

33. How do you tell the browser that a particular style declaration should override all others in situations where duplicate rules apply to the same element?

    A. Use the !important declaration.

    B. Add *preferred to the end of the declaration.

    C. Put the preferred declaration in the external style sheet.

    D. Place the preferred declaration before all others in the style sheet.

34. Which style sheet property can display text in small caps?

    A. font-style

    B. font-effect

    C. font-family

    D. font-weight

    E. font-variant

35. Which style sheet property is used to turn off the default underline of links?

    A. link-color

    B. link-border

    C. text-underline

    D. text-transform

    E. text-decoration

36. **Which property is used to specify the buffer space outside of the box's border?**

    A. float

    B. border

    C. margin

    D. padding

    E. whitespace

37. **Which property defines the horizontal alignment of text and block-level elements?**

    A. text-align

    B. font-align

    C. text-horizontal

    D. horizontal-align

38. **When fixed positioning is used, how is the element placed?**

    A. relative to its child object

    B. relative to its parent object

    C. relative to its current location

    D. relative to the viewable space in the browser window

    E. relative to where they would normally be on the page

39. **Which property defines whether a background image scrolls when the page is scrolled?**

    A. background-color

    B. background-scroll

    C. background-image

    D. background-position

    E. background-attachment

40. **Which HTML attribute allows you to attach a readable, searchable text description to the links on your page?**

    A. alt

    B. title

    C. desc

    D. caption

41. True or False: The content of meta elements is displayed to users when the page is viewed in the browser.

    A. True

    B. False

42. Which element functions as a container for paragraphs of text?

    A. p

    B. pg

    C. para

    D. paragraph

43. True or False: The br element is referred to as an empty element.

    A. True

    B. False

44. Which type of HTML list puts bullets before each list item by default?

    A. starred

    B. ordered

    C. numbered

    D. unordered

    E. definition

45. Which type of HTML list puts numbers before each list item by default?

    A. starred

    B. ordered

    C. numbered

    D. unordered

    E. definition

46. Which HTML attribute is used to specify in which browser window a link should display?

    A. link

    B. name

    C. target

    D. tabindex

    E. accesskey

47. Which HTML attribute is used to define a specific destination *within* a webpage so that you can link to that section of the page's content?

    A. link

    B. name

    C. target

    D. tabindex

    E. accesskey

48. Which HTML element is used to add check boxes to a web form?

    A. form

    B. input

    C. select

    D. textarea

49. Which HTML element is used to add multiple-line text fields to a web form?

    A. form

    B. input

    C. select

    D. textarea

50. Which HTML element is used to add radio buttons to a web form?

    A. form

    B. input

    C. select

    D. textarea

51. Which HTML attribute is used to define the initial value of a form's input control when the page is first loaded?

    A. title

    B. type

    C. name

    D. value

52. True or False: The GIF file format is most commonly used for images of a photographic nature and those that feature color gradations.

   A. True

   B. False

53. Which HTML attribute is used to specify the keyboard shortcut for an HTML element?

   A. type

   B. name

   C. value

   D. tabindex

   E. accesskey

54. Which two HTML elements are used specifically to structure form input controls into labeled groups?

   A. table and tr

   B. name and value

   C. group and label

   D. form and method

   E. fieldset and legend

55. Fill in the blank: When viewed in a browser, all images are displayed in the standard screen-based _____ color mode.

   A. spot

   B. RGB

   C. CMYK

   D. web-safe

   E. four-color process

56. True or False: Web file types that support transparency fall into two categories: binary and variable.

   A. True

   B. False

57. Which allows certain pixels within a web graphic to be partially transparent or partially opaque when viewed in a browser?

    A. interlacing

    B. an alpha channel

    C. lossy compression

    D. the JPEG file format

    E. the CMYK color mode

58. True or False: Dithering does not increase an image's file size.

    A. True

    B. False

59. Fill in the blank: Photoshop's Save for Web feature allows you to compare up to _____ versions of an image at once.

    A. 2

    B. 3

    C. 4

    D. 5

60. When a partially transparent image is saved as a GIF, it will only display appropriately if the background of the page matches the matte color. Why?

    A. GIF files don't support dithering.

    B. GIF files don't support transparency.

    C. GIF files only support one level of dithering.

    D. GIF files only support one level of transparency.

61. Which type of style sheet is helpful for making quick changes to a single page, but isn't suited to styling a website with multiple pages?

    A. inline

    B. shared

    C. linked

    D. external

62. Which line of HTML code is correct in syntax and form to create a link?

    A. <ahref="http://www.google.com" link="Search Google">Search</a>

    B. <a link="http://www.google.com" title="Search Google">Search</a>

C. <a href="http://www.google.com" title="Search Google">Search</a>

D. <a link="http://www.google.com" href="Search Google">Search</a>

63. **Which line of HTML code is correct in syntax and form?**

   A. <em><strong>Don't Miss This!</em></strong>

   B. <em><strong>Don't Miss This!<em><strong>

   C. <strong><em>Don't Miss This!</strong></em>

   D. <strong><em>Don't Miss This!</em></strong>

64. **Which line of HTML code is correct in syntax and form?**

   A. <p css {font-family:verdana;}>

   B. <p css="font-family:verdana;">

   C. <p style {font-family:verdana;}>

   D. <p style="font-family:verdana;">

65. **In the following style declaration, which is the selector?**
   p {border-left:2px;}

   A. p

   B. 2px

   C. border-left

   D. border-left:2px

66. **In the following style declaration, which is the property?**
   p {border-left:2px;}

   A. p

   B. 2px

   C. border-left

   D. border-left:2px

67. **In the following style declaration, which is the rule?**
   p {border-left:2px;}

   A. p

   B. 2px

   C. border-left

   D. border-left:2px

68. True or False: Image-based text doesn't require specific fonts to be loaded on a user's system because an image is essentially a "snapshot" of the text.

    A. True

    B. False

69. How many colors are included in what is referred to as the "web-safe" color palette?

    A. 144

    B. 216

    C. 256

    D. thousands

70. Fill in the blank: Viewing colors in grayscale can help identify problem areas with the _____ of the page.

    A. fluidity

    B. structure

    C. contrast

    D. bandwidth

    E. navigation

71. What are tabs, vertical navigation bars, and sliders are all examples of in terms of web design?

    A. multimedia

    B. form fields

    C. photographic elements

    D. visual navigation metaphors

    E. text-based organizational tools

72. What is the primary purpose of eye-tracking studies for web designers?

    A. which headline is read first

    B. whether the navigation is effective

    C. where users look when viewing webpages

    D. whether users read left-to-right or right-to-left

73. **Which web browser is the most widely used among traditional computer users?**

    A. Safari

    B. Firefox

    C. Chrome

    D. Internet Explorer

74. **What does the acronym HTML stand for in web design?**

    A. Hypermedia Language

    B. Host Terminal Modal Link

    C. Hypertext Markup Language

    D. High-speed Transmission Meta-Language

75. **What do we call a script that runs on the web back-end system?**

    A. a host-side script

    B. a client-side script

    C. a server-side script

    D. a browser-side script

    E. a database-side script

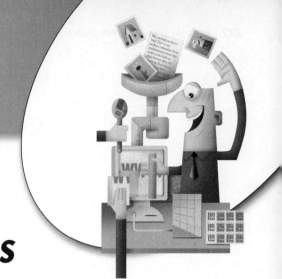

Answers to Quizzes and Final Exam

Chapter 1	Chapter 3	Chapter 5	Chapter 7
1. C	1. B	1. A	1. B
2. A	2. E	2. D	2. C
3. C	3. A	3. D	3. B
4. D	4. B	4. B	4. C
5. A	5. C	5. E	5. A
6. C	6. B	6. E	6. E
7. B	7. D	7. A	7. D
8. A	8. A	8. D	8. A
9. B	9. C	9. A	9. C
10. C	10. A	10. C	10. D

Chapter 2	Chapter 4	Chapter 6	Chapter 8
1. B	1. C	1. A	1. C
2. C	2. D	2. B	2. D
3. D	3. B	3. D	3. B
4. D	4. C	4. D	4. B
5. D	5. B	5. A	5. A
6. D	6. D	6. D	6. D
7. E	7. A	7. A	7. B
8. B	8. E	8. A	8. D
9. B	9. C	9. E	9. C
10. C	10. D	10. D	10. D

Chapter 9	Chapter 10
1. C	1. B
2. D	2. D
3. A	3. D
4. D	4. A
5. B	5. B
6. A	6. D
7. A	7. A
8. C	8. B
9. E	9. D
10. B	10. D

Final Exam

1. B	16. B	31. A	46. C	61. A
2. D	17. A	32. B	47. B	62. C
3. E	18. A	33. A	48. B	63. D
4. C	19. C	34. E	49. D	64. D
5. B	20. B	35. E	50. B	65. A
6. C	21. D	36. C	51. D	66. C
7. A	22. A	37. A	52. B	67. D
8. C	23. E	38. D	53. E	68. A
9. B	24. A	39. E	54. E	69. B
10. A	25. B	40. B	55. B	70. C
11. B	26. A	41. B	56. A	71. D
12. D	27. D	42. A	57. B	72. C
13. B	28. A	43. A	58. B	73. D
14. D	29. B	44. D	59. C	74. C
15. E	30. C	45. B	60. D	75. C

Index

Symbols

A

B

DeMYSTiFieD®

Hard stuff made easy

The DeMYSTiFieD series helps students master complex and difficult subjects. Each book is filled with chapter quizzes, final exams, and user friendly content. Whether you want to master Spanish or get an A in Chemistry, DeMYSTiFieD will untangle confusing subjects, and make the hard stuff understandable.